Political Games
Mathematical Insights on Fighting, Voting, Lying & Other Affairs of State

Macartan Humphreys

W.W. Norton & Company
New York • London

W. W. Norton & Company has been independent since its founding in 1923, when William Warder Norton and Mary D. Herter Norton first published lectures delivered at the People's Institute, the adult education division of New York City's Cooper Union. The firm soon expanded its program beyond the Institute, publishing books by celebrated academics from America and abroad. By midcentury, the two major pillars of Norton's publishing program—trade books and college texts—were firmly established. In the 1950s, the Norton family transferred control of the company to its employees, and today—with a staff of four hundred and a comparable number of trade, college, and professional titles published each year—W. W. Norton & Company stands as the largest and oldest publishing house owned wholly by its employees.

Copyright © 2017 by W.W. Norton & Company, Inc.

All rights reserved
Printed in the United States of America
First Edition

Editor: Ann Shin
Associate Editor: Emily Stuart
Project Editor: David Bradley
Editorial Assistant: Shannon Jilek
Managing Editor, College: Marian Johnson
Managing Editor, College Digital Media: Kim Yi
Production Manager: Ben Reynolds
Media Editor: Spencer Richardson-Jones
Associate Media Editor: Michael Jaoui
Marketing Manager, Political Science: Erin Brown
Design Director: Debra Morton-Hoyt
Designer: Anna Reich
Composition: MPS North America LLC
Manufacturing: Sheridan Books—Chelsea MI

ISBN 978-0-393-26333-6 (pbk.)

W. W. Norton & Company, Inc., 500 Fifth Avenue, New York, NY 10110
wwnorton.com

W. W. Norton & Company Ltd., Castle House, 75/76 Wells Street, London W1T 3QT

1 2 3 4 5 6 7 8 9 0

CONTENTS

INTRODUCTION   VII
What Game Theory Is and Isn't   vii
A Primer on Games   xi
A Guide to Graphs   xxii
Reading Guide   xxv
Outline for Specific Areas of Study   xxvi

Acknowledgments   xxix

PART 1   DILEMMAS OF COLLECTIVE ACTION   1
1   The Tragedy of the Commons (The Prisoner's Dilemma) ⊞   2
2   Strategic Substitution (The Game of Chicken) ⊞   4
3   Strategic Complementarities (The Assurance Dilemma) ⊞   6

PART 2   SOLUTIONS TO SOCIAL DILEMMAS   9
4   The Shadow of the Future (The Folk Theorems) ⛁ ☉   10
5   Playing with Your Progeny (Overlapping Generations) ⛁   12
6   Playing with the Wrong Goals (The Evolution of Preferences) ⊞ ☉   14

PART 3   WHAT GROUPS WANT   17
7   The Problem with Utilitarians (The Robbins Critique) ≳ ☉   18
8   Irrational Majorities (Condorcet's Paradox) ≳   20
9   There Is No General Will (Arrow's Theorem) ≳ ⊘ ☉   22

PART 4   MAJORITY RULE   25
10   Majority Rule Aggregates Knowledge (Condorcet's Jury Theorem) ≳   26
11   What's Special about Simple Majority Rule? (May's Theorem) ≳   28
12   Why the Middle Matters (The Median Voter Theorem) ≳ ⊞   30
13   Voting Weight and Political Influence (Power Indices) ≳   32

PART 5   THE INSTABILITY OF MAJORITY RULE   35
14   You Can't Satisfy All the Majorities Any of the Time (Plott's Theorem) ≳ ⛁ ☉   36
15   Naive Majorities Are Capable of Anything (The McKelvey-Schofield Chaos Theorem) ≳   38
16   How Sticky Are Sticky Rules? (Nakamura's Theorem) ≳ ☉   40

PART 6 MANIPULATION 43

17 Sophisticated Majorities Might Also Do Anything (Agenda Manipulation) ⋔ 44

18 Power from Proposing Proposers (Legislative Bargaining) ⋔ 46

19 It's Hard to Get People to Vote Honestly (The Gibbard-Satterthwaite Theorem) ≳ ⊙ 48

PART 7 STRATEGIC VOTING 51

20 Is It Rational to Vote? (The Rational Voter Paradox) ⊞ 52

21 Strategic Abstention (The Swing Voter's Curse) ◁ 54

22 Conformist Voting (Information Cascades) ◁ 56

PART 8 ARGUING 59

23 Listening to Pain (Costly Signaling) ◁ 60

24 When to Listen to Threats (Cheap Talk) ◁ ⊘ 62

25 Deep Democracy among Strategists (The Limits of Deliberation) ◁ ⊘ 64

26 You Can't Agree to Disagree (Aumann's Agreement Theorem) ◁ ⊘ ⊙ 66

PART 9 BARGAINING 69

27 The Bargaining Problem (The Nash Bargaining Solution) ≳ ⊘ ⊙ 70

28 Alternating Offers (The Ståhl-Rubinstein Solution) ⋔ 72

29 The Benefits of Constraints (The Schelling Conjecture) ⋔ 74

30 Changing Fortunes Threaten Negotiations (The Commitment Problem) ⋔ 76

PART 10 SELLING 79

31 Let the Market Decide (The Coase Theorem) ≳ 80

32 Auctions (The Revenue Equivalence Theorem) ◁ ⊘ ⊙ 82

33 The Missing Market for Lemons (Asymmetric Information and Market Failure) ◁ 84

34 The Impossibility of Informationally Efficient Markets (The Grossman-Stiglitz Paradox) ◁ 86

PART 11 INSTITUTIONAL DESIGN 89

35 Solomon's Dilemma (Maskin Monotonicity) ◁ ⊘ ⊙ 90

36 How to Choose a Policy (The Clarke-Groves Mechanism) ◁ 92

37 Not Getting to Yes (The Myerson-Satterthwaite Theorem) ◁ ⊘ ⊙ 94

PART 12   POLITICAL ECONOMY   97

38 Throw the Rascals Out (The Logic of Political Accountability)   98
39 Why More Inclusive Governments Produce More Public Goods
        (The Selectorate Model)   100
40 Redistribution and Inequality (The Meltzer-Richard Model)   102
41 Redistribution and Inefficiency (The Dixit-Londregan Model)   104

PART 13   REVOLTING   107

42 Small Is Beautiful (The Logic of Collective Action)   108
43 Surprised by Revolt (Threshold Models)   110
44 Dashed Expectations (Psychological Games)   112
45 Feigning Tough (Reputation Models)   114

PART 14   LIMITED RATIONALITY   117

46 Strategy without Strategizing (Evolutionary Stability)   118
47 Adaptive Play and the Dominance of Fear (Stochastic Stability)   120
48 Too Clever by Half (The k-level Model)   122
49 The Irrationality of Others (A Theorem on Imitation)   124

APPENDIX A: FOUNDATIONAL RESULTS IN THE THEORY OF GAMES   127

A1 Reasoning Backward (Zermelo's Theorem)   128
A2 Solving Zero-Sum Games (The Minimax Theorem)   130
A3 A Beautiful World? (Nash's Theorem)   132

APPENDIX B: GLOSSARY   135

APPENDIX C: NOTES   145

REFERENCES   171

INTRODUCTION

Social scientists have been trying to use mathematics to make sense of politics for more than two hundred years. They have ignored objections that politics is an art, not a science, and that political agents are unique and unpredictable. They have ignored complaints that mathematics forces a simplification that does violence to the inherently complex nature of political action, that you cannot explain a bloody phenomenon with a bloodless theory. And they have made a lot of progress.

But unfortunately for everyone, something funny happened on the way to uncovering the fundamental laws of social behavior. It was soon discovered that simple models of individual action do not lead to simple models of social action. The deeper the analysis went, the clearer it became that when people value different outcomes differently, and can act independently, simple individual decision making can lead to horrendous social complexity.

As formal theorists—who include game theorists and various close cousins such as social choice theorists, public choice theorists, and others—made progress in understanding when and how this complexity arises, their work also became more and more obscure. Although approaches and insights generated by formal theorists now permeate thinking in many corners of social science, the most important results go almost entirely unreported outside of specialized journals. In fact, the world of formal theory seems almost deliberately inaccessible.

My aim in this book is to help make some of it accessible. I am helped by the fact that, at bottom, game theory really is a collection of stories—stories of the *if-then* variety not unlike classic tales, each one seeking to impart a simple message. If you wander from the path, then you might get eaten by a wolf. If you try to be too clever, you will fall victim to your own machinations. Good stories resonate not because they accurately capture the details of a particular case but because they touch on something that is more universal. You can see your own situation in the stories you read.

This book focuses on the stories that lie at the heart of mathematical analyses of politics and uses them to present forty-nine of the deepest insights from the formal study of political economy. Collectively, these results reveal profound connections between seemingly disparate social problems and lay bare common logics underlying them. But collectively they also tell a cautionary tale for anyone hoping to decode human behavior: seeing past the details of a social situation to the underlying game focuses attention on critical logics. But it does not guarantee simple conclusions. Games, like stories, generally have many interpretations and many possible endings. While game theoretic tools deepen our understanding of social processes, they also cast a cold light on the limits of our knowledge.

WHAT GAME THEORY IS AND ISN'T

The basic principle of game theory is that social situations, even the most serious social situations, are structurally a lot like **games.** Different people have different choices and everyone cares about the choices everyone else makes. But different people generally want different things. Each game is a story and the question behind the story is what will people do or perhaps what *would* different types of people do in situations like this? The conclusion generally comes in the form of an **equilibrium**—a point at which people settle on a set of strategies.

The key plot elements you need to study games are a description of who the key players are, what they value, and a description of what actions they have available to them. Everything else follows from these. Contrary to common belief, you don't need to make *particular* assumptions about what people want or how they think. Although in many applied game theoretic models there is an assumption that people are driven solely by the pursuit of personal wealth, game theory does not require any assumptions about whether or not people are selfish. The type of selfishness or selflessness of the players determines *what* game they are playing but not *whether* they are playing a game. And although extreme cunning is often assumed in game theoretic analyses, it is also not required. The stories in this book include characters with all kinds of preferences and capabilities, with sometimes extreme limitations on their ability to strategize, and who are operating in a sea of confusion. In part because of this flexibility with respect to human motivations and behavior, game theory is not really a *theory* at all; it is a family of ways of thinking about strategic problems with tools that can be marshaled in support of all kinds of contradictory claims and stances. In its short history, game theory has been used to support arguments across the ideological map, including those made by anarchists, Marxists, and free-market capitalists.

As with any good story, game theoretic analyses involve deliberate departures from reality. Some critics bemoan what they see as an oversimplification inherent in game theoretic analysis. But game theorists generally don't share this concern. For them, the value of an analysis lies not in its realism but in the insights it can produce. The power comes from identifying a common core that is shared across different environments even as other details change. Some of the theoretically arresting results (like the Coase Theorem [§31] or the Revenue Equivalence Theorem [§32]) depend on such precise conditions as to have really no literal application. And some models (like the model of the Missing Market for Lemons [§33]) make predictions that are patently false. But that is not the point. The models serve as parables, seeking to isolate forces at work that shape reality even if they never tell the full story.

GAMES ARE EVERYWHERE

People are playing games all the time. In life, and in politics. Sometimes the game-like nature of politics is obvious. The president and Congress create a doomsday scenario for themselves in the form of a "fiscal cliff" in order to put pressure on each other to reach a deal. They then start fighting over different combinations of taxes and spending cuts, engaging in offers, counteroffers, walkouts, and bluffs until at the eleventh hour some deal is struck and everyone goes home to prepare for the next round. That game has a somewhat clear set of rules that determine what different actors can do. In other situations, the rules—if there are any—are much less obvious. In October 1962 the United States imposed a naval blockade in response to attempts by the USSR to install nuclear missiles in Cuba. Soviet ships prepared to run the blockade while the United States gave orders to respond with force. Both sides recognized the prospect of an escalation to nuclear war but both wanted the other to be the one to back down. The stakes during the missile crisis were much more momentous than the stakes during the fiscal cliff negotiations and there was much less agreement about the rights each side had to employ different types of strategies. But the two situations still share a common core: at the heart of each lies the simple, if fundamentally frustrating, logic of the Game of Chicken [§2].

Sometimes it is a lot less clear what game is being played. Consider O. Henry's story *The Gift of the Magi*. Jim and Della are poor. All Jim has is a watch and all Della has is her beautiful hair. Della loves her hair and Jim loves his watch but they love each other more. Seeking to make the other happy, Jim sells his watch to buy combs for Della's hair. Della sells her hair to buy a chain for Jim's watch. Their individual attempts to get nice things for the other result in both being worse off—at least in terms of their possessions. Had they just looked out for themselves each would have had something and could have been happy that the other did also.

It's a beautiful story partly because of its ambiguities. What is the meaning of their sacrifices? Do they really end up in a bad place? It's clear that things end up badly in terms of their possessions; it's also clear that the problem lies in part in their independent efforts to make the other happy. But it is not so clear that they made the wrong choices individually or collectively.

Figuring out what game is being played helps make sense of the story and reveals the connections to similar problems in very different settings. One reading of the story is that the primary purpose of the gifts was to communicate Jim's and Della's love. From a game theoretic perspective that turns the problem into a "signaling" problem, which is often resolved by sending *costly* signals [§23]. If so, Jim and Della would *not* both be better off if they had not made the sacrifices, since then the other would have lingering doubts about whether he or she was loved. Though they want to communicate love, their problem is strategically akin to enemies who want to communicate military resolve. In both cases the need to communicate convincingly can require suffering. Another possibility is that Jim cares about Della and knows that Della's happiness depends in part on how happy he is. In that case, if he suspected that Della would sell her hair, the greatest sacrifice Jim could make might be to *keep* his watch. If Della is thinking similarly, they might be caught in a Game of Chicken [§2]: a sacrifice is to be made by one of them and the tricky thing is to figure out who will get the chance to make it. Their problem shares elements with the Cuban crisis but in this case they failed to coordinate their way out of the dilemma. A third possibility is that there is some narcissism in their selflessness. It could be that Jim might still prefer to sell his watch even after finding out that Della had sold her hair. He may feel sad that Della has sold her hair but still feel compelled to an act of sacrifice, even though (or perhaps, if he is competitively selfless, *because*) it frustrates Della's attempts to make him happy. Della might be thinking the same way. Under that interpretation their particular brand of selflessness gets them caught in a Prisoner's Dilemma [§1] and dooms them to a life of tragedy.

More generally, the promise of game theory is that if you can figure out what games people are playing and if you know something about how people think, then you can get a handle on how people's individual strategizing translates into social outcomes, and, perhaps, what can be done about it. Representing social problems as games lets you see connections among all kinds of diverse interactions. Figuring out who is going to order the groceries presents some related challenges to figuring out whether the United States or the European Union will send troops to Libya. The difficulties of communicating seriousness of purpose can have similar implications for the type of grandstanding that despots engage in and the choice of methods that might be employed in an attempted suicide. The problem of busting a cheating cartel generates similar challenges to the cartel's problem of making sure their members *really do* cheat. The dilemma facing two prisoners is strategically akin to that facing major polluters worried about climate change. The same dilemma also has connections to a fundamental problem of political philosophy: how to reconcile the goal of protecting individual rights of action with the goal of ensuring desirable social outcomes. At the heart of the matter in each case is the problem of other people.

THE PROBLEM OF OTHER PEOPLE

What all the games in this book have in common is a focus on the problem of other people. What happens when people who disagree with each other have to interact with each other? How do they figure out how to make joint decisions? When do they end up making decisions that are good for them collectively and when do they fail? How can you even speak about when outcomes are good for collections of people? The problem of other people is not that other people are terrible, but that in social settings you can't avoid having to deal with them. Their actions and strategies affect your well-being and yours theirs. While any one player might have freedom in choosing among strategies, she often has very little control over actual outcomes.

As is clear from Jim and Della's dilemma, the problem of other people lies in their autonomy, not their decency. Outcomes are generated by societies, but societies are not like people. The games I describe in this book highlight three critical ways in which properties of individuals are not inherited by groups. First, even if you think all individuals put effort into getting the best outcomes they can, that does not mean that societies will choose good outcomes. That point is shown in the analysis of the Prisoner's Dilemma [§1], but it resurfaces in many other games. Second, even if you think individuals will act predictably in a given situation, that does not mean that societies will. In the Cuban missile crisis you might believe that you know exactly what is the best response of each country to any actions taken by the other, but that does not mean that you know what anyone is going to do. That point is shown in the discussion of the Game of Chicken [§2]. Third, even if individuals have **rational preferences** (which implies that if they like A more than B and B more than C, then they will like A more than C), that does not mean that their societies have rational preferences. That point is made in the discussion of Arrow's theorem [§9] and related work.

Business school gurus sometimes describe how understanding game theory helps you succeed in life and business: understand the strategic logic and you can predict what others will do. But those conclusions seems to fly in the face of what game theorists have actually found when they have taken strategic problems seriously. If there is a single conclusion, it is that once strategy comes into play, things are a lot less simple than we like to pretend. Living with others is tough and predicting how others live is tougher still. Many of the most important results from the study of games are negative. There is no meaningful notion of a "general will"; majorities almost never have preferences you can make much sense of; negotiations can fail even when everyone wants them to work; people hide their true preferences when they vote and talking before voting doesn't help much, even when people fundamentally agree about outcomes; you generally can't set up institutions in order to guide people toward socially beneficial outcomes. More applied models sometimes make sharper predictions but these predictions are often extremely sensitive to details of the problem analyzed. Even the most positive results have a dark side.

These conclusions are frustrating for anyone seeking simple truths because they represent not just a failure to find simple answers but a claim that simple answers are not to be had. The point is all the more striking since the complexity of the conclusions are often generated under the assumptions that individuals face relatively simple problems and engage with them in reasonably simple ways. But the simplicity of individual decision making does not add up to simple social outcomes. When people disagree but can act autonomously, all hell can break loose. Predict at your peril.

A PRIMER ON GAMES

Game theorists think that you can describe any situation as a game. Whether it's voting decisions, social customs, arms races, falling in love, lobbying, or terrorism. If you can write down and solve the game, you can understand the world.

So what is a game and can any situation really be described as one? For a game theorist to describe a situation as a game you only need to know three things: who the actors are ("the players"), what they can and cannot do (the "possible actions" or strategy sets), and how they value different outcomes (the "payoffs"). With these in hand you can produce what's called the **normal form** representation of the problem. In this book I use the symbol ⊞ to mark games in normal form.[1]

Normal Form Games

Here's an example: rock-paper-scissors. Two players each decide at the same time whether to choose the rock, the paper, or the scissors. The scissors beats (cuts) the paper, the rock beats (breaks) the scissors, and the paper beats ("covers," apparently) the rock. Each player just wants to win. That's a full description of the game.

You can represent games like this using a simple figure, or **payoff matrix**, like that in Figure A. I use many payoff matrices like this in this book. In the payoff matrix, the *players* are each represented by a dimension, the *possible actions* are the labels on the dimensions, and the *payoffs* are numbers in the cells that are formed by the dimensions, one number per player in each cell.

You can see in Figure A that the players "control" different dimensions: the vertical dimension is controlled by Jack—Jack decides which row will be selected; Jill decides which column will be played. Once both make their choices, you know which cell

	Jill Rock	Jill Paper	Jill Scissors
Jack Rock	0 / 0	1 / −1	−1 / 1
Jack Paper	−1 / 1	0 / 0	1 / −1
Jack Scissors	1 / −1	−1 / 1	0 / 0

FIGURE A PAYOFF MATRIX USED TO ILLUSTRATE ROCK-PAPER-SCISSORS
The numbers in each cell show the payoffs to Jill (upper-right numbers) and Jack (lower-left numbers) when Jill chooses a given column and Jack chooses a given row. The matrix fully describes the game.

---

1 Note that these elements do not fully capture possibly important features such as the role of information and time (more on these below) but on their own they can still provide a coherent—if not complete—description of a social problem, whether or not these features are important.

Introduction xi

they are in and the numbers in the cell then give the payoffs (or **utilities**) received by each player from each combination of strategies. Each of the nine cells in the matrix corresponds to one combination of strategies by the two players. For example, the top-right cell is the situation in which Jill chooses scissors while Jack chooses rock. The two numbers in each cell are the payoffs; they represent the *subjective* rewards that the two players get depending on what happens. Since the payoffs are part of the definition of the game, if you change the payoffs, you change the game. Within each cell the top-right number is the payoff to Jill (column player); the bottom-left number is the payoff to Jack (the row player). For example, when Jack chooses rock and Jill chooses scissors, you can see that Jack gets a payoff of "1" while Jill gets "–1." Good for Jack, bad for Jill.

This basic description of a game can be used to describe many situations including almost any traditional game you can think of. Say instead of just three objects, Jack and Jill could choose any one of a hundred objects. The payoff matrix would look similar, though a lot more dense, as you would need to give payoffs for each one of the 100 × 100 possible outcomes. Say that instead of two people playing that there were three people playing. Then instead of two dimensions, making a square, you would need three dimensions, forming a cube. With four players you would need a four-dimensional "hypercube" or else resort to some tricks to display the payoffs. But the basic idea is still the same: different people control different dimensions and everyone's payoff depends on everyone's actions. Even much more complex games like chess in which people take whole *sequences* of moves can be represented in this way. In this case each label would be very complicated (for example, "I move my king's pawn first, and then if you do x_1 I will do y_1, but if you do x_2 I will do y_2 ..."). Although these all describe actions that take place during a game, you can think of these as plans worked out by players in advance of play. Of course any numbers can be put into the cells, as long as they capture how people feel about different outcomes. These numbers are part of the game definition. Rock-paper-scissors is a **zero-sum game** (the numbers in each cell literally sum to zero) but the same structure can be used for what's sometimes called "variable-sum" games or "mixed-motive" games in which there are some outcomes that are better than others for *both* players.[2]

So that's the description of the game. Being able to describe a game is useful but the goal is to *solve* it. What's a solution? Most of the time, by solution people mean something like "What strategies will people play if they are trying to win?" But if your goal is to explain the world, then you should think of a solution as being a claim about what is likely to *happen*, given different assumptions about how people play.

In rock-paper-scissors, if two smart people are both trying to win and are thinking hard about how other people are playing, then they will quickly see that relying on any single action is not a good strategy. You can indicate this thinking by adding arrows to the matrix, as in Figure B. Here I have added arrows emanating from the different cells. The arrows show the set of *improvements* that can be made by different players given any outcome. For example, if both say "rock" (top-left cell), then there is a horizontal arrow pointing to paper, which means that Jill would be better off switching to paper; there is also a vertical arrow pointing to paper, which means that Jack would be better off shifting to paper. In game theoretic terms these arrows point to "best responses"—the best things that you can do given what other players

---

2 A game can be "zero sum" even if the numbers in the cells do not sum to zero for the simple reason that these **utility** numbers do not carry as much meaning as you often associate with numbers (see the Robbins Critique [§7]). Any game in which $u_1 + a + bu_2 = 0$ for some a and $b > 0$ has all the same properties as a zero-sum game.

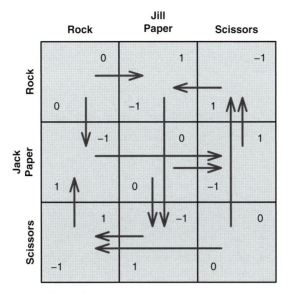

FIGURE B The same **payoff matrix** as shown in Figure A but here arrows are added to indicate improvements that can be made by each player: horizontal arrows for Jill and vertical arrows for Jack.

are doing.[3] The key feature of this game is that *there is an arrow pointing out of every cell*. That means that there is no cell you can point to and say, "That is what will happen when players play optimally."

There is a solution, however, for optimizing players. But to find it you have to make some assumptions about how people value risky prospects. The standard, though much challenged, approach is to assume that people satisfy what are known as the axioms of the **expected utility hypothesis**. This means that if they face a 50% chance of getting an outcome that they value at 1 and a 50% chance of getting an outcome that they value at −1, then the value they place on the risky situation is the *expected* (i.e., average) value, or 0. Or, more generally, the value to a player of a situation in which they have a p probability of getting an outcome they value at x and a $(1-p)$ probability of getting an outcome they value at y, is just their expected utility: $p \times x + (1-p) \times y$.

Under that assumption, you can identify a set of strategies that no one can improve on: let both players choose each of the three options randomly, with equal probability. If both players do that, then each wins with a one-third probability, and with a one-third probability there is a draw. Follow any other strategy and your opponent could choose strategies that force you to do worse than this. Obviously, if your strategy was just to play rock all the time, then you would get covered all the time. If you randomly alternated between two things (say rock and scissors), you could be forced to a loss half the time and a draw half the time (for example, if the other played rock all the time). So with two very strategic people playing, neither can employ better strategies than playing each option one-third of the time. That solution is called a **Nash equilibrium**, meaning simply that no one can benefit from changing her strategy given everyone else's strategy. The Nash equilibrium is a solution that makes sense if people are optimizing.

---

3 If no horizontal arrows point out of a cell, then that cell is a best response for the column player to the row action of the row player.

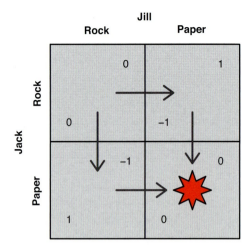

FIGURE C ROCK-PAPER-SCISSORS WITHOUT THE SCISSORS
Here all arrows point to the cell for which both players play paper. This cell is marked with a star indicating that it is a **Nash equilibrium**.

None of this means that the optimizing solution is necessarily the solution you should care about. A couple of years ago my five-year-old daughter was playing rock-paper-scissors with a friend. The two of them shifted around among the different possible strategies, sometimes winning, sometimes losing. They seemed to be playing the optimizing solution. Then I asked them to play a modified game: they were to keep playing but *they were not allowed to choose scissors*. Only paper and rock.

The modified game is shown in Figure C. What is strategically different about this game is that this time there is a cell with no arrows pointing out. In other words, there is an outcome that neither player can improve upon—in the same way that no one could improve upon the randomizing strategies in the full game. So this is the Nash equilibrium of the modified game. It is marked here with a star and corresponds to a set of strategy options such that when everyone is playing using those actions, no one player can do better by doing anything differently.

My daughter and her friend understood the rules of the modified game perfectly and started to play, this time alternating between rock and paper; paper always won of course and over time it looked like each played paper with increasing frequency. But rock continued to make an appearance every once in a while, in the futile hopes of a surprise victory. So with these two at least, the Nash equilibrium solution was a reasonable but not perfectly accurate solution to the modified game. A better solution might have assumed a baseline propensity to play randomly. Or it might have used information about play in previous games—before the rule switch—rather than assuming each game could be analyzed in isolation. A lot of game theory tends to assume optimizing action by everyone and many of the results in this book assume that also, but in general this is not necessary. In later sections of the book, I look at results that try to predict what is likely to happen when people are not fully rational.

So much for rock-paper-scissors. The big idea of game theory is not that now you can solve rock-paper-scissors but that very serious social actions look a lot like simple games such as rock-paper-scissors. Social struggles also consist of players, possible actions, and payoffs.

Consider for example this game: A captain stages a coup and now starts to worry whether he can get the rest of the army to support him. An older general thinks that he could do well by subverting the captain and taking control directly. They both

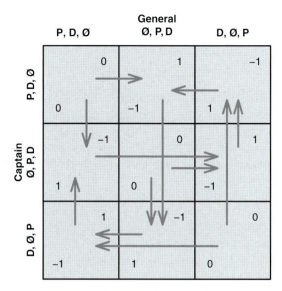

FIGURE D A POLITICAL ROCK-PAPER-SCISSORS GAME
Two players can offer a big prize (*P*), a small prize (*D*), or no prize (Ø) to each of three groups. Action "*D*, Ø, *P*," for example, means that *D* is offered to group 1, nothing to group 2, and *P* to group 3. Players want support from as many groups as possible and groups support whichever player offers them the most. This means, for example, that playing "*D*, Ø, *P*" wins against an opponent playing "Ø, *P*, *D*," as it is preferred by the first and third groups.

decide to send out messages to the army describing how they plan to set up their governments.

Let's assume the army is divided into three groups, the north, south, and central units. The captain and the general can each offer a major prize (such as the presidency, *P*) to a member of one faction and a smaller prize (minister of defense, *D*) to a member of another, while offering nothing (Ø) to the third faction. Assume that factions back whomever offers them the most and that you want as many factions to back you as possible.

This game is shown in Figure D. Here, strategy labels of the form *P, D,* Ø mean "presidency for the north, defense for the south, and nothing for the center." Have a look back at Figure A and you will see that the captain and the general are playing rock-paper-scissors, albeit with much higher stakes.[4]

If you know that the basic logic is like rock-paper-scissors, you know a lot. In particular, you know that if the general and the captain are playing optimal strategies, then there will be some randomness to their actions. In a sense, this means that you know that you have no idea what they are going to do. But you still understand the situation well. It's not just that you cannot predict, you can now confidently predict that the outcome is unpredictable. What would be odder in a way is if you *did* know what they were going to do. If, say, they simply chose to offer positions to their closest friends, they would be bound to lose. It would be like always choosing rock because you like rocks. Similarly, if they predictably *avoided* their closest friends, they would also lose.

While a lot of the games in this book are represented using payoff matrices like this, some strategic settings require us to take richer information into account. Two

---

4 Or nearly: In this analysis I focus on just three possible strategies but in fact each has six possible strategies. How different would the game look if you put all six into the matrix?

features of strategic interactions require special consideration: how the game unfolds over time, and what information people have about each other.

Consider time first. Imagine playing rock-paper-scissors but instead of playing at the same time, one player played first and the second played second. Then it's a bit obvious that the second mover will win (researchers in robotics have developed a winning robot with such a quick eye and rapid movement that it moves second every time without you noticing). So information about time matters. But how exactly does time matter?

Formally, if people are playing rock-paper-scissors sequentially, then the second player does not choose just one of three options, they have twenty-seven (3^3) options to choose from. For example, one option is for 2 to just do whatever 1 did: "If 1 chooses R, I will choose R; if 1 chooses P, I will choose P; and if 1 chooses S, I will choose S." A much better option of course is "If 1 chooses R, I will choose P; if 1 chooses P, I will choose S; and if 1 chooses S, I will choose R." This new game could then also be represented as a matrix, this time with three rows and twenty-seven columns. If you did that and drew arrows like the ones in Figure D, you would see that everything would point to three outcomes (try it!); in all of these, 2 plays the optimal strategy and so it does not matter what 1 does.

But for some games, time matters in a more profound way. Take the following game. A militant group is contemplating whether to take hostages. The government has to decide whether to make a payment if the militants do take hostages. The government's stated policy is never to make payments to militants. What will happen?

First you can represent the game using a payoff matrix as in Figure E. Filling in the arrows and stars you see that there are *two* Nash equilibriums in this game. One in which the militants do not take hostages and the government would not pay if they did. And another in which they do take hostages and the government pays.

There is something troubling, however, about the first equilibrium. The problem is that even though it is a Nash equilibrium (since no one wants to change their strategy given other people's strategies), the militants might reasonably think that if they did change their strategy (and took hostages) that the government would then change its

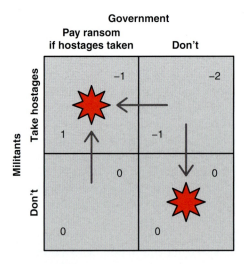

FIGURE E THE HOSTAGES GAME
Militants can choose whether to take a hostage and demand a ransom. A government decides whether or not to pay. Two **Nash equilibriums** are marked. But are both reasonable?

strategy and decide to make payments. They could call the government's bluff. But what sort of equilibrium is it if it's transparently a bluff?

The fundamental problem here is that time does more than expand the set of options available to people (which can be captured in a payoff matrix); it also changes strategic dynamics (which cannot). With people playing at different points in time they can select their strategies based on what actually happened, which means that early-moving players can take actions to manipulate later movers. To capture the strategic dynamics you need to be able to represent the game as it is played out over time. To do this you drop the normal form representation and switch to what's called the **extensive form** representation. The key feature of the extensive form is that you can make use of a **game tree** to represent play over time. I use the ⋔ symbol to indicate when games are in extensive form.

Figure F shows a game tree for the hostages game. This contains all the information found in the payoff matrix—the players, the strategies, the payoffs. In addition it has information about the structure of play. So while you can represent the situation in "normal form" using a payoff matrix, the "extensive form" representation is actually richer and may make it possible to get more refined predictions.

The game tree is read much like a decision tree. You start at the beginning, here the open circle on the left, and then at each node of the tree you read off who gets to move at that node. There is always only one person moving at each node. The branches coming off each node give the strategies available to whomever is moving at that node, and over the span of the tree these chart out all the possible patterns of play that might arise. At the very end of the tree you mark the payoffs that show what each person gets at the end of a particular history of play.

At this stage when you see the hostages game tree you might start wondering about how complete a representation this is. What will the militants do after the government pays the ransom? Will the government face more hostage takers in the future? These are great questions and extensions later in the book deal with both of them (reputation-forming gets discussed in §45; keep reading for what the hostage takers do). The main point for now is that you have to run with a game in order to solve it. Figure F might not fully describe some problem you have in mind but it still gives a complete representation of a simple game. Once you can figure out how to solve this simple game you can move on to more elaborate ones.

Extensive Form Games

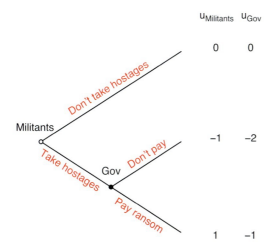

FIGURE F **THE HOSTAGES GAME IN EXTENSIVE FORM**

Games in extensive form like this are generally "solved" by starting at the final nodes of the tree, figuring out what will happen there, then pruning off all the branches that will not be pursued at the end; then moving to the new final set of nodes and figuring out what are the choices that will be made there (conditional on the other branches being pruned away) and continuing like that until you get to the beginning of the tree. This process is called "backward induction" and the set of actions that are identified using this approach are a subclass of Nash equilibriums called **subgame perfect Nash equilibriums**. The key feature of a subgame perfect equilibrium is that it is not just a Nash equilibrium of the overall game, it is also a Nash equilibrium of all the **subgames** that can be formed when you clip the tree at any node and treat the collection of branches following that node as its own game. As with the normal form, there can be many possible subgame perfect solutions even when you assume that people are optimizing, and there may be many more possibilities under different assumptions. In this case, though, the focus on backward induction (or, more generally "sequential reasoning") lets us rule out the noncredible equilibrium in which the government precommits to a strategy of not paying, no matter what the militants do.

If you go to the end of the hostages game (where the government gets to move), you can see that if the government gets there it will make a payment (preferring −1 to −2); then, moving up, you can see that the militants just have to compare the 0 from no taking of hostages to the 1 from taking hostages (given that the government will make a payment). So, if all are playing optimally, then there will be hostage taking even though the government would much rather have everyone believe that there will be no payment no matter what.

A second thing to worry about, that is still not captured in these games, is the information available to players. In the games above there is complete information, which means that everyone knows who else is playing, what they *can* do, and what they want (though they might not know of course what other people *will* do). But in real situations players might not know much about each other, what actions the other person took or how they value different outcomes. We need some way to represent this uncertainty and some solution concept that can make sense of it.

In practice, imperfect information of various kinds can be represented in a simple way. In general, uncertainty can be thought of as a player not knowing which node in a game tree she is at. Has the other side already started mobilizing for war? Has the magnate already backed the other candidate? Is the electorate forgiving or unforgiving? You represent this uncertainty by including all nodes over which there is uncertainty inside a dotted net or oval (or sometimes, if possible, by just connecting nodes over which there is uncertainty with a dotted line). Then players have to figure out what strategies to employ *given* their uncertainty.

Figure G illustrates the approach using a seemingly simple but really intriguing example—based on one given in Piccione and Rubinstein (1997)—in which there is only one player whose job is to figure out how to get home. He knows that he has to take the second left turn to get home ("left") but when he gets to a left turn he simply cannot remember whether he has already passed the first left or not. These turns look identical and he is a very forgetful type. It's worth spending some time with this problem. Assuming Jack is very smart, despite his failing memory, what strategy should he use to get home? Given his strategy, when he sees a left turn with what probability does he think it is the second turn? Does it make sense for him to follow his optimal strategy when he reaches a given intersection?

Often games are most interesting when some players know something that other players do not, such as whether the other player is honest or how they value different

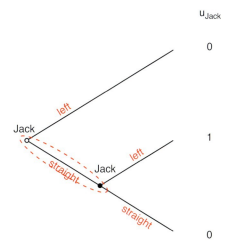

FIGURE G A MEMORYLESS MAN TRYING TO GET HOME
In this game there is only one player, Jack. Jack wants to take the second left to get home but the problem is that when he gets to a left turn he cannot remember whether or not he has already passed a turn. This uncertainty is represented by the dotted ellipse.

types of outcomes. This kind of game is called a game of *incomplete* information. I use the ◁ symbol to indicate when a game is of this type. Formally these games are represented as games in which "Nature" gets to make the first move, choosing the types of the different players. Everyone has a common expectation about what Nature *might* do, but only some people see what Nature in fact does. For example, people might have a common belief about how likely it is that a typical person is honest, but people only know for sure whether they themselves are honest. This simple analytic move makes it possible to study a huge range of otherwise complex problems including, for example, the possibility of player *unawareness* of the actions available to them, or uncertainty about who they are playing with (Meier and Schipper, 2014).

Figure H gives an example of this kind of game. The idea in this game is that the government is uncertain about whether the militants are hard-line or not. Perhaps if they are not hard-liners they will release the hostages even if the government refuses to pay? But if they are hard-liners and the government refuses to pay, it will have made a terrible mistake. This uncertainty is captured by Nature taking a first move to decide the militants' type. You treat Nature as if it chooses randomly. In this example I assume that Nature confronts the government with hard-line hostage takers with a 1 in 4 probability. Nature's move is observed by the militants (they know whether or not they are hard-line) but not by the government. The government cannot tell right away whether Nature has confronted it with a hard-line or soft-line set of hostage takers. The only difference between the hard-line and the soft-line militants is how they feel about not releasing a hostage when the government refuses to pay. The soft-liners would prefer to release the hostage anyway while the hard-line types prefer some more drastic action.

So what does a solution to this type of game look like? Will the government pay? Will the militants take hostages? Can the government learn anything about the militants based on the actions they take?

In these games the equilibriums have to specify not just what everyone *does*, but also what everyone *believes*. Just as the actions have to be optimal, the beliefs have to

Games of Incomplete Information

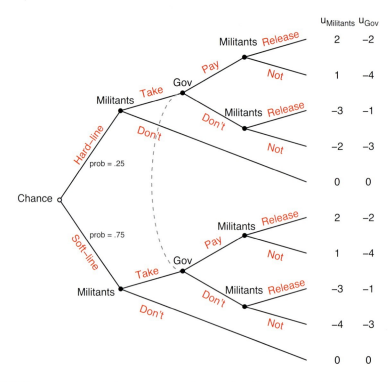

FIGURE H The government does not know whether the militants are hard-line or soft-line. If they are hard-line, they would be better off making a payment but if they are soft-line, the government could resist. What should it do? It starts out believing the militants are probably soft-line. But what should it infer when it sees the militants taking hostages?

be optimal in a well-defined way: they should conform with the dictates of **Bayes' rule** whenever that can be applied (see the glossary for more on this rule). This means, for example, that if **in equilibrium** a hard-liner does A and a soft-liner does B and I have a nonzero prior belief that I am up against a hard-liner, then when I see A I had better now believe that I am up against a hard-liner. Or, more tricky: if "in equilibrium" a hard-liner does A with probability q_H and a soft-liner does A with probability q_S and I have a prior belief of p that I am up against a hard-liner, then when I see A I had better now believe that I am up against a hard-liner with probability $\frac{q_H p}{q_H p + q_S (1-p)}$. This is the inference that one *ought* to draw if indeed people were playing according to the strategies specified by the equilibrium.

Back to the case at hand, one possible equilibrium is this: neither the hard-line nor soft-line militants take hostages. If in fact hostages *are* taken, the government puts this down to an error on the part of the militants and continues to believe that there is only a 1 in 4 chance that the rebels are hard-line. Since the government believes that the militants are probably soft-liners it makes no payments. Knowing this, neither the hard-line nor the soft-line rebels want to take hostages in the first place. In this equilibrium, the hard-line militants give up on hostage taking for the simple reason that they know that the government will not budge in its belief that they are probably a soft-liner group.

But there is another more intriguing equilibrium. Say when the government sees hostage taking they think there are even odds that the militants are hard-liners. Say it randomly decides whether to make the payments or not, choosing to pay with a 0.6 probability. Given these strategies, hard-line militants will always take hostages. But soft-line militants will be on the fence (can you see why?). Say that these on-the-fence soft-liners take hostages about a third of the time. Then, given these strategies, when the government sees no hostage taking, it knows for sure that the militants are soft-line; but if it sees hostage taking, then it has to figure out the probability that the militants are hard-liners. If the government is smart, then it should be able to figure out that the militants are hard-line with probability 1/2. You work out the probability the militant is hard-line given that they took hostages using **Bayes' rule**, but the key thing that is doing the work here is that you expect to face hard-line hostage takers with a one-quarter probability and you *also* expect to face soft-line hostage takers with a 1 in 4 probability (that is, $\frac{3}{4} \times \frac{1}{3}$). So, it's even odds, as we supposed above. Since they are even odds, the government is indifferent between paying (which gives it a reward of −2) or not (which gives a reward of −3 if the militants are hard-line and −1 if they are not), and for this reason is willing to play randomly.

In this example, soft-line militants sometimes successfully trick governments into thinking that they are likely to be hard-line; as a result they have a reasonable chance of getting payments, even though they would release the hostages if payments did not come through. The government gets tricked sometimes, but sometimes, it successfully calls the bluff of soft-line militants; sometimes, however, it mistakenly tries to call the bluff of hard-line militants with disastrous consequences.

In such games, bluff, trickery, and tragic error are all possible even with the most sophisticated of actors. Far from bloodless automatons choosing neat and **efficient** outcomes, the social actors studied in modern game theory can be both cunning and confused; they can plan meticulously but make the most tragic mistakes.

In summary, a very wide class of problems can be set up and solved as if they were games. Even still, not all formalizations of social problems focus on the strategic features that are so central to game theory. Some approaches seek to operate at a more abstract level, and sometimes at a normative level, trying to figure out what kinds of outcomes have desirable properties given the preferences of different actors or when different actors will have incentives to take different actions, whether or not you expect them to do so. Perhaps chief among these are what are called **social choice** problems. I describe some of the most important contributions to the study of social choice in Parts 3, 4, and 5. You will see these marked with the symbol that theorists use to indicate a preference relation: ≿.

Social Choice

GAME-THEORETIC REFLEXES

As you make your way through the various items in this book you will encounter a number of surprising logical twists. Things that seem obvious get called into question and things that seemed complicated suddenly appear simple. However, despite the huge variation in the type of insights across games there is an underlying set of approaches to thinking about strategic problems that are characteristic of game-theoretic reasoning. These are principles worth internalizing.

- **Backward reasoning.** You solve games by looking forward to the end of the **game tree** and reasoning backward, not by starting at the top and guessing at responses as you go down the tree.
- **Focus off the equilibrium path.** The equilibrium path is defined by what would happen if you stray off it. To understand what happened you have to understand what didn't happen.
- **Credibility.** Judge the plausibility of an action based on the incentives people have to take the action when it comes to making the decision and not based on their sincere desire to take the action ahead of time.

- **Optimization.** You need a reason for why individuals do not choose optimal actions. If people consistently choose badly, they should figure that out.
- **Efficiency 1.** You need a reason for why social interactions are inefficient. Why would people fail to make a deal when there is a deal to be made?
- **Efficiency 2.** You need a reason for why social interactions are efficient. Just because an outcome is good for everybody doesn't mean that everyone has an incentive to contribute to that outcome.

A GUIDE TO GRAPHS

Beyond the **payoff matrices** and **game trees** introduced already I will make heavy use of a small tight-knit family of graphs.

Scatterplots

The most basic graph is the *scatterplot*, which shows a set of points, with each point having a value on two dimensions. Look at any point and you can read off the values that that point takes on two dimensions. For example, if the horizontal dimension represents possible tax rates (ranging from 0 to 1) and the vertical dimension represents the hawkishness of foreign policy (also ranging from 0 to 1), then a single point (such as point "A" in Plot 1 of Figure I) describes a package, a bundle that consists of a specific tax rate and a specific stance on foreign policy. The set of feasible negotiation points in Figures 4 and 31 can be thought of as scatterplots similar to that in Plot 1.

Functions

Most of the other graphs can also be thought of as special types of scatterplots. Plot 2 in Figure I shows the graph of a *function*. Here rather than seeing a bunch of points you see a curve, though you can think of the curve as just a very large number of points sitting beside one another. The special feature about this graph is that there is one *and only one* point in the graph corresponding to every possible value on the horizontal axis. That means if I choose any point on the horizontal axis (such as 0.7), the graph will tell me what point of the vertical axis corresponds to that point (0.71, in this example). That gives me a mapping from one dimension to another. This mapping does not have to be nice and smooth like the one in this example and might sometimes look more like a collection of many line segments and not a simple curve. The only important condition is that there is one and only one point corresponding to every possible value on the horizontal axis. You can spot quickly if a curve represents a function by checking that it spans the entire horizontal range (with no doubling back), even if it does not span the vertical.

Graphs like this might be used, for example, to say what is the utility that a given person associates with each possible option on the horizontal axis. Note there is no guarantee that some point on the line will correspond to each possible value on the vertical axis, and it is also possible that multiple points have the same value on the vertical axis. With plots like these it is easy to pile up a number of lines, representing different mappings. One line, for example, might represent Jack's utility over options while another one represents Jill's utility. Figure 24 shows a plot that represents multiple functions at the same time. Figure 10 shows a special type of function, a density function, which shares the properties of other functions with the additional restrictions that the curves are always positive and the "mass" under the curves sums to one. This kind of function is used to show how probability is spread out over different possible outcomes.

Correspondences

The third plot shows a *correspondence*. This is also a kind of scatterplot but one in which there is at least one point on the vertical axis corresponding to every point on the horizontal axis. This is a lot like a function except that to be a function there should be only one point on the vertical axis corresponding to each point on the

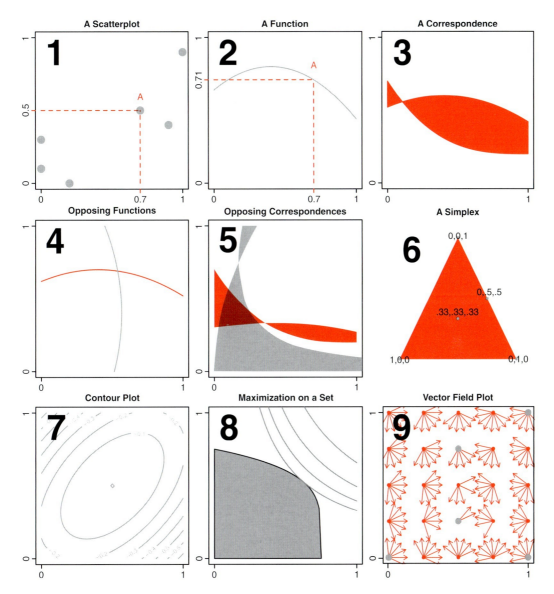

FIGURE I CRITICAL FIGURES
Nine standard types of figures used in this book.

horizontal axis.[5] The idea of a correspondence is more general than the idea of a function, so every function is a correspondence, but not vice versa. In game theory, correspondences are often used to represent best responses, since given any action by other people you can generally expect that there will be at least one, but possibly more than one, best response for any given person. That situation is represented by putting the actions of one person, say, on the horizontal, and then picking out all the possible responses by someone else on the vertical.

---

[5] Note that there are multiple definitions of a correspondence. The one used here is that it is a mapping from all points in a set X to all nonempty subsets of a set Y.

Double Functions/ Correspondences

Functions and correspondences are often shown as mappings from the horizontal to the vertical. You can graph functions from the vertical to the horizontal dimensions just as easily; you would do this if you had a situation where for every point on the vertical axis there was one (and only one) corresponding point on the horizontal. If you do this you are basically flipping the graph around and you will have curves that cover the entire vertical range but not necessarily the entire horizontal range. Sometimes it is useful to have graphs that show functions going in both directions—one that maps from the horizontal to the vertical and another that maps from the vertical to the horizontal. In such cases the intersections of these curves can sometimes have special importance. As an example see the curves on the fourth panel of Figure I. Here the red curve might represent the response you expect the "row player" (that is, the player whose actions are represented on the vertical) to give to any action by the "column player" (the player whose actions are represented on the horizontal). It is a function, which means in this case that you have exactly one prediction for the player's actions given the actions by the other player. The gray curve is the opposite—it shows the column player's reaction to any strategy by the row player. The point of intersection here is then a set of strategies such that the actions of each player at this point are their best responses to the actions taken at this point. Although this figure might not look like it, it is structurally the same as the payoff matrix in Figure C and the point of intersection of the lines picks out a Nash equilibrium in the same way as the star did in Figure C. The same idea holds (plot 5) if players have multiple best responses. In this case the intersection of correspondences can pick out multiple *sets* of Nash equilibriums. I use a plot of intersecting correspondences like this to identify equilibrium in the Second Price Sealed Bid auction (Figure 32).

Plots 1–5 all demonstrate ways of showing relations between two dimensions. The rest of the graphs in Figure I try to get beyond two dimensions in various ways.

Simplices

Plot 6 shows a *simplex,* which is used to plot points that have three values for the special case in which those three values all sum to 1 (or to some other constant). For example, if I want to think of all the ways of dividing $100 among Jack, Jill, and Jeff, each division will have three numbers (such as $50, $30, $20), but all divisions add up to $100. The constraint that divisions add up to a constant forces the set of admissible divisions to lie on a two-dimensional surface. In this case though the surface is best represented as a triangle, rather than points on a square or rectangle. The corners of the triangle represent the extreme points such as (0, 0, 1), (1, 0, 0) and (0, 1, 0), which in distribution problems represent the cases where everything is given to one person. Central points represent more equal divisions. I mark a few of these to give the idea.

Contour Plots

Plot 7 shows a *contour plot*, which is used to represent a relationship among three dimensions. The contour plot should be read much like a map in which the contours link together all points that have the same altitude. So, as with plot 2, plot 7 depicts a function, but this time it is a function that tells you what the value on some third dimension is given any values on the horizontal and vertical dimensions. You cannot actually see the third dimension in the graph because you are looking straight down at it, but the contour lines give a sense of how things are changing on that dimension. In this example, numbers are also added in for different lines to tell you exactly what the value on the third dimension is. Contour plots like this are sometimes used to show utility over two dimensions. For example, the point in the middle here—the top of the mountain—might represent the point of maximum utility given policy in two dimensions, and the contours how utility declines as you move away from that point. Figure 20 shows an alternative way of representing a function over two dimensions. This time, instead of contour lines showing elevation, circle sizes are used to indicate height. Figures 36 and 41 use contour plots like this to map out best-response functions in order to identify equilibriums.

Plot 8 does something similar but here I also mark off sets of the two-dimensional space that have particular properties. Here the gray space might be the set of two-dimensional options available to one person, or perhaps the set of one-dimensional payoffs available to two people. Often this set might be some kind of "feasible set"—a set of options over which a choice can be made. Contour lines superimposed on this same space can be used to represent preferences over the space and in particular over the feasible set. Here the key thing to look for is the point of tangency between the preference contours and the feasible sets; a point of tangency often has the interpretation of being the point on the feasible set that hits the highest possible contour. In a choice setting the point of tangency is the point you might expect to get chosen. I use this kind of graph in Figure 7 to illustrate how social choices are made given options available to a society and again in Figure 27 to illustrate bargaining outcomes.

Maximization on a Set

The last plot shows a way to map from two dimensions into the same two dimensions using *vector field plots*. Here you take a given point and use arrows to show what other point or points are associated with the point in question. You might think of the beginning of each arrow as representing a possible outcome today and the end of the arrow telling you the outcome tomorrow given where you started today. If there are many arrows, that means that there are many places you might end up tomorrow. In this book I use figures like these to identify stable points, where a stable point is a point that maps only into itself. If you were here today, you will be here tomorrow. This sort of figure is used in combination with a scatterplot in Figures 14–17 to show possible movements of policies given various ideal policy points. Figures 8 and 18 show vector field plots like this but where the vectors are defined over a simplex.

Vector Field Plots

READING GUIDE

There are probably good reasons that so many of the results from game-theoretic and related analyses of politics are so poorly known. Perhaps chief among these are the technical language, the Greek, the rampant jargon, and the sometimes excessive formalism.

I have tried here to keep the language jargon-free (and a glossary explains the most egregious hangers-on, including false friends like **efficient** or **expectation**). The simplification means some loss in precision and some loss in depth, but not all that much. For many of the results the endnotes provide more precision and more depth. A warning though about the language: the simple language sometimes masks treacherous turns of logic. I have added some signposts along the way to indicate when results are especially deep and when the logic behind them is especially tricky. If you see a it is a warning that a result or step is mathematically subtle or tough; if you see a that's an indicator that a result is particularly deep or general.

I often use figures to try to show the key steps and intuitions. Most interesting problems have many moving parts, however, and the graphs are static. I invite you to manipulate the graphs and see how they change as you change different features of the different models. All the figures are produced using relatively simple code in the free **R** language. You can simply download the code for the figures from my website www.macartan.nyc/hop and with small modifications you can create variations of any of the figures in this book. The endnotes provide some pointers to variations you might want to try.

Last, I provide puzzles for each item. These puzzles are meant to push you to think through implications of the logic (and sometimes limitations of the logic) and to help you check your intuitions. In some cases they could be answered in different ways depending on specifics of how models are set up and fleshed out. Use them as starting points for a conversation, not as problem sets.

Beyond the foreign language issues there is another problem. Game theorists seem to share an approach to thinking that outsiders find frustrating. They sweat over minutiae of models that anyone with a bit of distance knows to be obviously wrong from the get-go. The key thing here though is to know that theorists aren't in the business of being realistic: they are very deliberately trying to create simplified representations of aspects of the world in the hopes that these representations will be useful.

An analogy that is often used but is still very helpful is the idea of a model as a map. A city map, say, distorts reality in lots of ways. The scale is wrong, detail is missing, the colors are off. But if the map is useful, it is not despite the fact that it is wrong; it is *because* it is wrong. An accurate map of New York would be as large as New York and useful to nobody. It needs to be wrong. But it still matters how it is wrong. A subway map is wrong in different ways to a walking map but they are differently wrong in deliberate ways that make them useful for different purposes. People are often more reluctant to simplify the social world or to maintain hypotheticals about human behavior that they know not to be true. But here's the thing. To get anywhere with formal modeling you have to be prepared to swallow the *if*s. All the results are of the *if-then* variety. If you can't make believe, at least temporarily, that the *if*s are true, then you won't be able to see how *if* yields *then*. After you swallow the *if*s and see what they get you, you can step back and assess whether the exercise was worthwhile. So swallow the *if*s.

OUTLINE FOR SPECIFIC AREAS OF STUDY

All 49 games and results discussed in this book give novel angles and insights to help understand strategic thinking and political behavior. But I think some of them, for some areas of study, are *must*-knows. Here follows a listing of what I think are must-knows for scholars focused on different parts of politics.

COMPARATIVE AND AMERICAN POLITICS

Collective action: § 1, 2, 3, 4, 42. Students of comparative politics and American politics deal with collective action problems *all the time*, whether it is how to establish order, or how people organize into unions, clubs, rebel groups, parties, or coalitions. For this know the Prisoner's Dilemma, Assurance Dilemma, and Game of Chicken and be able to tell which game best matches different social problems. Know the solutions and challenges provided by the folk theorems and group structures.

Bargaining: § 18, 27-31. Policy deals, peace deals, and wage deals are all hammered out through negotiation. Must-knows on negotiation are Nash's solution to the bargaining problem and the solution from the alternating offers models. Know too the logic of legislative bargaining.

Voting: § 12, 13, 17-22. Know the properties of voting systems and how these affect outcomes. Know that weighted votes do not translate simply into voting power. Know the median voter theorem and key results on strategic voting.

Policy choice: § 12, 14, 15. Know the spatial model and the seminal results from Plott and McKelvey-Schofield, which suggest that in all democratic systems the status quo is always under pressure.

Political economy: §38-41. Know the canonical models of the politics of political accountabilty, redistributive taxation, distribution to swing voters, and the politics of maintaining core supporters.

Institutions: § 4, 19, 35-37, 39, 47. Game theorists think of institutions in two ways. One is as rules of the game. With this lens you should know how outcomes can change as the rules of the game change. Know the abstract results on what rules can produce particular outcomes and more applied results on institutional variation. A deeper notion of institutions—see Shepsle (2006)—thinks of institutions as being the equilibriums of underlying games—the behaviors that make rules rules. With this lens you can look to fundamental results (such as the folk theorems) to assess when the rules assumed in other games that presuppose strong institutional environments (such as in alternating offers bargaining) are **credible**.

Of particular importance to students of comparative politics:

Rebellion: § 22, 42-45, 47. Know the big arguments for when and why people participate in risky collective action. Be able also to distinguish between big social changes that are due to changes in information about others' beliefs (Information Cascades [§22]), about others' preferences (Threshold Models [§43]), or about others' actions (Stochastic Stability [§47]).

Of particular interest to students of American politics:

Lobbying and strategic communication: § 23, 24. Know the core models for when different branches of government are able to credibly convey policy positions.

Agenda setting: § 17, 18. Know when and why control of the agenda leads to control of outcomes.

INTERNATIONAL RELATIONS

Anarchy: § 1-5, 42. Realist scholars emphasize the difficulties of cooperation in anarchic systems. The problem of anarchy and the challenges of "security dilemmas" depend on the nature of the underlying conflicts. To understand the classes of basic conflict be sure to understand the Prisoner's Dilemma, Assurance Dilemma, and Game of Chicken and solutions to them.

Negotiation: § 23, 24, 27-30. Understanding negotiation, whether over security or over trade deals requires understanding bargaining and who gets what when opposing parties sit down to negotiate. Must-knows are Nash's solution to the bargaining problem as well as the solution from the alternating offers models. Students of international relations should also know the logic of the Schelling conjecture, which highlights the role of domestic politics in determining international agreements and when the logic of cheap talk and costly signals kicks in to get groups to conform. Know too the role of credible commitment and why states might be willing to have bargains fail in order to preserve their reputation for being tough.

Peace: § 4, 26, 30, 37. Maintaining peace requires reaching and enforcing agreements. Be sure to understand the logics of bargaining *failure* resulting from imperfect information, formalized in the Myerson-Satterthwaite theorem, as well as from the absence of commitment devices, which can lead to incentives to engage in preemptive strikes. You should also understand the folk theorems to understand when agreements can become sustainable even when there is no outside group to enforce them. Know too the agreement theorem on the difficulty of maintaining asymmetries of information once conflict starts.

POLITICAL PHILOSOPHY

Establishing social order: § 1–4. Hobbes, Rousseau, Hume, and others sought to understand the establishment of political order as a kind of escape from different types of fundamental social dilemmas. For the logic of the problems be sure to understand the Prisoner's Dilemma, Assurance Dilemma, and Game of Chicken, as well as the many solutions described by the folk theorems.

Justice: § 7, 9. As background for assessing accounts of justice that seek to determine what is socially right on the basis of the values and beliefs of different individuals be sure to know the Robbins critique and Arrow's theorem.

Democracy: § 10, 19, 20–22. For an argument on the epistemic virtues of democracy know the Condorcet jury theorem as well as the strategic challenges to it arising from strategic rationales against voting (the rational voter paradox and the swing voters curse) and against voting sincerely (the Gibbard-Satterthwaite theorem and the logic of information cascades).

Deliberation, truthfulness, and toleration: § 19, 25, 26, 35. Students of deliberation and toleration should know the results on the difficulties rational actors have engaging in deliberative decision making and of eliciting transparent communication in general, as well as results on the difficulty of maintaining differences of opinion when there is common understanding.

ACKNOWLEDGMENTS

This book was meant to be a weekend project, first inspired by a lovely little volume called *101 Things I Learned in Architecture School*. The idea was to sit down and pen a collection of single-sentence insights from formal political theory. For better or for worse, I soon found out that the insights from game theory require a bit more building up before they start making sense. So it has taken longer than planned. It has also taken a lot more consultation to figure out what it is exactly game theorists know that not everyone else knows. I have many people to thank. First, Bernd Beber and Neelanjan Sircar played a key role in the early stages of this book, helping draw up a first table of contents and thinking through approaches to presentation. I thank them especially for their quiet insistence that having **R** code included in the main text was not the key to making everything accessible to everyone. Neelan also developed the base code for the command `gt_bimatrix` used to generate all the payoff matrices in the book. Bernd developed beautifully elegant code to help calculate the Banzhaf power index [§13] as well as code for representing the transition matrices used to illustrate stochastic stability [§47]. A number of talented students read and commented on large chunks of the text, providing thoughts on applications and presentation, as well as spotting errors. Really big thanks to Tinghua Yu and Kunaal Sharma and especially Anna Wilke, who worked through every item and improved every figure. Amazing students in game theory classes and comparative politics classes helped me see new angles to the issues covered by the items; deepest thanks to them. Now more than ever I am conscious of the huge debt I owe to my own teachers who first exposed me to some of these ideas. Deep appreciation to Eddie Hyland who first introduced me to many of these ideas in the context of reflections on political philosophy; Mik Laver really got me invested and has been a constant inspiration ever since; Ken Shepsle and Bob Bates continued to expose me to new ideas and new ways of thinking. A good share of my takes on these results I inherited from them. Other colleagues have given suggestions and guidance along the way; big thanks especially to Antje Ellermann, Andy Gelman, David Hecht, John Huber, Alan Jacobs, Dan Posner, Dan Rubenson, and Dustin Tingley. I also owe a debt to Robert Carroll, Kevin Esterling, Jens Grosser, Indridi Indridason, Paul Johnson, Jenn Larson, Jesse Richman, Tyson Roberts, Branislav Slantchev, Mark Souva, and Robert Trager who sent terrific reflections on focus and pitch. Fair chunks of this book were written while I sat at the market behavior group of the WZB Berlin Social Science Center, and I benefited from input from the many smart theorists around me—thanks especially to Dorothea Kübler, Steffen Huck, and Justin Valasek. Ethan Bueno de Mesquita, Salvo Nunnari, and Peter Buisseret, all extremely sharp theorists, gave especially detailed and generous comments. Really big thanks to Thomas Leavitt who teamed up with Lorraine Glennon to give the full manuscript a close read and made sure I was always writing correct. One of the few nonexperts to read through the full thing (twice!) and give comments was my dad, Niall. Certainly there's no one like him. Kind comments from Eileen also, as ever. Many people to thank at Norton, a staff-owned publishing house where they are in it for the books. Roby Harrington first picked up the project and Lisa McKay ran with it. Ann Shin and Emily Stuart saw it through, providing wonderful guidance on text and style. Thanks for your thoughtfulness. Thanks for going for red. David Bradley led the copyediting: warm thanks for your patience and care. Last words for family. Aoife and Finbar, it's not for you now but if you pick it up in a couple of years and leaf though it, I hope you'll find something interesting here. Jacobia, thanks for so many games of chicken. My brothers Stephen and Ciarán have sharpened my thinking in innumerable ways over many years; this book is dedicated to you.

PART 1
DILEMMAS OF COLLECTIVE ACTION

A wide range of social situations are shaped by the strategic logic of just three canonical social dilemmas. Each of these dilemmas can be described in simplest form as a game in which two players face a choice regarding which of two actions to take. In each case, people can do collectively well or collectively badly, but in all cases, how they do depends in part on the different ways in which their happiness depends on the actions of others.

In the best known of the three, the Prisoner's Dilemma [§1], one person's action always helps another but at a private cost that makes it individually not worthwhile. Generally, you can expect everyone to end up in a bad place when playing this game. The other two games differ in the ways that cooperative strategies interact with each other. If they are "substitutes" as in the Game of Chicken [§2], then it might become a question of which player is the more effective free rider. If, however, strategies are "complements" as in the Assurance Dilemma [§3], cooperation becomes a kind of coordination problem, in which case people could end up in a good or bad place depending on how they expect other players will play.

You can be sure that you are playing some version of these three games every day. With your friends, with strangers on the street, with your colleagues, with your kids. Every time you make a deal, at every traffic intersection, in every project. After you master the logic of these three dilemmas you can start figuring out which ones you are playing when.

The two main concepts you need to understand to make sense of these games are the payoff matrix and the Nash equilibrium.

1 The Tragedy of the Commons (The Prisoner's Dilemma)

The United States and China account for about half of the world's greenhouse gas emissions. A switch to greener technologies, while costly for each, would bring benefits for both. So if both are better off reducing emissions, you might expect both to do so. But they don't. Why not?

One reason might be that the United States and China are stuck in what game theorists call a "Prisoner's Dilemma." Their pollution problem is strategically identical to the strategic problem faced by two prisoners who are separated and offered a deal of reduced sentences in return for giving evidence. Each would be better off giving information about the other ("defecting"), *no matter what the other does*. But still, compared with both giving evidence, both would be better off if they *both* cooperated with each other and kept their mouths shut.

Applied to the emissions problem, while they would be *jointly* better off polluting less, they might be *individually* better off continuing to pollute. And in trying to do the best they can for themselves they end up in a collective mess. As articulated by Senator Marco Rubio: "America is not a planet. And we are not even the largest carbon producer anymore, China is. . . . So the bottom line is, I am not in favor of any policies that make America a harder place for people to live."

A particularly depressing feature of Prisoner's Dilemmas is that communication between the prisoners will not help much. To see this, imagine that the United States made an overture to China: "China, things are getting out of hand, let's fix this mess. If we both go green, things will be a lot better for both of us." China agrees. But as she walks away she thinks to herself: It's really great that the United States is going to stop polluting; that alone makes things so much better. But given that the United States is stopping it's not so clear that it really makes sense for me to stop. As the United States walks away she starts reasoning in a similar way. She was quite enthusiastic about getting both of them to stop polluting, but when it comes down to it, the real benefits come from having gotten China to stop polluting. The next day everyone pollutes as much as ever.

The Prisoner's Dilemma is probably the best-known problem in the study of **games** of strategy. It's an extremely simple problem with wide resonance and deep implications. Applications might include the decisions to:

- *cheat on taxes*: I'd rather live in a world where everyone pays taxes, but if I can dodge undetected, should I?
- *disarm*: I wish there were no weapons in the world but can I really risk being defenseless?
- *place sheep on common land*: each addition by me means yours eat less, but my first priority is to grow my flock

The common feature of all these problems is that the cooperative action is akin to contributing to the production of what economists call a **public good**—a good whose benefits are shared by all whether or not they contribute to them. For all these problems, the key result is that the outcomes of individually rational action can be socially irrational. Simple as that sounds, it goes directly against what might be the single most influential idea of market economics in the last 200 years: an invisible hand ensures that the social good is well served by all individuals acting in their own interests. The Prisoner's Dilemma shows how that logic can break down in even the simplest settings.

Principle: In some games, if everyone chooses optimally, everyone does badly.

Puzzle: Might the players be able to solve their problem by reasoning that since the other side *reasons* similarly to them they will also *act* similarly to them? If a reasonable person cooperates, expecting the other to follow suit, as a reasonable person, aren't the two more reasonable than a pair that fails to cooperate? Isn't that reason enough to cooperate?

Reference: Hardin, G. (1968). The tragedy of the commons. *Science,* 162(3859), 1243–1248.

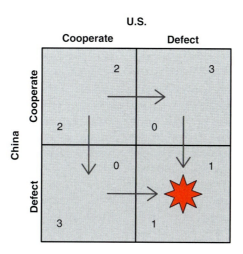

FIGURE 1 THE PRISONER'S DILEMMA
This figure uses a **payoff matrix** to illustrate the dilemma. The key feature needed to make this a Prisoner's Dilemma is that each person benefits a lot from the cooperation of the other but pays a net cost for her own cooperation. You should see this logic reflected in the payoff matrix. The arrows show the incentives different players have to change strategy, given any combination of strategies: thus the arrow from the top left to the top right cell indicates that the column (U.S.) player would do well shifting from cooperate to defect given that both players are cooperating. Comparing across cells you see that with these payoffs, each has an incentive to defect *no matter what the other person does*. All arrows point to the "all defect" outcome. The tragedy is that you end up with no one cooperating and getting a payoff of 1 even though all would be better off if all cooperated, in which case they would each get a payoff of 2. In this **game** the situation in which no one cooperates is a **Nash equilibrium** and is indicated by the star in the lower right cell of the matrix. See Appendix §A3 for more on the Nash equilibrium.

2 Strategic Substitution (The Game of Chicken)

There are massacres in the Central African Republic and France considers intervening. Calculations suggest that the cost of a light intervention is €20m but the value of the stability gains for French investors is €30m. Intervention makes sense it seems and so the Ministry of Defense argues for it. The Ministry of Finance is not so sure. Before deciding on intervening, France should think about what *others* might do. Perhaps the United States will intervene? If the United States intervenes, then that will bring stability but without putting the costs on France. So better for France not to intervene. The argument seems sound. But if it is sound, then perhaps the United States is thinking similarly? If the United States thinks that France will intervene, then the United States might *not* intervene, so then France had better intervene after all.

So who, if anyone, will intervene?

Here France and the United States are playing a Game of Chicken, strategically identical to the high-risk **game** in which two cars speed at each other hoping the other will swerve, or the version in *A Rebel without a Cause,* in which two cars race for a cliff and whoever jumps out first is the chicken. There are various possible outcomes to the Game of Chicken. If one expects that the other will swerve (intervene), then they should go straight (not intervene). In that case there will be one winner and one chicken and no one, not even the chicken, would want to change their strategies, given what the other person is doing.

There is also a more subtle and much more dangerous outcome in which people deliberately play randomly so no one can be sure what the other one is going to do. In game theory that's called a **mixed strategy** because rather than simply driving or swerving, you play a random mixture of the two. Say France sat back and said, "I am going to let fate decide. I will toss a coin and will intervene if it comes up heads." If the United States knows that that's what France is up to, the United States might not have a clear preference between intervening or not: if she intervenes, then there is a reasonable chance that it will have been for nothing and a reasonable chance that her intervention will have been critical; if she doesn't, there is a reasonable chance that she can free-ride on France, but also some chance of disaster. If France sets the probabilities just right, the United States might also be happy to play randomly, which in turn makes France willing to play randomly in the first place. That makes this pair of random strategies a symmetric but dicey **Nash equilibrium**. In this equilibrium, everyone is playing rationally but everyone is playing with death and there is a real chance of disaster.

The game captures some of the logic of high-stakes diplomacy: Who'll fund a bailout? Who'll accept refugees? This logic kicks in hard for environmental dilemmas—who will pollute up to the tipping point? What all these problems have in common is that strategies "substitute" for each other, like two hats: the benefits from taking some action decrease if the other player also takes that action. In the classic Game of Chicken there is no point in swerving if the other person is going to swerve; for **public goods** problems there is less reason to contribute if others are contributing. When games have this structure they can produce a surprising pattern that forms a key insight of political economy: when actions substitute for each other, the incentive to free-ride can make the risks of cooperation failure greater when more people care about the outcome.

Principle: If people's actions can substitute for each other, then collective action dilemmas can be about who gets to free-ride on whom. In these cases optimal individual action can lead to unpredictable but possibly catastrophic outcomes.

Puzzle: In the Prisoner's Dilemma [§1] the equilibrium depended only on the ordinal rankings of the payoffs, not the specific numbers in the **payoff matrix**. Do the specific numbers matter in this game? Does it matter how catastrophic the "all defect" outcome is?

Reference: Taylor, M., & Ward, H. (1982). Chickens, whales, and lumpy goods: Alternative models of public-goods provisions. *Political Studies, 30*(3), 350–370.

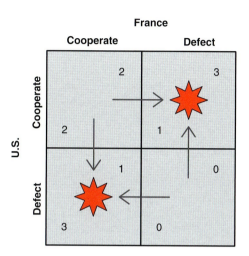

FIGURE 2 THE PAYOFF MATRIX FOR A CHICKEN GAME
This **payoff matrix** should be read the same way as the Prisoner's Dilemma matrix [§1] with numbers indicating payoffs, and arrows showing the incentive of each player to shift between cells. In this game, each player has an incentive to provide a public good (cooperate) if the other person is *not* doing so, but an incentive not to (defect) if the other is. These incentives produce two Nash equilibriums (marked with stars) in which one player cooperates and the other free-rides. While it is obvious what each person should do given what the other person is doing, it is not at all obvious what they *both* will do.

There is also a third less obvious ("mixed strategy") equilibrium in which players toss a coin and cooperate with a 50% probability; in this case if you expect the other person to cooperate with a 50% probability, you can calculate your ***expected*** **utility** from cooperating to be $.5 \times 2 + .5 \times 1 = 1.5$ and your expected utility from defecting to be $.5 \times 3 + .5 \times 0 = 1.5$. Since both give you the same expected payoff you too cannot do better than to toss a coin. In that case if everyone is cooperating with a 50% probability, no individual can do better by doing anything else; because of this, these random strategies form an equilibrium. Note that while in this case the probabilities work out to 50%, they need not in all cases: if, for example, the "all defect" outcome was much worse for everyone (say it is −8 rather than 0), then in the mixed strategy equilibrium everyone would put much more weight on cooperation (90%, rather than 50%).

3 | Strategic Complementarities (The Assurance Dilemma)

Organizers prepare for a demonstration to protest against their dictatorial government. They are wondering whether to include their most radical, violence-prone fringe. The government prepares its response. Should it bring in the army? The government reckons it will need the army if hardline protesters will be there, but no need otherwise. But will the protesters bring in the hard-liners? The government knows the protesters don't like bringing in the hard-liners; but it also knows the protesters will bring them if they think the government is going to use the army. What should each side do?

Here the protesters and the government are playing what's called the "Assurance Dilemma" or "stag hunt" **game**. In the classic account, two people set out to catch a stag. They take up positions on either side of a path and wait. As they wait one spots a hare in the brush behind him. He starts thinking. If I sneak off to catch that hare I won't go hungry tonight. But it does mean that the stag would get away. So I should probably stay. Then he starts thinking some more: What is my partner going to do? She is also hungry. If she sees a hare will she run after it? If she does, then I'll be left sitting here like a fool while the stag escapes. But surely she wouldn't do that to me. Then again she might if she thinks that I will run off after this hare. . . .

The stag hunt logic is simple enough—if you think your partner will stick to the plan, then you should too; if you think they won't, then you shouldn't either. So it depends on what you expect. So what should you expect? You should expect that the other person will try to get the stag if she expects that you will too. But if they expect you will quit for the hare, then they will quit too. So it all depends on what you expect they expect you expect. How frustrating.

Lots of problems have this structure. Should you go out and protest against human rights abuses by your government? Maybe not on your own, but perhaps if others will also. Should you race to move your savings out of your favorite bank? Perhaps if others are also going to abandon the bank, but otherwise maybe not. Should you trust people from other countries? Should you trust the police?

What all these problems have in common is that the strategies of different players "complement" each other, like a left sock complements a right sock. A given strategy for one player becomes more attractive if the other player is also using that strategy. If these complementarities are strong enough, then (unlike the Prisoner's Dilemma [§1]) these games have more than one plausible outcome. The multiplicity of **equilibriums** seen in this game and the Game of Chicken [§2] is actually very common in strategic situations and suggests that there are basic limitations on our ability to predict strategic behavior even in the simplest strategic environments.

Principle: If people's actions complement each other, then getting good outcomes depends not just on what people value but on how they expect each other to behave.

Puzzle: The equilibrium of the Prisoner's Dilemma is the same whether people play simultaneously or sequentially. How about with this game? If one player went first and the second followed, what outcome would you expect?

Reference: Sen, A. (1974). Choice, ordering and morality. In S. Körner (Ed.), *Practical Reason*. Oxford, UK: Blackwell.

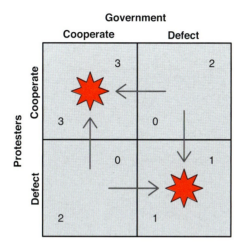

FIGURE 3 THE ASSURANCE DILEMMA GAME

This **payoff matrix** should be read the same way as the Prisoner's Dilemma matrix [§1]. The difference between this game and the Prisoner's Dilemma is that the "all cooperate" payoff and the "free-rider's payoff" are reversed. This has large strategic implications, however, and results in multiple possible equilibrium outcomes. The figure shows two possible equilibriums: in one, all players defect, as in the Prisoner's Dilemma; in the other, all cooperate. The latter is an equilibrium in this game since when all cooperate neither has an incentive to try to free-ride on the other.

Again, there is also a third less obvious (**mixed strategy**) equilibrium in which players toss a coin and cooperate with a 50% probability; in this case if you expect the other person to cooperate with a 50% probability, you can calculate your *expected* utility from cooperating to be $.5 \times 3 + .5 \times 0 = 1.5$ and your expected utility from defecting to be $.5 \times 2 + .5 \times 1 = 1.5$. Since both give you the same expected payoff you too cannot do better than to toss a coin. We then have that if everyone is cooperating with a 50% probability, no individual can do better by doing anything else; because of this, these random strategies form an equilibrium.

PART 2
SOLUTIONS TO SOCIAL DILEMMAS

Some social dilemmas end in tragedy, but some get solved. The most powerful solution is the embedding of "one-shot" dilemmas within a larger context of strategic interactions [§4, the Folk Theorems]: when people engage not just once but over and over they can use behavior in future play to affect the play of others today. In the long run, cooperation becomes possible, even if in single encounters it would not be. A similar logic holds even if people are short-lived but the societies they live in are long-lived [§5, Overlapping Generations]. A third solution solves the problem by suppressing it. The key idea is that even if in some material sense cooperating is costly for individuals, *evolutionarily*, people might be individually better off if they wrongly thought that cooperation was good for them (individually) [§6, the Evolution of Preferences]. Having the wrong preferences sometimes makes sense. A fourth solution dodges the dilemmas by leaving them to the market to solve. I discuss that solution much later (see §31, the Coase Theorem).

4 The Shadow of the Future (The Folk Theorems) ♏ ☉

Countries at war often respect the rights of their prisoners and sometimes even engage in prisoner swaps. Even though they are devoting resources to destroying each other, they still share a commonality of interest—both would prefer if both had their prisoners returned than if neither did. Their decision how to treat prisoners, or whether to swap them, itself creates a Prisoner's Dilemma [§1] (where the states are the prisoners in the dilemma). But how can they succeed in cooperating? Following the logic of the dilemma, why not always cheat and renege on promises to return prisoners?

One reason is that even when states are at war, they are in a *relationship*. The fact that they fight a lot means they expect to engage with each other many, many times over similar issues. This means they can condition behavior in one situation on behavior by others in past situations. There are different ways to do this. One approach is to use "tit-for-tat" strategies and do whatever the other person did last time. If the other state mistreated the prisoners last time, then you do so this time. The "shackling crisis," in which Britain and Germany mistreated each other's prisoners in response to each other's mistreatments may be an instance of this.

Will such strategies solve the problem?

Let's work through the logic. Say two players were to play a Prisoner's Dilemma **game** on Monday, Tuesday, and Wednesday and they agreed to cooperate every day with a threat of no future cooperation if either ever cheats. Though it sounds promising, this will only work if neither thinks too far ahead. The problem is that endgame behavior kicks in on Wednesday: on Wednesday, with no future keeping them disciplined, no one will cooperate. But then no matter what they do on Tuesday they know that no one will cooperate on Wednesday. So no point in cooperating on Tuesday. And clearly Monday cooperation is similarly pointless.

This type of unraveling always happens if strategic players only meet a *finite* number of times (at least for situations in which the single period game has a unique **equilibrium**). But things look a lot better if they meet up indefinitely. In that case there are no distinct endgame incentives: each day they compare the gains from free riding today coupled with failed cooperation forevermore, to the benefits of eternal cooperation. If they are sufficiently patient, then the latter is better than the former.

The "Folk Theorems" (of obscure origin) map out the set of equilibriums that can be achieved in this way. It turns out to be a huge set. For any repeated game *every payoff combination that is an average of the payoffs of the simple game and that gives each as much as they could get with no cooperation can be achieved* **in equilibrium**.

The key implication is that with indefinite interactions, cooperation can be achieved. This is perhaps the single most positive result in all of game theory. It is also an example of a beautifully *general* result since it applies to *any* **normal form game**, not just the Prisoner's Dilemma. But there is also a dark side to the Folk Theorems: with enough interaction, almost anything is possible. If cooperation is an equilibrium outcome, it is only one of many. Repeated interactions can result in the worst outcomes being repeated over and over and in equilibriums with all sorts of seemingly consensual exploitation.

Principle (The Folk Theorems): If people interact indefinitely—and are patient enough—then lots of outcomes become possible in equilibrium even when the single-period game has only one possible equilibrium outcome. Gains from future interactions can provide incentives to make people act well in *every* period. But if they only interact a finite number of times, people might not act well in *any* period.

Puzzle: If two countries can cooperate enough to respect each other's prisoners of war, why can't they cooperate enough to stop fighting altogether?

Reference: Fudenberg, D., & Maskin, E. (1986). The folk theorem in repeated games with discounting or with incomplete information. *Econometrica: Journal of the Econometric Society, 54*(3), 533–54.

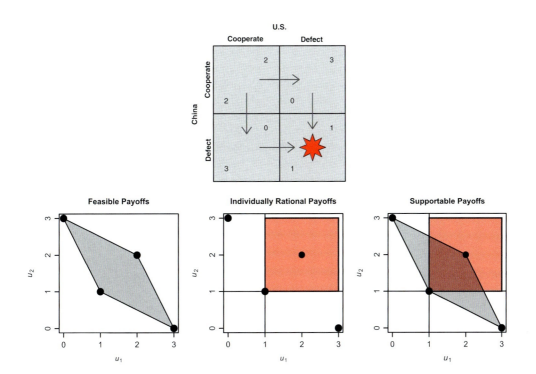

FIGURE 4 **THE FOLK THEOREMS**
The shaded diamond (lower left figure) shows the average payoffs that can be achieved through repeated play of the Prisoner's Dilemma [§1] shown at the top. These include all averages of payoffs from the original game such as "1 for China and 2.5 for the United States" (achievable by alternating between "all cooperate" and "the United States free-rides"). The colored square (lower center panel) shows the payoff outcomes that are "individually rational"—that is, the payoffs that people can guarantee themselves without trying to coordinate with others. Here, since by not cooperating each person can guarantee themselves a payoff of 1, no equilibrium that gives people less than 1 would be individually rational. The kite-shaped intersection of these gives the set of payoffs that can be supported as **Nash equilibriums** of the repeated game. This includes all cooperating all the time, which gives every player a payoff of 2 for all periods. But it also includes more exploitative outcomes. For example, there could be an equilibrium here in which players alternate between "cooperate-cooperate" and "cooperate-defect" in a way that guarantees one player an average payoff of 1 over time while the other player enjoys an average payoff of 2.5.

5 Playing with Your Progeny (Overlapping Generations)

When Samuel Doe took control of Liberia in 1980 he killed President Tolbert and then lined up Tolbert's cabinet on the beach and executed them by firing squad. Ten years later another aspiring president, Prince Yormie Johnson, captured Samuel Doe and began to torture him. Doe pleaded, "Yomi, two people fight, one win. Spare me, please." Johnson ignored the pleas and killed Doe, brutally. Could things have been different? Should you expect vicious leaders to eliminate their predecessors? Or might it sometimes make sense for an incoming dictator to treat an outgoing dictator well in the hopes of being treated well when his own time comes?

This kind of problem can be represented as a curious type of Prisoner's Dilemma [§1], one played by *sequences* of people over time. Imagine a string of dictators succeeding one another in office. Each outgoing dictator is a threat to the new dictator and so there are reasons to dispose of them. But clearly all dictators would be better off if they were all allowed to enjoy their retirement, than if they are executed as they exit office.

One might imagine the incoming dictator reasoning: "Why would I treat you well when you are a threat to me?" The outgoing dictator might respond: "If you dispose of me, you can only expect to have the same treatment yourself when you are older." But the argument seems uncompelling. Why would a future dictator punish the new dictator for an action taken against a past dictator that the future dictator does not care about?

Odd as it sounds though, it is possible to reach agreements in **games** of this form. The dictators could make use of the fact that a society of short-lived dictators can itself be long-lived. The outgoing dictator could argue: "You should treat me well even though I am a threat to you because if you don't, the next dictator will surely treat you badly, and then where would you be?" But, the incoming dictator might counter: "Why would I expect them to spare me?" "Aha," says the outgoing dictator: "They will want to do it because if they don't, then they will be treated badly by whomever replaces *them*." And so on.

The solution is surprising and it helps resolve concerns that achieving cooperation in the manner identified by the Folk Theorems [§4] depends on implausible assumptions of longevity. Although the outgoing dictator cannot threaten any future sanctioning by himself, cooperation can still be achieved through the threat of sanctioning by future generations of dictators.

This type of intergenerational calculation might be in operation for much more commonplace problems. The elderly, for example, can count on their pensions being paid out not necessarily because they can punish younger generations that try to rob them but because they know that if younger generations rob them, then the younger generations will not be able to expect to benefit from security when they are old.

Principle: Cooperation can be achieved by short-lived individuals if they are embedded in long-lived institutions.

Puzzle: Does a growing population make it easier or harder to maintain intergenerational cooperation?

Reference: Samuelson, P. A. (1958). An exact consumption-loan model of interest with or without the social contrivance of money. *Journal of Political Economy, 66*(6), 467–482.

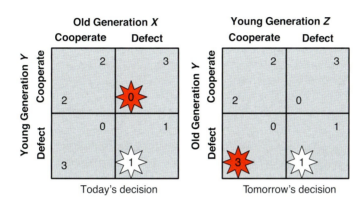

FIGURE 5 OVERLAPPING GENERATIONS
Here I show two rounds of a repeated Prisoner's Dilemma. What's unusual here though is that different people are playing in each round. Each person plays twice, once when they are "young" (against an "old" player) and once, later, when they are "old" (against a "young" player). I show a snapshot here of play that involves three players, generation X, generation Y, and generation Z. Clearly since each old player is at the end of their game there is no incentive for them to cooperate. This means that an all-cooperate **equilibrium** cannot be sustained. However, a *sometimes* cooperate equilibrium can be. In particular the following strategies form an equilibrium: cooperate when you are young (unless the person you are playing with did not cooperate when they were young) and defect when you are old. The key thing to check here is that if everyone is playing these strategies, it makes sense for young players to cooperate—even though the person they are playing with will not. Given these strategies, the choice the young player faces is one between everyone defecting both today and tomorrow (which yields 1 and 1, marked with white stars), and getting the sucker payoff today (0), and the free-rider's payoff tomorrow (3), marked with red stars. If you care enough about the future, then the red payoffs are a better deal. To give confidence that taking the risk makes sense, you just have to note that *if* every generation were going to behave in this way, *then* it would make sense for each generation to behave in this way.

6 | Playing with the Wrong Goals (The Evolution of Preferences) ⊞ ⊙

Successful leaders often exhort citizens to think beyond their own narrow self-interest. "Ask what you can do for your country," said Kennedy. Might players solve the Prisoner's Dilemma [§1] if they started valuing the good of the group rather than what's good for them individually?

That solution sounds a little naive. Even if people do better in the short run by playing with the "wrong" preferences (recall that the numbers in the Prisoner's Dilemma are *by definition* the right preferences), aren't they setting themselves up to be exploited? You sometimes hear that if firms don't focus on maximizing their profits, then they will not survive. Doesn't that kind of evolutionary logic apply more generally?

In fact that is a misapplication of evolutionary logic. In strategic environments, having the wrong preferences—valuing outcomes that do not increase your chances of surviving—can sometimes be a big help. The key insight is that in strategic environments—unlike simpler choice environments—your preferences affect your actions but also the actions that other people take. While making the wrong choices might make things worse for you, the responses by *others* to the possibility that you will make these choices may make things better for you. This basic idea is evident in the hostage-taking **game** discussed in the introduction. Consider a situation in which negotiating with hostage takers would be beneficial for a government but it falsely believes that this is not the case. Then the government's false belief might do it harm if hostages are taken, but its false belief will also ensure that it doesn't get into that position in the first place.

By similar logic, having the wrong preferences might help you solve the Prisoner's Dilemma. Say that according to some metric (such as profit, electoral viability, evolutionary fitness) you are better off defecting whether or not someone else cooperates, but you, and others, mistakenly believe that you are better off cooperating if someone else cooperates. Then if you play strategically you will reach the cooperative outcome when you play with people like you and you will do better than people who have the right preferences when they play against each other. Critically though, you won't be exposed to exploitation since when playing against someone with the correct preferences, you will correctly expect them to defect and you will also defect.

The surprising thing here is that having the wrong preferences is good because of strategic responses not because it pays to be naive. The benefits of having the wrong preferences extend to a very large class of games and it has been shown that generally nature selects for people who get it wrong.

Principle: If people are strategic, then nature selects for people who do not value outcomes that are best for their survival.

Puzzle: Does this result also mean it makes sense to select political representatives who do not have your interests at heart?

Reference: Heifetz, A., Shannon, C., & Spiegel, Y. (2007). What to maximize if you must. *Journal of Economic Theory, 133*(1), 31–57.

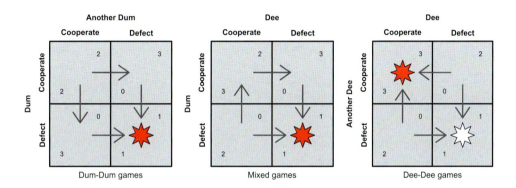

FIGURE 6 **THE EVOLUTION OF PREFERENCES**

Say a population of people is playing lots of Prisoner's Dilemma games together—in the sense of games that have material or "survival" payoffs like those in the Prisoner's Dilemma [§1]. Say though that half the players, the Dums, have preferences that are exactly in line with the material payoffs of the game while the other half place more value on cooperating when others cooperate. This half, the Dees, have preferences like those characteristic of an Assurance Dilemma [§3]. Then interactions look like one of the three games shown above. In Dum-Dum games the only **equilibrium** involves all defecting. The same holds for mixed games. But in Dee-Dee games there is an equilibrium in which all cooperate. If this equilibrium is played, then for any share of Dums and Dees in the population, Dees outperform Dums and, in evolutionary terms, will drive them out.

PART 3
WHAT GROUPS WANT

Behavior in social dilemmas tells us something about what groups will or should do. There is a related, though somewhat more philosophical, question of what groups *want*. Answering this question, or figuring out when it is answerable, has been the focus of *social choice theory*—a close cousin of game theory. There are two ways to think about the question. One is as a practical question about whether you can make any statements at all about what groups desire; the question here is not whether groups literally think as units but whether there is a way to make meaningful summaries about the desires of a group given the possibility of internal disagreements. The second is more normative: Is it possible to decide what is good for a society based on what individuals in the society value? You might be willing to make a judgment about what is good for society based on your religious beliefs, or based on principles following some fundamental values you cherish. But what if you were a "welfarist" and wanted to make that determination based on what the individuals in a group value? Would you be able to do it?

Historically there have been lots of answers to this question. Maybe simplest is the utilitarian answer: just figure out what outcome makes "most people most happy" (maximizes utility) and choose that. There have been various moral objections to that idea and obviously it's easier said than done. But it does seem to show that the question is answerable, at least in theory. A shock to this way of thinking was delivered by Lionel Robbins [§7], who argued that the calculations required were not just hard, they were meaningless. They rely on specific information about something—utility—that doesn't actually exist. Alternative strategies make use of weaker information on preferences, for example, just whether individuals prefer *A* to *B*. But a paradox attributed to the Marquis de Condorcet two hundred years ago [§8] suggests that this approach might also fail to give meaningful answers. The general problem was taken up by Kenneth Arrow in the mid-twentieth century. Arrow's seminal "possibility theorem" [§9] really challenges the idea that you can talk sensibly about what is good for groups, at least if you want to base your claims on the individual values of group members.

7 The Problem with Utilitarians (The Robbins Critique) ≿⊙

An idealized description of policy making is that policy makers choose the policies that are objectively best for their polity. But the most interesting political problems are about the more grubby question of who gets what. Distribution and redistribution. Protecting agriculture is good for farmers but bad for industry. Increasing estate taxes is bad for the very wealthy but good for everyone else. So given that different people benefit and lose from different options (and personal calculations to the side for the moment), how should you decide what is the right thing to do?

The classic answer is to commit to a set of moral principles and then figure out how the distributive outcomes of each policy rank given the principles. Utilitarians advocate maximizing the greatest happiness of the greatest number—just see how happy each outcome makes each person, convert the happinesses to numbers and add them up. Then choose the top scorer. Egalitarians want to maximize happiness provided all do equally well. Followers of John Rawls want whichever option would make the worst-off person as well-off as possible.

These all sound good and people apply logics like this all the time when they try to figure out moral conundrums or what sorts of policies are optimal. The problem is that they place too much meaning in numbers. The problem is not that you can't use numbers to represent happiness but that you start believing that those numbers mean the same thing for all people. We might both be able to rate our happiness on a scale of 1–10 but who is to say that when I say 7, I am happier than you when you say 6? Who's to say we are using the same metric? If you refuse to allow such "interpersonal comparisons of **utility**," however, then the utilitarian, egalitarian, and Rawlsian predictions become unintelligible—what you think society should do just comes down to how you weight the values of one person against those of another.

Principle (The Robbins Critique): If you don't have a way of comparing levels of happiness across people, then you shouldn't try to decide what is right based on classic principles like maximizing the happiness of the greatest number.

Puzzle: How about this solution: if there are *n* options, why not just let each person's preferred option be given the score *n* and the least preferred option the score of 1 and let every other option take scores in between based on the rank (ties allowed). Can you then meaningfully apply a utilitarian calculus to these numbers?

Reference: Robbins, L. (1938). Interpersonal comparisons of utility: A comment. *The Economic Journal, 48*(192), 635–641.

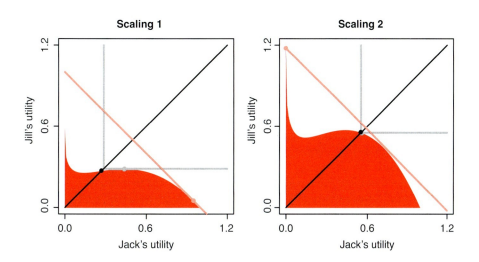

FIGURE 7 THE ROBBINS CRITIQUE
The shaded regions in the lower left of each panel show the set of potential utility ("welfare") outcomes for Jack and Jill that could be achieved through different policy choices "in some imaginary world." The shapes of the two regions are identical in the two panels, the only difference is the scale of Jill's payoff: in the second panel the scale is twice that of the first panel. The figure shows what options would be chosen by the utilitarians, egalitarians, and Rawlsians under the representation of preferences in each panel. The egalitarians would choose the highest point available on the upward-sloping 45-degree line; the utilitarians would choose the most outward point on a line like the downward-sloping line; the Rawlsians would choose the most outward point on an L-shaped line like the gray one. Each choice is marked for each scaling. The problem is that each scaling implies entirely different optimal policies. So without knowing which representation is correct you just can't know what these approaches recommend.

8 | Irrational Majorities (Condorcet's Paradox) ≿

In 1994 a Danish polling firm asked a thousand voters to say what they thought about three potential prime ministers. Among those answering, a majority of 51% preferred former foreign minister Uffe Ellemann-Jensen to the incumbent Poul Nyrup Rasmussen. A 51% majority in turn preferred former minister of justice Hans Engell to Ellemann-Jensen. You might think that this means that Hans Engell comes out ahead and the incumbent in the worst position, at least among this sample. Awkwardly though, the polls also found that a 53% majority preferred Rasmussen to Engell. What was going on?

The problem is that even if every voter has **rational preferences** (which implies that for each of them if they prefer x to y and y to z, then they also prefer x to z), this does not mean that they collectively have rational preferences—it is quite possible that they "majority prefer" x to y and they majority prefer y to z and also majority prefer z to x.

Condorcet made the point in 1785 with examples like this: imagine three friends have one $10 bill and one $5 bill to divide among them. Say they are considering the three alternative ways of dividing the money shown in the table below:

	Jack	Jill	Jeff
x	$10	$5	$0
y	$5	$0	$10
z	$0	$10	$5

Say they all prefer getting more money than less money. Then Jack and Jill both prefer division x to division y. And Jack and Jeff prefer y to z. So x is majority preferred to y, which is majority preferred to z. You might then expect that x would also be majority preferred to z, but in fact both Jill and Jeff prefer z to x. That's Condorcet's paradox.

The paradox shows the difficulty of making statements about group preferences but it also raises the prospect of some odd behavior by politicians. For example, with preferences like these you could find members of parliament might vote for policy z then replace it with y then replace that with x and then replace that with y, with all votes supported by majorities. Three votes later they are back where they started without anyone ever changing their positions.

Principle (Condorcet's Paradox): Majorities of groups are not like people. If a majority of a group prefers A to B and a majority prefers B to C, there is no reason to expect that a majority will prefer A to C.

Puzzle: Can you construct a version of the paradox with three options and four players?

Reference: Condorcet, M. J. A. N., Marquis de [1785] (1972). *Essai sur l'application de l'analyse à la probabilité des décisions rendues à la pluralité des voix.* New York, NY: Chelsea Publishing Co.

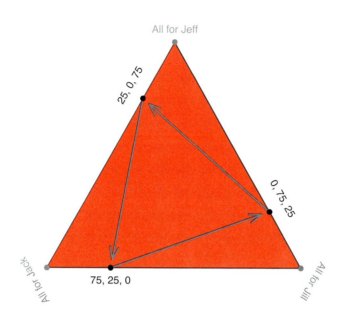

FIGURE 8 **A CONDORCET CYCLE**
The triangle in the figure represents *all* the possible ways of dividing $100 among Jack, Jill, and Jeff. This is a simplex like the one shown in panel 6 of Figure I in the introduction. The apexes award the whole amount to one person, so "All for Jeff" corresponds to a (0, 0, 100) split; the edges split it in different ways between two people, for example (0, 50, 50) or (20, 80, 0); the center point divides it equally among three (33⅓, 33⅓, 33⅓), and so on. Assume that everyone likes outcomes that give as much to them as possible. Then an allocation beats another allocation (under majority rule) if it is simultaneously closer to any two vertices of the triangle. Condorcet paradoxes arise constantly in "divide the dollar" problems like this; in the figure above you should be able to see that every allocation is beaten by some other allocation, which means that some Condorcet cycles exist (I have marked one with arrows).

9 There Is No General Will (Arrow's Theorem) ≳∅⊙

Political philosophers and elder statesmen are sometimes asked to advise on the drafting of a constitution. A constitution should reflect the collective values of a group, but, more fundamentally, it should outline the mechanisms through which those changing values can be elicited. Drafting a constitution can be a contentious affair, and historically these processes have sometimes been marred by violence (as happened with the race riots in Louisiana in 1866) and have ended in failure (as in Europe's failed attempt in 2005).

Say a constitutional convention sought in a disinterested way to generate procedures that can be used to determine the collective values of a people. Will it be able to do that?

Condorcet's Paradox [§8] showed that statements about the preferences of groups can sometimes be tricky, at least if **majority rule** is used to determine group preferences. So you might wonder what sort of method *can* be used to turn statements about the values of individuals into statements about the values of societies.

Kenneth Arrow worked on answering that question. He started looking for all possible methods that:

a. return "**rational**" results (unlike majority rule);

b. can handle any set of individual preferences;

c. determine society's preferences over pairs of options using only information on how individuals value those options;

d. are minimally representative in that if *everyone* values A over B, then the method reports that society values A over B, and;

e. reflect the values of more than just one person ("no dictator").

His "possibility theorem" says that there are no such methods. No matter how cunning you are you can't design a procedure that meets these goals. Every nondictatorial rule either sometimes produces intransitivities (violates *a*), has to exclude some sorts of preferences (violates *b*), assesses whether groups prefer A or B based on what people think about other things (violates *c*), or sometimes says that A is better than B even though everyone prefers B. The implication is that if you are brave enough to say you know what society wants, then you must be willing to drop one of Arrow's goals.

Principle (Arrow's Theorem): There is no method that can be used to reliably make claims about what groups want based on the diverse preferences of all the individuals in the group.

Puzzle: The rationality requirement in Arrow's theorem is that if society likes A at least as much as B and B at least as much as C, then it has to like A at least as much as C. Imagine the following weaker requirement: if society likes A more than B and B more than C, then it cannot like C more than A. Are there any rules that satisfy this plus requirements *b* through *e*?

Reference: Arrow, K. J. (1963). *Social choice and individual values.* New York, NY: John Wiley & Sons, Inc.

Group D	All Others		D (part 1)	D (part 2)	All Others
x	y		z	x	y
y	z		x	y	z
z	x		y	z	x
(i)			(ii)		

FIGURE 9 ARROW'S THEOREM

The key parts of the proof of Arrow's Theorem (tricky). I use the following notation: $x \geq y$ means society likes x at least as much as y; $x > y$ means society likes x more than y. The strategy is to show that a rule that satisfies goals *a* through *d* must be a dictatorship, in violation of goal *e*. I use the concept of a "decisive group" *D*—group *D* is decisive over x and y if the rule says society values x over y in situations in which all members of *D* value x over y even if everyone else values y over x. From condition *d* you know that such a group exists since society as a whole is such a group. The strategy now is to show that there is a decisive group with just one member—also known as a dictator.

There are two big steps:

Step 1: The left panel shows that if *D* is decisive over one pair, then it is decisive over all pairs. To see why, note that with these preferences (goal *b* says the rule has to be able to handle these as well as all other preferences) you have $y > z$ (from goal *d*), now suppose that *D* is decisive over x and y, then $x > y$ and so (from goal *a*) $x > z$—and so *D* is also decisive over x and z. That means that from here on out I can just talk about a group being decisive in general, rather than being decisive over particular pairs.

Step 2: The right panel then shows that if a group is decisive and has more than one member, then a subgroup of that group is decisive. Why? Say $z > y$, then "part 1" of *D* would be decisive. Say instead that $y \geq z$, then since $x > y$ (since *D* is decisive), it must be (from goal *a*) that $x > z$, which implies that "part 2" of *D* is decisive. The implication is that some parts of *D* are not critical to the decisiveness of *D*.

Repeatedly applying the logic of these two steps you can keep cutting *D* down until you have a decisive group of size 1—a dictator.

PART 4
MAJORITY RULE

Majority rule is one of the most cherished methods for determing what groups want. There are at least two distinct types of formal justifications for majority rule, as opposed to other types of democratic rules. The first, due to Condorcet [§10], points to *epistemic* benefits—that majority rule is especially good at aggregating information about the value of different policy choices. The second, due to May [§11], emphasizes the neutrality implicit in majoritarian decision making. Majority rule seems to imply a kind of procedural egalitarianism. The choices resulting from majority rule also seem egalitarian in some ways: in some conditions, described in the Median Voter Theorem [§12], majority rule produces "middling" outcomes.

But not all is well with majority rule. Power Indices [§13] shows that the egalitarian benefits might also be overstated at least in situations where the voting units are groups. In these situations the voting weights assigned to different blocks may say very little about the underlying contributions different groups make to decision making. In the later sections other results show why the selection of middling outcomes may not, in general, be guaranteed (see the Chaos Theorem [§15]) and why the epistemic benefits may be questionable (see the Swing Voter's Curse [§21] and Information Cascades [§22]).

10 | Majority Rule Aggregates Knowledge (Condorcet's Jury Theorem) ≳

Condorcet gave an early mathematical defense of majority rule. Say that everyone in a society was in fundamental agreement about outcomes but nobody was really sure what the right policy was to get those good outcomes. Then say in a choice between two alternatives each individual was more likely than not to know what the right policy was (for example, their probability of being right might be just 51%); then, assuming everyone votes based on their own belief about what is best, the option selected by majority rule is *much* more likely than not to be the right one. Moreover, as the size of the electorate grows, the probability that people will be collectively right will get close to 100%. The result is a direct application of the "law of large numbers"—the bigger the sample the closer the average of the sample is to the average of the population from which it is drawn.

Unfortunately, if everyone has a reasonable chance of being wrong, then *for the same reason*, pooling individual views will lead just as neatly to collectively terrible choices.

Principle (Condorcet's Jury Theorem): If people are fundamentally in agreement but err independently in their judgments, then with large electorates, the right option is likely to be selected under majority rule.

Puzzle: Is the logic of the jury theorem specific to simple majority rule or does it work just as well for supermajoritarian rules, such as rules that require two-thirds support to change a policy?

Reference: Condorcet, M. J. A. N., Marquis de [1785] (1972). *Essai sur l'application de l'analyse à la probabilité des décisions rendues à la pluralité des voix.* New York, NY: Chelsea Publishing Co.

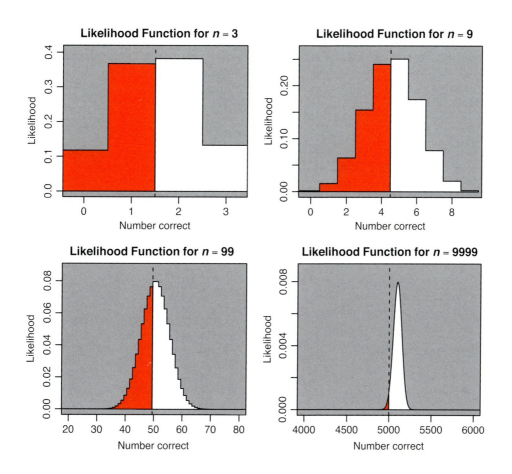

FIGURE 10 CONDORCET'S JURY THEOREM

The figures show the probability that a given number of people are "correct" for different population sizes given that each has a 0.51 probability of being correct. In all cases it is possible that only a minority are correct (colored areas in each graph), and with small numbers of voters this probability is about 50%. But the probability of getting it wrong shrinks rapidly as the number of voters goes up. In statistical terms this is an application of the "law of large numbers"—as the numbers go up, the distribution of the number of people getting it right gets tighter and tighter around the mean of 51%, with, eventually, almost no probability that less than a majority will be correct.

11 | What's Special about Simple Majority Rule? (May's Theorem) ≳

Under majority rule, narrow margins can lead to the adoption of decisions that are opposed by nearly as many people as support them. If the goal is for each person to live under rules that they created, majority rule fails royally. Aristotle said that majority rule is implied by a principle of numerical equality—treating all people equally. But that's not right. There are after all many other ways a group could choose between two options, or instead declare a tie. It might, for example, require that say 66% of members support an option before it is declared the winner. Or it might randomly choose one person to make the decision.

So: Is there anything special about majority rule?

Kenneth May argued that there is. Suppose a decision is to be made over A and B: some want A, some B, and some don't care. Say now you want some rule to be *decisive*—for any set of opinions, it should unambiguously determine whether to call for A, B, or a tie; *anonymous*—be sensitive to how many people support different positions, but not who they are; *neutral*—no particular outcome (neither A nor B) is privileged; and *monotonic*—if there is a tie or if A is winning and one person switches to A, then A will surely win again. Then according to May you have to like majority rule.

Majority rule certainly satisfies these four desiderata, but May's theorem says something stronger: *only* majority rule satisfies these four goals. If you value these goals, then you have no choice but to use majority rule.

Principle (May's Theorem): Simple majority rule is the only procedure for choosing between two outcomes that can determine a choice in a way that is positively responsive to preferences and that treats voters and options equally.

Puzzle: *Should* a decision rule treat all options equally?

Reference: May, K. (1952). A set of independent necessary and sufficient conditions for simple majority decision. *Econometrica: Journal of the Econometric Society, 20*(4), 680-684.

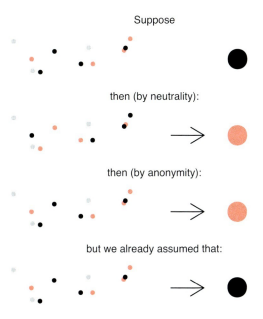

FIGURE 11 MAY'S THEOREM
Here the colored dots represent people supporting different options, with gray indicating indifference. The figure shows that a rule that satisfies May's properties must declare a tie whenever votes are split down the middle (not all rules do this!). Say instead that an equal number support one of two colors but one of them gets selected for the rule; then by neutrality the rule would have to choose the *other* color if you swapped the color labels; but then it would also have to choose that other color if you swapped the *player* labels, but this second swap gets us back to the original case in which the original color was selected. So to satisfy anonymity, neutrality, and decisiveness any rule has to call a tie when facing an even split. Adding the monotonicity requirement forces any admissible rule to be simple majority rule.

12 | Why the Middle Matters (The Median Voter Theorem)

Condorcet's Paradox [§8] gave some reasons to worry about the predictability of outcomes arising from majority rule. In some circumstances, however, the outcomes from majority rule decision making might be very predictable.

Say there are an odd number of voters and that available policy options are such that it is possible to put them into some order with the property that each person has some preferred ("ideal") outcome from all the options and the farther away you move from that ideal outcome the less happy the person is. Technically preferences like that are called "single-peaked." The assumption that preferences are single-peaked violates the second desideratum from Arrow's [§9] list. But it does seem reasonable in some circumstances. For example, it's hard to imagine a voter supporting universal health care coverage but still preferring no coverage to partial coverage (though it's not so hard to imagine someone thinking that a half-hearted military intervention is worse than a large-scale intervention and also worse than no intervention).

If voters have single-peaked preferences, then the option that is preferred by the "median voter"—the one whose preferred point is in the middle of the distribution of preferred points of all voters—is guaranteed to be the unique unbeatable option. The reason is simple enough: if the policy in place is to one side of the median, then the median plus all voters to the other side of the median would prefer a shift toward the median. These all collectively form a majority, by definition of the median. This logic implies that no policy but the median policy can be unbeatable. It's also obvious that the median policy itself is unbeatable since a shift in either direction would be opposed by the median and by all those on the opposite side, who collectively form a majority.

This means that when preferences are single-peaked, the median voter effectively controls the policy. That's why when political scientists hear about a vote of a committee, or of a panel of judges or a council, the first question is often: Who is the median voter? That it all comes down to the median voter does not, however, mean that others don't matter. They matter because it is the positions of others that make the median the median in the first place. If the median changes preferences and shifts far from her original position, she might soon find she is no longer the median and her control has vanished.

Principle (The Median Voter Theorem): If choices can be laid out on a line such that everyone prefers options closer to the option they like best (their "ideal point") to options farther away, then the option preferred by the median voter cannot be beaten by any other option under majority rule.

Puzzle: Say that each person had a unique *least* favorite point and preferred things farther away from that in any direction. Would there be an unbeatable point? What would it be?

Reference: Black, D. (1948). On the rationale of group decision-making. *Journal of Political Economy, 56*(1), 23–34.

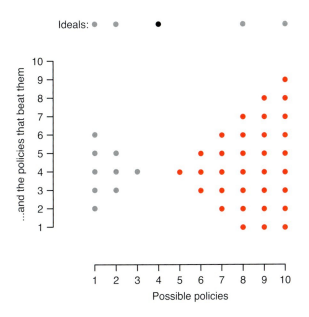

FIGURE 12 MEDIAN VOTER THEOREM

The top part of the figure shows a distribution of "ideal points" of five voters with respect to ten policies, with the median marked in black. Voters like their ideal best and like policies less and less the farther they are to the left or right of their ideal. The lower dots show, for each possible policy, the set of policies that are majority preferred to it. The gray dots correspond to rightward shifts in policy (from 1 to 2), the red dots to leftward shifts (from 6 to 5). Three important facts are implied by the pattern of dots. First, every policy, other than the policy preferred by the median, is beaten by the median policy (Policy 4). Second, the median policy is beaten by nothing. Third, nonmedian policies are often beaten by many policies, including policies on either side of the median. The bow-tie shape illustrates variation in the scope of policy volatility: the farther from the median the *status quo* starts out, the farther from the median, on the opposite side, it may end up.

13 | Voting Weight and Political Influence (Power Indices) ≳

In 1990 the German Party of Democratic Socialism (PDS), the rump of the former communist party, won 17 of 662 seats. Just 2.6%. But still there were lots of ways in which that 2.6% might—in principle at least—be put to good use. For example, if the social democrats and the liberals tried to form a coalition, they would have had 48% between them; the PDS could have taken them to a majority. In fact the liberals went with the conservatives to form a center right government. The PDS might have felt it was in a stronger position in 1994, when it nearly doubled its seat share to 4.5%. This time though its votes were *entirely* useless—there was no collection of parties that would have needed the PDS in order to form a majority. In a word, the PDS had votes but seemed to have no voting power. So it continued for the PDS; in the 1998 election they rose to hold 5.4% of seats. But they were still strategically irrelevant. Forget their policy positions; they just didn't have the numbers to be pivotal players in coalitional politics.

The problem isn't being small. Small parties are often pivotal. The problem has to do with the specific sizes of all the other parties. That's what determines whether you have power or not.

Is it possible to calculate power given information on voting weights? One approach was suggested by John Banzhaf. Banzhaf defined power in terms of the share of times that a person is pivotal across winning coalitions. Note that this notion does not use any information about what way a person is likely to vote on any given issue. For example, if there are four parties with seat shares of 48, 48, 3, 1, and simple **majority rule**, you can see that the smallest party is never going to be pivotal (any winning coalition that they are in is also winning without them), but the second smallest party is just as likely to be pivotal as the two biggest ones. By the numbers, 48 here is no better than 3.

Another approach, due to Lloyd Shapley and Martin Shubik, thinks in terms of random orderings of players and asks what is the probability of being pivotal to the outcome (in the sense of being the player that gets the coalition over a voting threshold) across orderings. Note that given any random ordering of players only one person will be pivotal.

A third approach tries to identify the *minimal integer weights* that represent the possible decisive coalitions. This approach, for example, would code a case with weights 48, 48, 3, 1, and 51 votes needed for a decision as strategically equivalent to one with weights 1, 1, 1, and 0 with 2 votes needed.

These different approaches sometimes produce different results. For example, imagine three groups: group 1 has 1 vote, group 2 has 2 votes, and group 3 has 3 votes. Assume simple majority rule. The winning coalitions are (1, 3), (2, 3), (1, 2, 3). Voter 1 is pivotal in the first one only, 2 in the second one only, and 3 in all three. So the Banzhaf power has to be proportionate to 1, 1, 3 and we get 20%, 20%, and 60%, respectively. In contrast, the possible *ordered* coalitions are 123, 132, 213, 231, 312, 321. Party 1 is pivotal in the fifth one, 2 is pivotal in the sixth one, and 3 is pivotal in the first four. So the Shapley-Shubik power index has to be proportionate to 1, 1, 4 yielding 17%, 17%, and 67%, respectively. The minimal integer weight representation is 1, 1, 2 with 3 votes needed, which suggests relative importance of 25%, 25%, and 50%, respectively.

Under all approaches, how size matters depends not just on the sizes of other parties but also on the particular voting rules that are used, which can make the decision to support or oppose a particular constitutional provision a calculated affair. It is possible, for example, that a small party punches well below its weight under majority rule but well above its weight under supermajority rule.

Principle: The number of votes you hold can be a poor indicator of your influence on voting outcomes.

Puzzle: Is it possible for a smaller party to have greater voting power than a larger party?

Reference: Banzhaf, J., III (1964). Weighted voting doesn't work: A mathematical analysis. *Rutgers Law Review,* (19), 317.

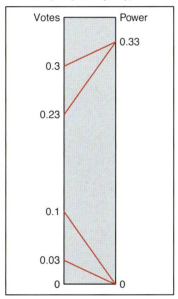 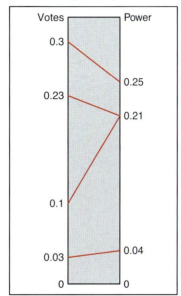

FIGURE 13 POWER INDICES
The voting power, as calculated according to the Banzhaf index, for six towns in Nassau county with voting weights of 1, 1, 3, 7, 9, and 9. In this example under simple majority rule the three smallest towns have zero power while the others do well. But under a two-thirds rule the smallest ones punch above their weights and the bigger ones punch below theirs.

PART 5

THE INSTABILITY OF MAJORITY RULE

Majority rule might have some nice properties, but it turns out that the paradox that Condorcet discovered in the late eighteenth century, far from being a curiosity, appears to be a generic problem facing majority decision making.

The Condorcet and Arrow results suggest that majority rule procedures cannot *guarantee* that you can talk sensibly about group preferences; but they say nothing about how often you end up making meaningless statements. Perhaps the problems only arise when people have unusually irreconcilable preferences. If people have "reasonable" preferences, can you reasonably make statements about group preferences? Plott's Theorem [§14] gives a negative answer to that question: if you use majority rule to determine whether a group prefers this to that, then *in any minimally complex environment you can be certain that there will be no outcome that all majorities think is best*.

The so-called Chaos Theorem [§15] pushes things one step further and shows that generally the intransitivities that Condorcet found to be merely possible are actually what you should be expecting all the time. Moreover *all* options get caught up in cycles of this form, not just a small number of otherwise desirable policies.

Perhaps it would help to have "stickier" rules like supermajority rules? Nakamura's Theorem [§16] gives a negative answer to that question and says that the sorts of rules people use in democracies to make things stickier aren't going to solve the problem unless they really involve giving some people veto power. Other findings go even further than this and say that every rule (that doesn't have veto players) is guaranteed to produce cycles in sufficiently complex policy environments.

14 | You Can't Satisfy All the Majorities Any of the Time (Plott's Theorem) ≳ ⋔ ⊙

A **game** for two players: Throw three gray stones onto a table. Now let Player 1 place a black stone anywhere. Then let Player 2 place a red stone down. Player 2 wins if the red stone is closer to any *two* (or more) of the three gray stones than the black stone.

If you try it a couple of times you will find that Player 2 always wins. No matter where Player 1 places his stone Player 2 can do better (some examples below).

That is bad for Player 1 but it also has drastic implications for democracy. Think of every point on the table as a package of policies (say tax policy is one dimension and foreign policy is another). And think of the three gray stones as representing the preferred policies of each of three voters. Say that voters like policies more the closer they are to their preferred policy. Then the fact that Player 1 never wins means that no matter what policy is on the table, there will be some *other* policy that some majority would prefer.

This holds for any number of dimensions (above 1) and any number of players (except 1, 2, and, surprisingly, 4 for the case with two dimensions). The result suggests a fundamental uneasiness at the heart of democracy. No matter what policy a government implements, a rival should always be able to find some alternative that a majority thinks is better.

Principle (Plott's Theorem): For any minimally complex set of policies, no matter what you choose, *some* majority is going to prefer something else.

Puzzle: How about if, against all odds, you threw the stones so that they landed in a perfect straight line? How about if they landed *almost* perfectly in a straight line?

Reference: Plott, C. R. (1967). A notion of equilibrium and its possibility under majority rule. *The American Economic Review, 57*(4), 787–806.

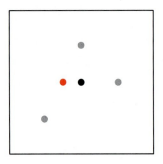 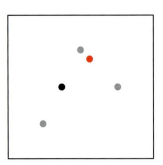 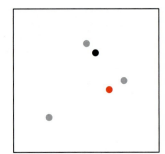

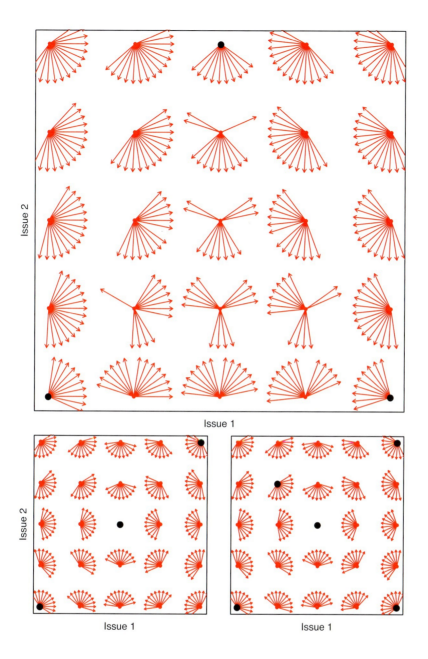

FIGURE 14 PLOTT'S THEOREM

The figure shows a "vector field plot" illustrating the sorts of policies that beat other policies. The rays emanating from the points show the directions of movement that would be majority preferred to the point of origin. Our interest is in finding points for which there are no such rays. In the first panel you see that every policy can be beaten by (generally many) different policies—that is, every point you look at has some set of rays emanating from it. There are some configurations of preferences that yield some unbeatable points, but they require extremely demanding conditions. The lower left panel shows that if your three stones landed in exactly a straight line, then it would be like being in a one-dimensional space in which case the "median" outcome would be selected (see the discussion of the Median Voter Theorem [§12]). Note that the very central point in the figure has no rays emanating from it. Other highly symmetric configurations also do the trick, such as the collection of five points arranged in radial symmetry in the lower right panel. But the problem returns with even the slightest deviation from these special configurations.

PART 5 | The Instability of Majority Rule

15 | Naive Majorities Are Capable of Anything (The McKelvey-Schofield Chaos Theorem) ≳

Plott's theorem suggested that majorities will generally have trouble reaching agreement. So you might be resigned to the idea that some amount of indecisiveness (or "cycling") is unavoidable in a democracy. Maybe not being able to identify a "best" option is not so bad as long as majority rule at least helps keep people away from indisputably bad outcomes. This line of thinking led researchers to try to figure out what the "top cycle set" looks like—is there a set of policies that might cycle with one another but that can still be separated from other worse policies that lie outside the cycle set?

But here comes more bad news. An extraordinary result due to Richard McKelvey and Norman Schofield tells us that not only is there (almost) never an "unbeatable" policy under majority rule, but that given any two policies (a and z) it is almost always possible to construct chains of policies (a, b, c, . . . , z) such that a majority prefers a to b, b to c, and so on, all the way to z. In other words, the top cycle set of options is the whole set of options. An implication is that if voters are myopic and just vote their preferences, a cunning agenda setter can always bring them to support her preferred outcome.

Principle (The McKelvey-Schofield Chaos Theorem): If there is no policy that is unbeatable under majority rule (which generally there is not), then majority preferences can cycle over *every* possible option.

Puzzle: Say that policy changes have to be "continuous" in the sense that a point can only be beaten by a point very, very close to it—hopping back and forward over the space is not allowed. Then is it possible to find a continuous path between any two points such that each small step on the path receives majority support?

Reference: McKelvey, R. D. (1976). Intransitivities in multidimensional voting models and some implications for agenda control. *Journal of Economic Theory, 12*(3), 472–482.

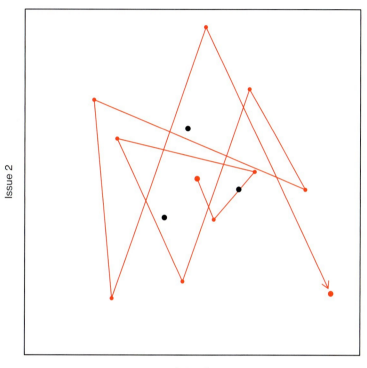

FIGURE 15 THE MCKELVEY-SCHOFIELD CHAOS THEOREM
This figure shows a sequence of motions, each supported by at least two out of three people on a committee. The set of steps takes the committee from some point that they all like to something very far away from their ideals. Convince yourself that each individual step (red circles) takes the policy to a point that is closer to the ideals of at least two voters (black circles).

16 | How Sticky Are Sticky Rules? (Nakamura's Theorem) ≿⊙

Groups often try to endow decisions with some stability by requiring that any changes have the support of a supermajority rather than a simple majority. Thus to keep some semblance of respectability on papal rivalries, the Third Lateran Council started using a two-thirds rule in 1179. In some places, for laws to get passed they have to get accepted by majorities in multiple separate houses of parliament and perhaps by parliaments and assemblies in other houses also. This sort of decision rule clearly stops some things beating other things. But is it enough to make sure that some things cannot be beaten by anything?

Surprisingly not. Supermajorities only stop cycling if the required supermajority is really *everybody*—absolute consensus. If absolute consensus is required, then everyone is a "veto player" and any veto player would stop cycles if policy ever ended up at their ideal point. If something less than consensus is required, then there may be unbeatable points in simple environments where only a few options are under consideration. But with sufficient policy complexity, there can be no unbeatable points. More generally, Kenjiro Nakamura shows that unless the rule is a unanimity rule, or some other rule with veto players, and if there are enough options (for example, if there are more options than players), then you can never guarantee that there will be unbeatable points. Later work has shown that things are actually even more chaotic than this: unless you have veto players, then it doesn't matter what your rule is; policy complexity alone is enough to guarantee that there will never be unbeatable options.

Principle (Nakamura's Theorem): Complex rules to make sure that complex outcomes can't be beaten by other complex outcomes only work if they provide some people with veto power.

Puzzle: In a "unicameral" system you need support from only one house to pass a bill. However, with a two-dimensional policy there is no guarantee that there will be a stable outcome in a unicameral system. Consider now a "bicameral" system in which a bill has to get majorities in two separate houses in order to pass. Should you expect there to be a stable outcome in a bicameral system in two dimensions?

Reference: Nakamura, K. (1979). The vetoers in a simple game with ordinal preferences. *International Journal of Game Theory, 8*(1), 55–61.

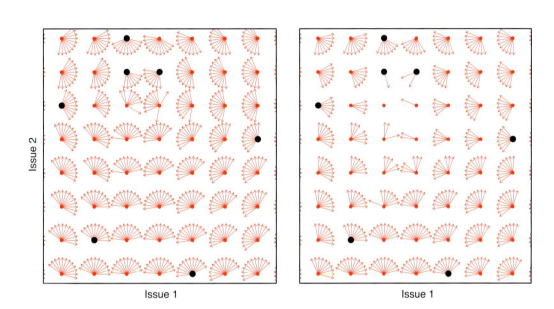

FIGURE 16 **VECTOR FIELD PLOT FOR SUPERMAJORITY RULES**

This figure can be read in the same way as Figure 14: for a selection of points the rays show the directions of movement that would be supported by all members of a winning coalition. The left figure shows movements that are possible under a 4/7 rule; the right plot under a 5/7 rule.

You can see that with the 4/7 rule there are no stable points (red arrows go out from every point on the grid in the left panel). But there are unbeatable points with a 5/7 requirement (see the top left blank space in the right panel, indicating a point from which there are no arrows emanating).

However, 5/7 or even 6/7 may not be enough with more dimensions. To see why, imagine dividing $1 among seven voters. You can quickly see that for this six-dimensional problem no division is unbeatable even under a 6/7 rule: to see why, consider any division and then note that it can be beaten by one in which one player's share from the original division gets divided among the rest.

PART 6
MANIPULATION

The social inconsistencies that arise when individuals disagree open the door for manipulation. The same logic that makes it impossible to identify socially optimal outcomes also makes it possible to exploit groups by playing subgroups against each other. From the chaos theorems you can see that if people are very unsophisticated, then you could construct agendas that would get majorities to support any outcome you like by simply walking them through the right sequence of choices.

Agenda Manipulation [§17] shows that sophistication does not protect voters from this kind of exploitation. A cunning agenda setter is able to set up a sequence of votes that will take majorities from any starting point to any point the agenda setter likes even though the voters can see exactly what he is up to. The scope for manipulation among strategic players also plays out when groups bargain with each other: Legislative Bargaining [§18] shows that the ability to propose deals can nullify any constitutional advantages that are given to groups by the careful choice of voting system.

The scope for manipulation extends to a much larger class of decision-making procedures. A remarkable theorem due to Gibbard and Satterthwaite [§19] shows that almost every decision rule is "manipulable" in the sense that sometimes a player can get the group to choose outcomes that she prefers by lying about what she really wants. (The problem of figuring out more generally when you can or cannot set rules so that people choose good outcomes is the subject of Part 11, Institutional Design.)

17 | Sophisticated Majorities Might Also Do Anything (Agenda Manipulation)

The king has died and left his kingdom to be divided among three greedy princes. The princes can divide it in three even parts or they can vote on any alternative proposals put forward by the king's brother.

The king's brother has been left with nothing but starts wondering whether he could get these princes to vote to give him the lion's share of the kingdom. The problem of course is that these are greedy princes, the decision is up to them, and, worse, they are not easily duped. Even still, he pulls it off. How does he do it?

In his plotting, he realizes that he can make use of the chaos result [§15], which says that for any reasonably loved policy, x_1 (here, an even split among the princes), and clearly terrible policy, x_n (here with nearly everything going to the king's brother), you can find policies in between $(x_2, x_3, \ldots)$ such that a majority prefers x_2 to x_1, a possibly different majority prefers x_3 to x_2 and so on all the way to x_n. That sounds promising.

Armed with this result, the brother gathers the princes and suggests a sequence of votes to decide on how to divide the kingdom: "Let's pit x_n (97% to me and 1% to each of you) against x_1 (a third to each of you)," he says. "I know no one likes my proposal much but let's try anyway; if x_n doesn't win, then let's pit x_{n-1} against x_1, if that fails, let's try x_{n-2}, and so on."

Reasoning backward (which is the strategic thing to do—see Zermelo's Theorem [§A1]), the princes figure that if it came to a vote between x_2 and x_1, then x_2 would win. But that means that if it came to a vote between x_3 and x_1, voters know that if x_3 loses they will end up with x_2, so they vote x_3. But then if it came to a vote between x_4 and x_1 they should go for x_4, which is better than x_3 for some majority and so on so that in the very first vote x_1 loses to x_n. The brother gets the kingdom. Which they all hate.

More generally: the set of outcomes that result from sophisticated voting is the same as the set of outcomes that cycle with one another.

Principle: If there is no unbeatable policy option, then it is possible to construct an agenda so that even very sophisticated voters will vote to support any outcome you like straight away.

Puzzle: See Figure 17.

Reference: Austen-Smith, D., & Banks, J. (2005). *Positive political theory II: Strategy and structure* (Vol. 2). Ann Arbor, MI: University of Michigan Press.

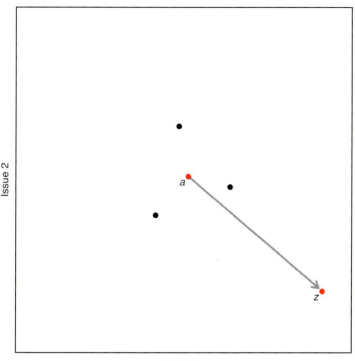

FIGURE 17 AGENDA MANIPULATION

The three dots represent the ideal policies of three players over issues 1 and 2. Say the *status quo* policy is at point *a*, that voters all prefer options closer to their ideal options than options farther away, and that voters are very strategic. Then can you construct an agenda such that in the very first vote a majority opts for option *z* over of *a*?

18 | Power from Proposing Proposers (Legislative Bargaining)

Another king has died and left his kingdom to be divided among three princesses. They can divide it whatever way they choose. Learning the lesson from the foolish king in §17 (Agenda Manipulation) this king does not leave his brother control over the decision making.

The princesses decide to proceed as follows. Consider some proposal. If a majority agrees, implement it. If not, then consider some alternative. This is the basic structure of legislative bargaining.

The princesses are in no rush and happy to carry on in this way until they reach a decision. The plan is simple but disaster soon strikes: they all shout out different proposals at the same time and no one can figure anything out. So they figure they need a way to decide who should make proposals.

They turn to the king's brother and ask him to randomly select one of them to make a proposal each time a proposal fails. He cannot make any proposals himself and he cannot vote, of course. How will the kingdom be divided?

It depends entirely on the likelihood with which the brother will favor any of the three would-be proposers.

If the brother were to choose each one of the three with an equal probability each time, then they should all expect to get the same share of the kingdom. This could be achieved, for example, if whenever anyone gets selected, they propose keeping 2/3 for themselves and randomly choose one of the other two to receive 1/3. If everyone does that, then (assuming patient princesses) it makes sense to accept the offer of 1/3 since that's exactly what you would expect to get if you said no and waited until the next round (more precisely, if you said no then, with a 1/3 probability, you would not get offered anything next time, with a 1/3 probability you would be offered 1/3 again, and with a 1/3 probability you would be the offerer and get to keep 2/3, which all adds up to 1/3).

However, if the uncle were to have favorites and call on some more often than others to make proposals then, *even though they all have the same voting strength*, they can expect very different shares of the pie. For example, say the uncle selects Princess *A* with a 2/3 probability to make offers and chooses the others with a 1/6 probability each. Then *A* could expect to get 50% of the kingdom and the others 25% each. This is achieved by *A* offering 25% to one sister while the sisters offer 25% to each other but nothing ever to *A*. In that case *A*'s expected value is $\frac{2}{3} \times \frac{3}{4} = \frac{1}{2}$ while the others expect $\frac{2}{3}\frac{1}{2}\frac{1}{4} + \frac{1}{6}\frac{1}{4} + \frac{1}{6}\frac{3}{4} = \frac{1}{4}$.

Tasos Kalandrakis showed that the scope to use proposal power in this way is enormous. If you can decide the probability with which different factions get to make the proposal, then you can set things up so that you can be sure that any division among them can result as an **equilibrium** in the resulting **game**. This holds not just for simple majority rule but for much trickier rules with veto players and voting weights and other provisions designed to protect various constituencies. The effects of these rules, he shows, can be entirely undone by inequalities in the ability to make proposals.

Principle: Proposal power can be more important than voting weights.

Puzzle: Imagine a dictator with no agenda-setting powers (no right to make proposals) bargaining with an agenda setter with no decision-making power over how to divide a dollar that loses half its value after every failed effort to reach an agreement. How much of the dollar will each end up with?

Reference: Kalandrakis, T. (2006). Proposal rights and political power. *American Journal of Political Science, 50*(2), 441–448.

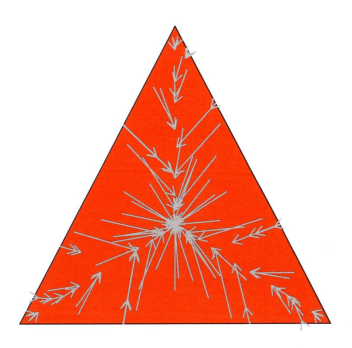

FIGURE 18 LEGISLATIVE BARGAINING

The figure shows mappings from proposal power weights to bargaining outcomes for the case of three bargainers deciding subject to majority approval. The figure shows a simplex (similar to that shown in Figure 8), which represents all possible ways of dividing a unit into three parts. The very center is the equal 3-way division, the vertices show the allocation that concentrates all weight on one person, the edges are divisions between two people with the third (the person represented by the opposite vertex) getting nothing. The simplex is also used to show all possible ways of dividing up proposal power (or "recognition probabilities"). The arrows show examples of mappings between recognition probabilities and the outcomes they produce. Many of these arrows point to the center implying that many power allocations produce equal splits (**in expectation**). In general the arrows point inward, but they don't all go as far as the center. Unequal outcomes can be fixed by the institution, but to achieve an unequal equilibrium allocation of a good you generally need an even more unequal distribution in proposal power. Notice also that arrows pointing from the edges have multiple heads: this means that multiple allocations can result from situations in which one person has no proposal power at all.

19 | It's Hard to Get People to Vote Honestly (The Gibbard-Satterthwaite Theorem) ≳⊙

The Liberal Democrats in the United Kingdom has been frustrated with the voting system in the country for a long time. The first-past-the-post system creates strategic incentives that work out very badly for them. Under first-past-the-post everyone votes for one candidate and the person with the most votes wins. The problem is that people who prefer someone other than the top two candidates might decide not to vote for their preferred candidate because they fear throwing away their vote. And worse: even if everyone liked one candidate the most, they might all not vote for that candidate if they expect (possibly correctly) that everyone else will be voting for one of two other candidates. In the United Kingdom this means that the seat share of the Liberal Democrats is lower than its vote share and possibly much lower than the share of voters that like it most.

Is it possible to design a voting system in which you can be sure that everyone has an incentive to vote their true preferences? Alan Gibbard and Mark Satterthwaite (independently) provided a negative answer to the question: you can demonstrate that unless the decision rule is a dictatorship (meaning that the rule just chooses what one particular person wants), or selects items even when everyone prefers something else, then every existing rule, and every rule that can ever be conceived, will be manipulable in the sense that people don't always have an incentive to vote their true preferences.

Principle (The Gibbard-Satterthwaite Theorem): There is no voting system that will always encourage people to reveal their preferences honestly.

Puzzle: The French presidential election system is set up so that the president ends up with majority support. The method has two rounds. The two candidates that get the most votes in the first round go into a second-round runoff; the winner of the second round (with an absolute majority, not just a plurality of votes) is then the winner. There is no point voting strategically in the second round. And in the first round you can vote your preferences without that necessarily determining the outcome. Does the French system escape the negative conclusion of the Gibbard-Satterthwaite theorem?

Reference: Taylor, A. (2002). The manipulability of voting systems. *The American Mathematical Monthly, 109*(4), 321–337.

Dee	Dum
a	b
b	a
c	c

(i)

Dee	Dave	Dim	Dum	Dan
a	a	a	b	b
b	b	c	a	c
c	c	b	c	a

(ii)

FIGURE 19 THE GIBBARD-SATTERTHWAITE THEOREM

These tables show the core logic of the theorem for cases in which the rule chooses one outcome for any configuration of preferences of voters. Say that Dum and Dee are deciding whether to choose *a*, *b*, or *c* using some nonmanipulable decision rule. Say now that option *a* would be chosen by the rule *if* Dum's and Dee's preferences over the three options were as in table (i) (the proof also goes through of course if *b* is chosen in this case). That means that for that particular configuration of preferences, Dee's preferred option is selected. There is nothing wrong with that. The key strategy of the proof though is to show now that in fact Dee's preferred outcome would be chosen *no matter what Dum thinks*. Dee is not just privileged for these particular preferences, she is in fact a dictator.

To see why, notice that, given Dee's preferences, there are six different preferences that Dum might have (focusing on strict orderings only). I have shown four of these six in table (ii), giving each different names. Say Dum's preferences were really like Dave's or Dim's. Then (since the rule should choose things that everyone likes best) *a* would be chosen again and everyone would be happy. But say Dum's preferences were like Dan's, then what? You can count on option *c not* being chosen (since both Dee and Dan prefer *b* to *c*) but the rule could not choose *b* either since *if it did*, then Dum would be better off pretending to have preferences like Dan's instead of admitting to having Dum's actual preferences (but since he has no incentive to lie since the decision rule used is non-manipulable this cannot be the case). So *a* gets chosen in this case also. That means that if Dum really did have preferences like Dan's he would do badly, getting his least-preferred outcome. Finally, if there were any other case in which anything *other* than *a* would get chosen, then someone with preferences like Dan's would have an incentive to claim to have preferences like those. But since Dan has no incentive to misrepresent his preferences, it must be that *a* is always chosen, no matter what.

The conclusion is that the rule *has to be* a Dee dictatorship (no one else's preferences can matter). Note the result extends to the case with many people and many options and to rules that allow ties.

PART 7
STRATEGIC VOTING

Voting is often thought of as the most important political act citizens can take. But awkwardly, although outcomes depend on votes, it is vanishingly rare that any one vote is ever pivotal, at least in sizable elections. In almost every midsize or large election the outcome would be unchanged if any one person decided to say at home.

Cold and calculating as the reasoning sounds, the mathematical case against voting is not quite as strong if you really start thinking strategically. The Rational Voter's Paradox [§20] discusses the implications of the obvious fact that if it doesn't make sense to vote and so no one votes, then *surely* it would make sense to vote. A more strategic analysis reveals that often it does make sense to vote with some likelihood even in bigger elections, and the optimal strategies are ones that result in elections being tight.

Once you start thinking strategically, other intuitions also get challenged. The logic of the Swing Voter's Curse [§21] suggests that people might often have a strong incentive not to vote at all—not because it is costly, but because they fear they will only make matters worse by voting for the wrong thing. The logic of conformist cascades [§22] suggests that sometimes strategic considerations make nonsense out of the epistemic virtues of majority voting—even with only two options voters might vote against the options that they privately think are best, if they see enough others voting the other way.

20 | Is It Rational to Vote? (The Rational Voter Paradox)

Election day, May 6, 2010, 7:28 P.M. Boris Johnson, mayor of London, sent out a mass e-mail: "Get down to the polling station and play your part in history. In an election this tight, your vote could be decisive." In the end, 65% turned out. Not huge perhaps, though still more than have turned out for any U.S. presidential election in the last hundred years.

Perhaps voters believe that the kind of argument Johnson was making is nonsense. Surely for large elections the odds of being pivotal are tiny. So while there may be lots of good reasons to vote, changing the outcome is not one of them.

You might think that voters thinking that way are too calculating, but in a way they are not calculating enough. Are they thinking through what would happen if everyone thought like that? It turns out the logic is a little more tricky than it seems at first.

Here's how it goes. Dum and Dee are running for president. Say the difference to citizens of a Dum versus a Dee presidency is $1,000. Say 1,000,000 people support Dum and 1,100,000 support Dee. Voting costs $2. With a cost of $2 and potential gains of $1,000, voting would be optimal if the probability of being pivotal were at least 2 in 1,000. What are the chances of being pivotal? If turnout were random, the chances of a tie would be truly tiny. For example, with a 10% turnout they would be about 10^{-118}, and this probability goes down rapidly for higher turnouts.

Things look a lot better though if people are really strategic. Say that everyone in Dum's party were to turn out to vote and all Dee supporters were to vote with a 10/11 probability (for a total 95% turnout). In this case everyone could calculate that there will be a 0.13% probability of a tie, and a similar probability of a difference of 1. That's small but nothing like as small as what you get under random turnout. In fact, combining these two chances to make a difference, it's just enough to make everyone willing to vote. The result: high turnout and a close election.

Principle: Close elections can be both cause and consequence of instrumental voting.

Puzzle: Say there are two parties each with two supporters and there is a vote to elect a leader. Say that the value of having your leader selected is $8 but that the cost of voting is $3. Say that you get $0 if there is a tie or if the other side wins. Is there any probability p such that if everyone voted with probability p the chances of being pivotal are such that everyone would in fact be happy to vote with probability p?

Reference: Palfrey, T. & Rosenthal, H. (1983). A strategic calculus of voting. *Public Choice, 41*(1), 7–53.

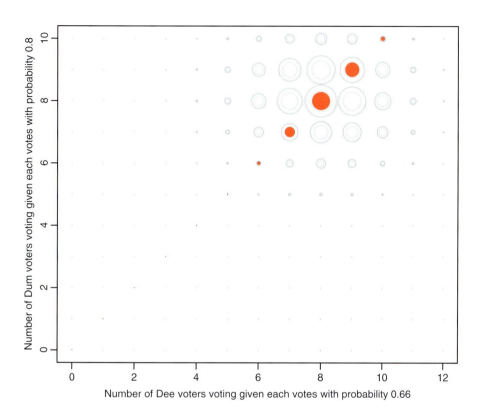

FIGURE 20 STRATEGIC VOTING

The probability of being pivotal when everyone (else) in your group votes with probability p_1 and everyone in the other group votes with probability p_2 can be calculated by adding up the diagonal elements of a "bivariate binomial" distribution: this statistical distribution captures the probability of observing different shares of people voting in the two groups given the strategies used in the two groups—for example, the probability of seeing exactly five people voting in each of the two groups given possibly different probabilities of voting within the two groups. The diagonal elements are all the possible ties. A distribution like this is shown here for a Dee supporter for the case in which Dee's 12 other supporters each vote with probability .66 and Dum's 10 supporters each vote with probability 0.8. Different combinations of p_1, and p_2 give different probabilities of being pivotal for members of each group. In order to figure out the **equilibrium** actions we need to figure out a combination of probabilities for participation such that pivotal probabilities are *just* high enough to make everyone willing to vote.

21 | Strategic Abstention (The Swing Voter's Curse) ◁

Voting changes outcomes only when your vote is pivotal. If, under majority rule, two out of three voters vote in favor of some change and one votes against, then the two voting in favor are pivotal and the third is not. If all three vote in favor, then none of them is pivotal (since the outcome would have been the same if any one of them had voted differently).

If you focus on pivotality, you can see an argument for why you might not invest in voting when you do not expect to be pivotal. That's discussed in §20 (the Rational Voter Paradox). But a more subtle logic suggests that there are reasons not to vote *especially* when you think that you *will* be pivotal.

The reason is that if it turns out that you are pivotal, that in itself tells you something: it tells you that all the other voters are split on the issue. But if they are split, maybe they know something you do not know. Consider voting to sanction someone. You might suspect a person to be guilty and be willing to vote for a punishment when everyone else is also voting to punish. But you might not think the same way if you find out that half your peers think the person is innocent. In that case you might prefer to abstain or even vote against conviction rather than take the risk of convicting an innocent person.

Reading that argument you might think that when you are voting you don't know what others think, so, given that logic, you should just vote your beliefs and let the best outcome emerge (inspired perhaps by Condorcet's logic in §10). But that would be missing the strategic logic of pivotal voting. The key principle of pivotal voting is that when you assess the effects of your vote you shouldn't be thinking of how your small voice can have a small impact on outcomes. You should be focused on the unlikely case of your vote having a very large impact on outcomes. That's the case that matters. If that ever happens, it is because the group is divided and the fact that it is divided has implications for whether or how you should vote.

This logic can lead to quite structured predictions regarding when strategic voters have incentives to abstain or even vote against their gut. Consider a large election in which 47% support party A no matter what, 45% support party B, and 8% are independents. Say that these 8% share political beliefs and so if they have good information about the candidates, they would agree on which is the right one to choose. Say that nearly a quarter of these independents are "informed independents" (that is, just shy of 2% of the voters) and have correctly figured out what would be best for independents in general. The others might have a strong leaning, but are not sure. These uninformed independents constitute just over 6% of the electorate. How should they vote (assume that voting is costless so that the decision is focused on how best to affect electoral outcomes)? In this case if all the uninformed independents voted for one party, that party would win. But really what they want is for the set of informed voters to decide. So maybe they should abstain? The problem with that is that if they all abstained, party A would win and the informed independents would have no influence. So the best strategy is to vote for the underdog with probability 1 in 3 and to abstain with probability 2 in 3. This strategy brings the race as close as possible to a tie (**in expectation**) and lets the informed voters make the determination.

Principle: If other voters share your preferences but understand the issues better than you, then you should either abstain or vote for the losing side.

Puzzle: Take the last example but say some late action by party B successfully wins over 2% of the uninformed independents prior to the election, bringing the race to a tie among the decided voters in the polls. How would this affect party B's expected final vote share? How would it affect total turnout?

Reference: Feddersen, T., & Pesendorfer, W. (1996). The swing voter's curse. *The American Economic Review, 86*(3), 408–424.

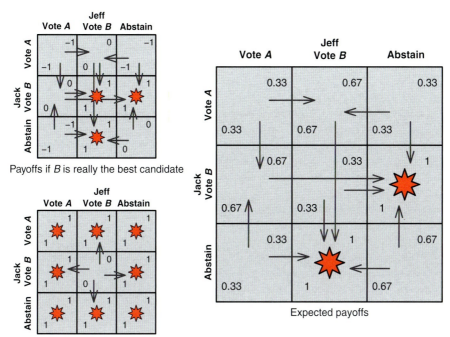

FIGURE 21 THE LOGIC OF STRATEGIC ABSTENTION

A and *B* are running for president and *A* has one more committed supporter than *B*. Jack, Jill, and Jeff are not partisans and simply want to elect the most honest leader. A good candidate is worth 1, a bad candidate –1, and a tie is worth 0. Jill does some investigation to figure out who is more honest. Jack and Jeff don't, but reckon there is a 2 in 3 chance *A* is the better candidate. How should Jack and Jeff vote? This problem can be represented as a simple **game** with **expected** payoffs that depend on who is most honest. The large matrix above shows expected payoffs generated by combining payoffs from the two smaller matrices. Payoffs are made under the assumption that Jill votes for the right person. In that case if *A* is the right person, then *A* will win unless both Jack and Jeff vote for *B*; if *B* is the right person, then *B* will win only if either Jack or Jeff supports her and neither votes against her. From the large matrix you can see that there are two simple **equilibriums**, both of which involve one of the uninformed undecideds staying at home and the other voting for the underdog, *B* (and *not* for the candidate that he thinks is most likely better). The one who votes has a 1 in 3 chance of being decisive: if he votes for *B*, then if in fact *B* is the better candidate, his vote combines with Jill's to get her elected. If (as he expects) *B* is not the better person, then there is nothing to worry about since *A*, enjoying Jill's vote, would win whether or not he votes.

22 Conformist Voting (Information Cascades)

In December 2010 a Tunisian street vendor set himself on fire in protest of mistreatment by his government. His action set off protests in the capital that spread throughout the region, launching the Arab Spring. The revolts took the regimes of the region by surprise. How could they have miscalculated the willingness of their citizens to confront them so badly? These revolts added to a growing list of major world events, including the collapse of the Soviet Union and the global financial crisis, that seemed to take everyone by surprise.

How could so many people be so wrong?

One reason is that when rational people listen to one another too much, they stop sharing the original information they have. Rational conformism can lead to collective ignorance.

To see how the phenomenon, sometimes called rational herding, or informational cascades, works, imagine this. A dictator wants to figure out whether there is a risk of a popular uprising. He gathers together a set of generals and asks them, in order, what they think. Each general sincerely wants to give the right answer, and doesn't just want to fall in line with what other people are saying. But none of the generals know, for sure. Say though that they all have insights into the situation; in particular they all know that they each (independently) have a two in three chance of having correct beliefs. Will the dictator benefit from their knowledge? Surprisingly, she might not. Here's what can happen.

The first general goes first and has only his own knowledge to go on so he gives his view. He may be right or wrong but still gives his best guess. The second general, when choosing his answer, can take account of what he knows but also the fact that the first general gave whatever answer he did. The first general had some information after all. If by chance the first general got it wrong, and the second general agreed with the first general, then the second general will repeat the first general's error. Then by the time it gets to the third general the third general has a lot of reason to doubt his own information, even if it is correct. He thus has incentives to conform (specifically he can calculate that the likelihood that he would think what he thought *and* the others would say what they said is $\frac{2}{3} \frac{1}{3} \frac{1}{3}$ if he is right, but $\frac{1}{3} \frac{2}{3} \frac{2}{3}$ if he is wrong). The same is true of every single general coming after him. The result is a unanimous, but possibly completely false, answer. Each statement by the late-speaking generals carries no new information at all.

The logic of information cascades can explain rational conformism and systemwide error, but it can also explain rapid *changes* of positions by groups. Say after a string of generals state that there is no risk, a general is consulted who has not yet heard everyone's responses so far. This new general cannot take into account the past statements by generals and so provides new information in what is in fact a very informationally poor environment. The fresh information can be enough to reverse the cascade, with the result that all subsequent generals adopt the position voiced by the new general.

The result seems to contradict the rosy picture painted by Condorcet [§10]. In Condorcet's account, if everyone has a little information, then when they voice their opinions this will point the group to the right answer. Here, rational individuals, also seeking the truth, make poor use of their collective information.

Principle: If individuals are under pressure to be right, their best efforts can lead to rational conformism and systemwide error.

Puzzle: Would you see the same conformism if instead of simply supporting or opposing a position, people could report how certain they are?

Reference: Bikhchandani, S., Hirshleifer, D., & Welch, I. (1992). A theory of fads, fashion, custom, and cultural change as informational cascades. *Journal of Political Economy, 100*(5), 992–1026.

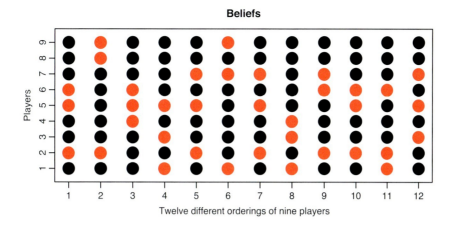

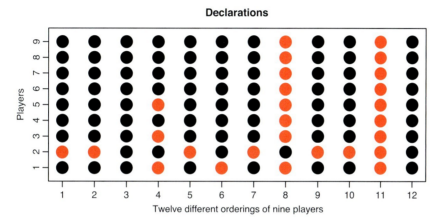

FIGURE 22 INFORMATION CASCADES

Nine people are each trying to decide whether to support a policy or not. They have no idea whether the policy is good or bad. Then each of them does a little research and gets a clue. Let's say that six get a *reliable* clue (marked as black here) but three unknowingly get a *misleading* clue (marked in red). Everyone knows that they all get misleading clues with a one in three probability. Then each is asked, in random order, whether they support the policy or not. That's the **game**. The upper figure shows twelve possible orders in which the nine are asked to express views. In some orderings people who happen to have reliable clues get to state their views early. In others, people with misleading clues get called on first. The lower figure shows the *statements* that people will make if they are all trying to make their best guess about whether the policy is good or bad. A black circle is a statement supporting a good policy and a red statement supports a bad policy. You can see enormous conformism for each ordering and in two cases the wrong decision is supported by a huge majority. What is going on? What's driving the results is sensitivity to the order in which people make their statements, particularly at the beginning. Take the last column. Here the first person got a clue supportive of a good policy, and since that is the only information they had, they went with it. The second happily supports the policy both because they got a positive clue and because they know that the first person also got a positive clue. Had the second person gotten a negative clue they would have been torn since they know that their research is inconsistent with what the first person found. Assume in such cases they go with their own clue. The third person in the last column got a signal *against* the policy; but since they know that the first two found evidence supporting the policy they rationally decide to ignore their own research. From this point onward *everyone* conforms since they all think that the evidence of others outweighs whatever they learned themselves. This conformism can lead to everyone supporting the wrong policy, following the exact same logic. See the second-to-last column for an example of this. In all you can see two tragedies: first a risk of massive support for the wrong policies (this arises about 10% of the time) and second a terrible use of research. If people are likely to ignore their own research, they might have little incentive to conduct any in the first place.

PART 8
ARGUING

If strategists find voting hard, they find talking even harder. In situations where people depend on one another but want different things, their power to persuade may be seriously compromised.

Costly Signaling [§23] and Cheap Talk [§24] show two ways in which political communication can be effective. One of these is through the imposition of costs on the side seeking to communicate. If I want to stop you from attacking me, it may be more effective to hurt myself to demonstrate my resolve than to hurt you to demonstrate my power. In some situations it is also possible to communicate your position by just talking, especially when interests are aligned. But the type of communication that is possible through talk is often noisy; you should not, for example, expect people engaging in collective deliberation prior to joint decision making to tell the truth. As demonstrated in §25 (Limits of Deliberation), under unanimity rules, people often have an incentive to misrepresent their position before the vote. Things can be better under majority rule, but not by much. The Agreement Theorem [§26] provides perhaps the most striking result from the game theoretic analysis of communication: if people are extremely sharp in inferring information from the arguments and actions of others, then they cannot agree to disagree. The theorem puts limits on the scope for tolerance but also threatens the viability of some types of markets.

23 | Listening to Pain (Costly Signaling)

As Angela Merkel and François Hollande started negotiations with Vladimir Putin to divert an expansion of the war in Ukraine, Russian helicopters started engaging in precision shooting practice right at the Ukrainian border. Amassing troops may be just that, preparations for war, but could it also be a form of communication? Can sending troops communicate seriousness of purpose? Could Putin's helicopter practices have been intended to strengthen his arm in negotiations?

If you think about the issue strategically, communicating resolve is a difficult business. If you could get an edge in negotiations by sending troops to the border, then couldn't someone do the same thing even if they were not really resolved to fight?

Interestingly, it might depend on the cost of amassing the troops.

Here's the logic. Dee threatens war if Dum doesn't give her his new rattle. Dum retorts that he will fight to the death for the rattle. Dee wonders how serious Dum is. If Dum is serious, then Dee would be better off walking away. Say the rattle is only worth $8 to her, fighting would cost them $6 each, and Dee would only have a 50% chance of winning. So when she does the math, fighting wouldn't make sense if Dum were really to fight back. But maybe Dum is just bluffing about fighting back? How to know?

Here are more details on the problem. Say that Dee is not sure how much Dum really cares about the rattle but she believes it equally likely that he values it anywhere between $0 and $24. You can figure out that Dum would be willing to fight if and only if he valued the rattle at $12 or more (since if he valued it at $12, then **in expectation** fighting would give $.5 \times \$12 - \$6 = \$0$). So Dum's question is: how to convince Dee that Dum thinks it is worth at least $12?

Dum comes up with an idea. He goes to Dee and says, "Dee, I am really serious that I will fight for this and to prove it I am going to burn $9." He flings the money into the fire. "Now leave me alone!" Should Dee be convinced?

Dum's strategy does make sense and Dee is rightly convinced. Dee figures that this crazy strategy would only make sense if Dum thought the rattle was worth at least $9. Otherwise why bother? So let's say that Dum thinks the rattle is worth at least $9, then what are the chances that Dum thinks it is worth $12 or more: 80% (or $\frac{24-12}{24-9}$). If that is right, then the benefits from an attack are now 80% $\times (\frac{1}{2} \$8 - \$6) + 20\% \times \$8 = 0$. She knows there is still a 20% chance that Dum is bluffing, but the risks of real resistance are too high to risk.

Critically, Dee is convinced that Dum cares about the rattle because burning money was costly to Dum. If instead of throwing the money into the fire, Dum had spent the money on a sandwich, then Dee wouldn't have been convinced at all. If Dee were to take such a signal seriously, then Dum would go off and buy a sandwich even if he didn't care about the rattle, and Dee would be back at square one. Burning money (unlike buying sandwiches) only makes sense if you care enough about how others will respond.

This type of reasoning might explain why militaries invest in costly air shows. It might also explain what penance is and why attempted suicides that are used as cries for help have to involve real risks.

Principle: Sometimes you have to suffer in order to send a signal.

Puzzle: Say amassing troops reduces the costs of going to war. Would that make amassing troops a more or less successful strategy for communicating a state's resolve to go to war?

Reference: Fearon, J. (1997). Signaling foreign policy interests tying hands versus sinking costs. *Journal of Conflict Resolution, 41*(1), 68–90.

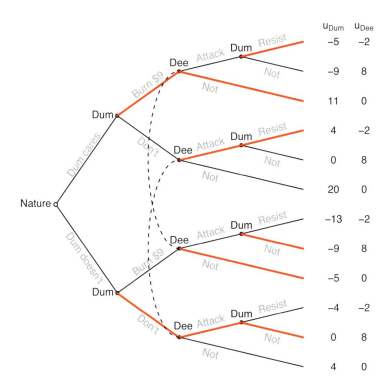

FIGURE 23 COSTLY SIGNALING
A **game tree** illustrating the logic of burning money to signal intent. I assume it's known that Dee values the disputed item at 8 but critically there is uncertainty over whether Dum thinks the object is worth fighting for. In the figure above this uncertainty is represented by assuming that "Nature" first chooses whether Dum really cares (valuing the object at 20) or not (valuing it at 4). When Dee gets to choose she does so not knowing what Nature did, which formally means that she does not know which node in the game she is at (is she in the top set of branches or the bottom set?). This uncertainty is represented by using dotted lines to connect two nodes that are indistinguishable for Dee. I use red on the tree to mark out the solution. Starting at the end: if Dee attacks, then Dum's decision to resist depends only on whether or not he cares about the object—it does not depend on whether he burned money or not. I assume resisting means a war, which costs $6 and yields a 50% chance of success. With these values, fighting makes sense for Dum if and only if he cares (red lines). Dee's **utility** over attacking does not depend on whether Dum burned $9 or not either, but it does depend on whether Dum will fight back or not. So the best responses for Dee are to attack if Dum cares and not if he doesn't. The problem is that this is information that Dee does not have. Say instead Dee took Dum's money-burning signal seriously and decided to attack if money is not burned and not if it is. This should work out all right as long as the signal is reliable. To be reliable it must be that Dum should burn the money if and only if he cares about the object (marked again with red lines). You can see from the tree that this is indeed the right strategy for him: if he burns the money there will be no war, but he will have lost the money; if he does not burn the money, he will be attacked and either give up the object or face the uncertain and costly option of fighting for it. The former outcome is better than the latter only if you care a lot about the object.

24 | When to Listen to Threats (Cheap Talk)

In his 2015 State of the Union address, President Obama declared what actions he would not accept from Congress. Any attempt to put new sanctions on Iran would be vetoed. Attempts to reverse policies put in place to promote "middle class economics"—such as moves against health insurance or the regulation of Wall Street—would be vetoed.

Politicians try to communicate their positions all the time. The hard thing though is figuring out when those communications carry content. Does Congress learn anything from these statements by the president?

For this kind of problem there are reasons to suspect that listening to the president's arguments about what he is going to do will be a waste of time. Often the costliness of signals [§23] can make them informative; but here talk is cheap so perhaps nothing gets communicated.

Here's a simple description of the problem and the reasoning for why efforts to communicate policy preferences would carry no content. Say Congress wanted to expand the energy sector as much as possible. In contrast, the president has a preferred rate of expansion of the energy sector. Call it x. Expansion beyond this rate is not desirable, to the point that an expansion larger than twice this rate ($2x$) would be considered worse than no expansion at all and would be vetoed. Say that everyone understands that but that Congress is not sure what exactly the president's ideal expansion is. Then, if he could, the president should try to convince Congress that his optimal expansion is only half as large as it truly is, anticipating that Congress will try to send a bill proposing much greater expansion than the president's ideal but still just within the bounds of acceptability (but in fact ending up proposing exactly what the president really wants). So, if the president can convince Congress that his ideal is $x/2$, he hopes they will push for x and that way he gets exactly what he wants. Of course if Congress is wise to the president's strategy, they will figure that they can safely send a bill proposing $2x$. Anticipating this, a crafty president would be better off saying that really his ideal is $x/4$. You see where this is going. With enough second guessing, communication breaks down.

It turns out, however, that a kind of crude communication is possible even among such incompatible political actors. Say the maximum expansion is 100 and that for Congress the more expansion the better, though the additional gain from expansion is decreasing (for example, say the value of one new field is 1, the value of 4 is 2, the value of 9 is 3, and so on). Say they reckon that the president's ideal was anywhere between 0 and 100, but they are not sure where. Then Congress could ask: "Is your ideal expansion below 75?." If the president answers "no," then Congress should put forward a bill to expand right up to 100. If "yes," then Congress should propose expanding to 50 only. With these numbers, there is a one-third chance the president will veto the bill, but it is still the best choice for Congress. Other options either involve weak expansions, from their perspective, or they run too high a risk of a veto. Given these strategies, you can check that the president will be willing to tell the (rough) truth. Here is why: if the president's ideal was really above 75, then he would say so since having 100 is better than having 50; if his ideal was really below 75, then he would be better off getting an offer of 50 (which he might veto if in fact his preference was below 25—a one-third probability conditional on being below 75) than getting an offer of 100.

Principle: When talk is cheap, communication is possible if there is enough commonality of preference among players.

Puzzle: The president had reason to tell the truth when asked if he prefers expansion above 75. But why is 75 the right number for Congress to ask about in the first place?

Reference: Crawford, V., & Sobel, J. (1982). Strategic information transmission. *Econometrica: Journal of the Econometric Society, 50*(6). 1431–1451.

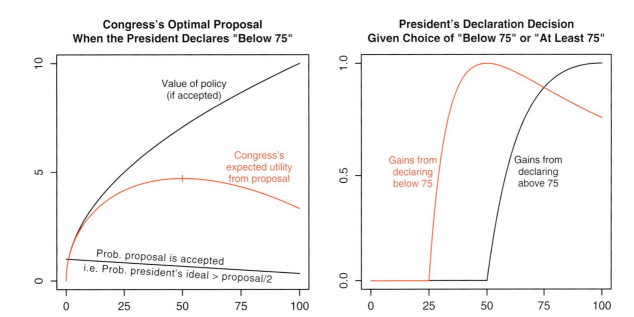

FIGURE 24 CHEAP TALK

The left graph shows the decision Congress faces under the assumption that the president has truthfully declared his valuation below 75. Now believing that the true valuation is anywhere between 0 and 75 and expecting a veto if they propose a policy greater than half the president's valuation, Congress can figure out that a proposal of 0 would be accepted with probability 1, a proposal of 50 would be accepted with probability 2/3 (since there is now a 2/3 chance the president had a valuation greater than 25), and so on. So the more aggressive the proposal, the greater the benefit if it gets accepted (gray line), but the less likely it is to be accepted (black line). This induces a trade-off (red line) that results in an optimal choice of 50. The right graph shows the president's incentives to tell the truth given how Congress will respond (and given that the president thinks Congress will think the president is telling the truth). The president expects that a declaration below 75 will produce a proposal of 50, whereas a declaration above 75 will produce a proposal of 100. For any president with a true valuation less than 25 they will end up vetoing both proposals and get a utility of 0. For a president with a valuation between 25 and 50, they would veto a proposal of 100 but accept, and be better off with, a proposal of 50. With a valuation between 50 and 75, neither proposal would be vetoed, but the president would be better off with the proposal of 50. For a valuation greater than 75 the proposal of 100 is preferable. The result is that the president can never do better than to tell the (rough) truth.

25 | Deep Democracy among Strategists (The Limits of Deliberation) ◁ ⊘

For many advocates of "deep democracy" there has been an unfortunate historical conflation of democracy with majority voting. Voting gathers only very coarse information about citizen knowledge and views, and provides limited scope for citizens to really learn from one another. It can also produce odd strategic incentives like those shown in §21 (the Swing Voter's Curse) where voters vote *against* what they believe to be the best choice for society. Perhaps a better alternative is a system in which rather than relying on majority votes, decisions are made through consensus voting, preceded by frank deliberations. Will such procedures work?

Return to the problem in §21. Say in that example that if all knew what each person believed about the accused, then all would come to the same conclusion regarding whether to convict or not. Deliberating would work, consensus would be achieved, and the right results could be expected.

Say though that people weigh the risks of convicting an innocent person differently. Then things fall apart. To be clear we are still imagining a situation with fundamental agreement in the sense that everyone would like to convict if and only if the accused is guilty. What they disagree on is how much evidence is enough to warrant a given decision.

Here's why things fall apart. Say some voters are "negative soft-liners," which means that the information they have suggests guilt but they also will not vote for conviction if others have contrary evidence. Others are "positive hard-liners," which means that their private information suggests innocence, but they would convict if there were any evidence of guilt. There might also be negative hard-liners and positive soft-liners, but these are not so strategically interesting since their decisions will not be affected by the discussion. Assume that people don't know whether the others are hard-line or soft-line or what information they have.

Say now that decisions are to be made by consensus—the accused is convicted only if everyone votes for a conviction—and everyone has to decide whether to tell the others what they know prior to voting. I will show how things fall apart by demonstrating that it cannot be **in equilibrium** for everyone to truthfully share the information they have. In particular if everyone else is telling the truth, then positive hard-liners have an incentive to claim they have evidence of guilt even when they do not.

Why is that? First note that if everyone else says that they think the accused is innocent, then a lying positive hard-liner, now convinced the accused is innocent, can always use their veto to prevent a conviction. The consensus rule provides a protection to ensure that lying will not lead to a false conviction. For positive hard-liners, however, lying can have an upside and ensure a conviction that might not otherwise have happened. The reason is that although lying won't change the positions of negative hard-liners or positive soft-liners, it can change the views of negative soft-liners. These are people who have evidence of guilt but who will not vote to convict if they hear that the positive hard-liner had doubts. However, if there are such people, then positive hard-liners want to see a conviction and need these soft-liners to vote for it. In other words, they need to lie.

People might have stronger incentives to reveal their true preferences in a discussion prior to a *majoritarian* vote, however. In that case positive hard-liners are taking more risks when they lie since if everyone else is a positive hard-liner, then the lie will lead to a majority conviction of an innocent person.

Principle: Unanimity decision making can remove the incentives for voters to share information truthfully before voting, even when all voters are in fundamental agreement.

Puzzle: What are the incentives of negative soft-liners under majority rule?

Reference: Austen-Smith, D., & Feddersen, T. (2006). Deliberation, preference uncertainty, and voting rules. *American Political Science Review, 100*(2), 209.

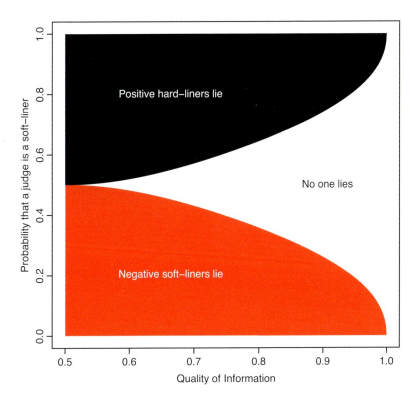

FIGURE 25 THE LIMITS OF DELIBERATION

Three judges are deciding whether to punish an accused murderer. The judges have each examined the evidence and in light of their experience have formed private opinions of the likely guilt of the accused. Each is more likely to form a *negative* view if indeed the accused is guilty and a *positive* view if not. All three want to punish the guilty but they differ in terms of how hard-line they are. Say *hard-liners* would punish if even one of them had formed a negative view; whereas *soft-liners* only seek punishment if all three had formed negative opinions. They now have to decide whether to share their opinions with each other before moving to a majority vote on the guilt of the accused.

Since they all want to punish the guilty you might expect that sharing their opinions would be best for all. But in fact it comes down to the incentives of the "negative soft-liners" and the "positive hard-liners." Negative soft-liners will want to hide their negative opinion if they suspect that the other judges are positive hard-liners (because they do not want to see the accused convicted based on their view only). Positive hard-liners might lie and say that they have a negative view if they thought the others were negative soft-liners (they would want a conviction because the views of others is suspicion enough). Overall it is possible to have everyone tell the truth only when the quality of information is good—and so if you think the accused is guilty, then others likely do too—and when there is uncertainty over whether people are hard-liners or soft-liners. The figure shows combinations of uncertainty and information quality that can make honest communication optimal under majority rule. See technical notes for more details.

If they were deciding by consensus, however (instead of using majority rule), then there is *no* situation in which everyone wants to tell the truth. In particular if everyone else were telling the truth, positive hard-liners would never admit their private belief that the accused was innocent as that would only change things if in fact the other judges had negative views, in which case the positive hard-liner would like to see the accused convicted.

26 | You Can't Agree to Disagree (Aumann's Agreement Theorem) ◁ ⊘ ⊙

Germany's conservative finance minister Wolfgang Schäuble exited talks with his radical Greek counterpart Yanis Varoufakis noting that the two had agreed to disagree about how to solve the Greek financial crisis. Varoufakis disagreed with Schäuble's summary saying, "We didn't even agree to disagree, from where I am standing."

Varoufakis's remark underlines the level of agreement needed to be able to agree to disagree. A remarkable theorem due to Robert Aumann suggests that if people really have a high level of understanding of each other's beliefs, then they will not in fact disagree about facts. Once they really understand where the other side is coming from, they will be coming from the same place.

To see the logic, consider an application to the decision by two parties to go to war. Say Jack and Jill are out to have a battle and both expect to win. Of course it is not possible that both have a greater than 50% chance of winning, but they might both think they do. Maybe each discovered the other's weak spot but neither knows that their own weak spot has been discovered. The problem arises, however, once they see the troops amassing and figure out that the other side believes it has a high chance of winning. If Jack knows that Jill thought that she had a good chance of winning, then he should infer that Jill found his weak spot and revise down his own belief about winning accordingly. If he continues to believe he has a greater than even chance of winning, and if Jill knows this, and knows that Jack knows her beliefs, then she should infer that Jack thinks he will win even though he knows that she has found his weak spot, which must mean he knows something really bad about her. In that case she should dial down her own expectations.

More generally Aumann's agreement theorem says that if people have "common priors"—that is, their beliefs and uncertainties about possible states of the world are the same prior to observing facts about the world—and are adept at making inferences from the beliefs of others, then, if they have **common knowledge** about the beliefs of one of them, they must both have the same beliefs at the end of the day.

A set of "no-trade theorems" on the impossibility of purely speculative trading follow from Aumann's result: if a buyer and seller have common knowledge that the buyer thinks a stock is worth buying, then the seller can't expect to turn a profit from the sale.

There are also implications for religious tolerance. If people really understand each other's religious beliefs and claim to base their beliefs on fundamentally similar stances then they have to have the same beliefs. If they don't have the same beliefs, then either they don't really have common knowledge about each other's beliefs, or they have fundamentally different world views, or, of course, they are not rational.

Principle (Aumann's Agreement Theorem): If rational people really understand each other's beliefs about the world, then they must have the same beliefs about the world.

Puzzle: Why might people *not* have common priors?

Reference: Aumann, R. (1976). Agreeing to disagree. *The Annals of Statistics, 4*(6), 1236–1239.

Jack's Partition

Jill's Partition

Meet of Jack's and Jill's Partitions

FIGURE 26 AUMANN'S AGREEMENT THEOREM

Each box shows an "information partition" and each point in each box represents a possible state of the world, corresponding to the probability that Jack will win the battle. Say the prior probability of each state is the same. Points in the same "cell" are indistinguishable to the individual in question. For example, if in fact there is a 0.5 chance that Jack will win, then both will believe they will win (Jack reckons it is either 0.5 or 0.6; Jill that it is between 0.3 and 0.5). But they certainly do not know that the other expects to win. If Jill found out that Jack thought he would win, then she would infer that the true probability is in fact 0.5 (since if it were 0.3 or 0.4, then she knows that Jack would know he was *not* likely to win). In turn, if Jack knew that, on finding out about his optimism, Jill concluded that the true probability was 0.5, then he would be compelled to agree that it is 0.5.

Partitions like these allow us to make quite complex statements about what sort of agreements are possible. Say Jack is certain to win. Then, although Jill does not know this for sure, both can agree that Jack has at least a 90% chance. But if in fact Jack had an 80% chance, Jill would know this but the two could not even agree that Jack thinks that he has a 50% chance! Rather, Jill could reason that Jack would think it *might* be 70%, in which case (if it were 70%) Jill *might* think it *might* be 60% and so think Jack might think it is 50%, in which case Jill *could* think it is 30%, and so on. . .

Events (collections of states of the world) that are "common knowledge" are those that do not allow this kind of back-and-forth movement between cells of the partitions. These can be identified by looking at the "finest common coarsening" (or the "meet") of the information partitions. In this example the events "the probability is at least 0.9" and "the probability is no more than 0.8" are both cells in the meet (last figure) and both can be common knowledge if they arise. If it were common knowledge that Jack thought the probability were at least 0.9, then they would both believe the probability was at least 0.9.

PART 9
BARGAINING

Lots of books give advice about how to bargain. Game theoretic work tries to answer more fundamental questions about when negotiations succeed and what properties bargaining outcomes are likely to have. Nash's bargaining theorem [§27] is perhaps the most important result in the study of bargaining, which states who is likely to get what, whenever bargaining is efficient. Nash's solution describes what an outcome will (or should) look like, but not how that outcome is achieved. The most important model for understanding *how* bargaining outcomes arise (and how this determines what they will be) is the alternating offers model [§28], generally associated with the work of Ariel Rubinstein. This model suggests that player patience is a critical thing for determining who gets what from negotiations. Schelling's Conjecture [§29] works through the counterintuitive logic of constraints showing how the absence of options can make you stronger. But the most interesting thing about bargaining is how often it fails and why people can't reach agreement on courses of action even when there are clear joint gains to be made. There are lots of reasons why negotiations fail but two are especially intractable. The first is the difficulty of making credible commitments to respect the terms of a deal. The second is the killer effect of imperfect information. §30 shows the logic of the credibility problem and why it sometimes makes more sense to fight an opponent than to seek peace if an effect of peace is that the opponent can grow stronger. §37, introduced later along with other results on mechanism design, presents the Myerson-Satterthwaite theorem, which shows how poor information can make the risk of bargaining failure unavoidable.

27 | The Bargaining Problem (The Nash Bargaining Solution) ≳⊘⊙

Labor leaders and employer representatives sit down at a table to discuss wages. Disaster awaits if they fail to make a deal. They have a bargaining problem. The problem is not that they cannot find a deal that is good for both sides. The problem, rather, is that there are lots of deals that are better than no deal, but they value each of those deals differently. They need to figure out which one to agree on before it's too late.

The bargaining problem is challenging for analysts for the same reason: there is generally a multitude of possible solutions. How can you begin to guess at what deal will be reached? In some accounts, who does well comes down to confidence, rhetorics, or the ability to interpret subtle clues from bargaining partners. The bargaining problem, with no markets or prices, seems so poorly defined as to be not amenable to mathematical analysis.

In 1950 John Nash provided a startlingly general answer to the bargaining problem. He assumed that people's preferences satisfied the **expected utility hypothesis** and then proposed that any reasonable prediction about outcomes should have four features:

1. **Efficiency:** An outcome (including bargaining failure) should not result from bargaining if there is an alternative that both bargainers prefer to it. Making this assumption means that you are willing to assume that a deal will be made, and you want to focus on what the deal will look like.
2. **Symmetry:** *If* the bargaining problem really is symmetric, then the outcome should be symmetric (so if, under some representation of preferences, for every deal that gives value *a* to Player 1 and *b* to Player 2 there is another that gives *a* to Player 2 and *b* to Player 1, then the two players should value the outcome equivalently).
3. **Invariance to utility representation:** The solution should not depend on the scales used to represent people's preferences.
4. **Independence of irrelevant alternatives:** If the outcome of some bargaining problem is *X*, then *X* should be the outcome of any bargaining problem for which *X* is available and no *new* outcomes are available. In other words if the United States and Iran can agree on some deal, they won't then move away from that deal if it turns out that some other deal that they didn't want is not available.

Nash then asked: What kinds of bargaining outcomes would satisfy these features? His answer was that there was just one possible outcome from bargaining that would do the trick. Say that each person receives a **utility** of 0 if bargaining breaks down; then choose the outcome that maximizes the *product* of their utilities.

Who does well in bargaining? Not people who care a lot about outcomes in general. Apathy in bargaining is not a problem. What matters is how much you care about risk. **Risk-neutral** people care the same about marginal gains whether or not they are doing well already; **risk-averse** types care more about marginal gains when they don't have much. The risk-averse types do badly in head-to-head bargaining.

Principle (Nash's Bargaining Theorem): Choosing the deal that maximizes the product of the bargainers' gains is the only procedure that is **efficient**, treats equals equally, and is not influenced by irrelevant options or irrelevant representations of preferences.

Puzzle: Does Nash's theorem provide a solution to the problem posed by Arrow [§9]? Can you think of the optimal **social choice** as just being whatever arises from bargaining?

Reference: Nash, J. F. (1950a). The bargaining problem. *Econometrica: Journal of the Econometric Society*, *18*(2), 155–162.

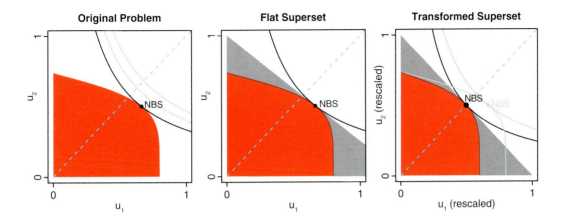

FIGURE 27 THE NASH BARGAINING SOLUTION

The left figure shows in red a set of possible payoffs for player 1 and player 2 from dividing $1 (the asymmetry of the shape comes from assuming that 1 is risk tolerant and 2 is risk averse). I have marked a number of "indifference curves," all of which are of the form $u_1 u_2 = k$; that is, for any two points (u_1, u_2), (u'_1, u'_2) on a given curve we have $u_1 u_2 = u'_1 u'_2$. The Nash point (NBS) is picked out as the point in the red set that is on the highest of these indifference curves. The challenge now is to show that this NBS is the only point that satisfies Nash's four conditions. I will do this with the help of some transformations of the possibility set.

The second figure shows the same situation but now has a new (gray, triangular) possibility set that includes all points in the set with surface tangent to the indifference curve that passes through the NBS. Note that the new possibility set includes the original set and also has the NBS point on its frontier. The slope of the surface is $-u_2$ (NBS)$/u_1$ (NBS). (Figuring out that slope is the hardest part of the proof. You can get it by working out the slope of the indifference curve.)

The final figure shows what happens when you reshape the triangle so that it becomes a *symmetric* possibility shape (that means that if it contains payoffs $u_1 = x$, $u_2 = y$, then it also contains $u_1 = y$, $u_2 = x$). You do this by dividing all the u_1 values by $2u_1$ (NBS) and all the u_2 values by $2u_2$ (NBS). This results in a possibility set whose frontier has a slope of −1.

Note now that in this final panel the (rescaled) NBS is located at the point (0.5, 0.5). This point is in fact the only point that is efficient (Condition 1)—since it is on the edge of the possibility set—and that satisfies the symmetry condition (Condition 2), which kicks in now because this final possibility set is symmetric. So, the NBS has to be the solution to the problem in the third panel. Working backward, it also has to be the solution for the problem in the second panel, since that is different from the third panel only through a rescaling of utilities, which shouldn't make a difference according to Condition 3. Finally, the NBS is the only acceptable solution in the first panel since it differs from the second only by excluding points that were not accepted as solutions in that panel, which shouldn't make a difference according to Condition 4.

28 | Alternating Offers (The Ståhl-Rubinstein Solution) ⊙

Nash's solution [§27] describes what successful bargaining outcomes might look like under a set of reasonable-sounding assumptions about bargaining processes. But it says nothing about *how* people bargain or why they would reach particular outcomes.

Studying how people bargain is difficult because bargaining is one of those situations where the rules are not very clear. Is there a well-defined sequence of actions that people can take to get to an agreement?

One approach is to just make up a set of rules, assume that people follow them, and see where they end up. You can then see how much the results you get depend on the specific rules assumed. The canonical approach treats bargaining as a sequence of offers and counteroffers. One person proposes a deal, the other person then either accepts or rejects it. If she rejects, it is her turn to make a proposal, which is either accepted or rejected and so on.

Represented like this you can see immediately that a couple of elements are introduced that are absent from Nash's formulation. Most obviously, time is now a consideration. The way game theorists generally think about time is to think in terms of **discounted utility**, with outcomes that are realized in the future valued less than outcomes realized now. One useful analogy is to think of players as splitting up some melting ice cream. They both want as much as possible, but the sooner they can divide it up and eat it, the better it is for everyone.

Having specified how players value time, it is easy enough to figure out what each person should do in each round. Go to the end of the **game** when there is not much ice cream left and the last offer is about to be made. Let's say that person A makes this final offer. A will offer as little as possible to B. B should say yes because something is better than nothing (in fact even if *nothing* is offered, she might still say yes since nothing is no worse than nothing!). A will then have most of not much. Go then to the offering decision *before* that final offer. At that stage B can figure out that she just has to offer A enough to be happy taking the offer now rather than waiting to see the ice cream shrink and taking most of not much. A would get the remainder, which is the amount that B should then offer her directly in the previous round and so on. Working backward you can figure out what the first person should offer. In (**subgame perfect**) **Nash equilibrium** you'll see that the first offerer always has her offer accepted right away and that how much she offers will depend on how long the game is and how much each player cares about time.

The outcome of this alternating offers game is **efficient** in the sense that deals get made right away with no waste. Does that mean that it will be the same as what is predicted by the Nash bargaining solution? Interestingly, it is not. The reason is that the solution does not satisfy Nash's symmetry axiom: even if the set of possible outcomes from bargaining is symmetric, the outcome of the bargaining might not be because there are asymmetries on dimensions—such as attitudes toward time—that Nash did not consider in his definition of symmetry. While Nash hoped to abstract away from the details of bargaining, it turns out that those details are needed to figure out when the Nash solution is appropriate.

Principle: More patient bargainers do better.

Puzzle: Consider the game in Figure 28. Say that instead of alternating offers between us, I got to offer in both periods. You then have the power to block a deal but not to propose a new one. What would the equilibrium be? What would it be if offers could be any number between 0 and 1?

Reference: Rubinstein, A. (1982). Perfect equilibrium in a bargaining model. *Econometrica: Journal of the Econometric Society, 50*(1), 97–109.

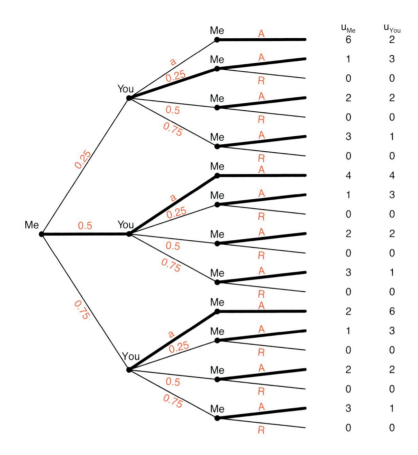

FIGURE 28 A TWO-PERIOD ALTERNATING OFFERS GAME
Here I get to offer first and can make an offer of 25%, 50%, or 75% of a pie worth $8. You can accept the split I propose or you can reject it. If you reject the offer, then the pie reduces in value to $4. At that point you get to offer some allocations. This simple game can be solved by backward induction. The equilibrium solution is highlighted with thicker lines. I can figure out that you know that in the last period I will accept any offer, which means that you can guarantee yourself $3 in the last period, with me getting just $1. To avoid this outcome I offer you $4 in the first period. Offering too little will result in us both being worse off; offering too much results in me being worse off. I make a fair-looking offer not out of any desire for fairness but because of the risks that arise if I take too much for myself.

29 | The Benefits of Constraints (The Schelling Conjecture)

In the middle of negotiations over a nuclear deal between the United States and Iran, forty-seven Republican senators wrote to the Iranian government advising that Iran should not think it was negotiating just with the U.S. Executive: any serious deal would have to get legislative approval or else it would surely be quickly reversed. Three months later, a set of supposed allies of the president—former advisers on Iran—wrote an open letter warning of the risks of a bad deal. Some supporters of the president worried that the letter gave ammunition to Republicans seeking to veto a deal.

This sort of meddling in negotiations seems to highlight internal divisions, which in turn could weaken the hand of a negotiator. Surely a united front is critical for success in negotiations.

Not according to an argument first put forward by Thomas Schelling. Schelling's idea was that division could actually strengthen a negotiator's hand by removing her ability to make concessions to the other side. If implementing a deal relies on support from other actors, then the positions of these actors start to matter. These others provide a way for a negotiator to credibly argue that deals that they might otherwise want to accept are simply not going to fly at home.

Ultimately, whether these constraints help or hurt depends on the structure of policy disagreements and the initial strength of the negotiator. The gains are particularly strong when constraints come from parties that are more extreme than the negotiator *on the dimension of disagreement* with the opposite side. And gains are particularly important for negotiators who are otherwise weak, and so liable to be giving concessions to the other side in the first place.

Principle: Ratification constraints can strengthen the hands of weak bargainers.

Puzzle: Say you can hire someone to engage in alternating offers bargaining [§20] on your behalf, while retaining the right to sign off on the resulting deal. Her fee is a share of your gains from the negotiations. Should you choose someone who is more patient or less patient than you? Or should you choose someone who has the same preferences as you?

Reference: Schelling, T. C. (1960). *The strategy of conflict*. Cambridge, MA: Harvard University Press.

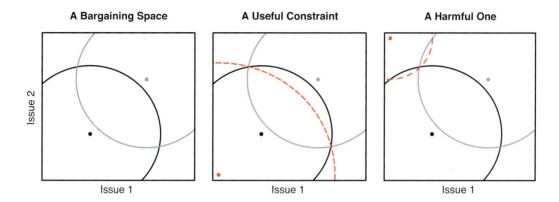

FIGURE 29 **THE SCHELLING CONJECTURE**

The first figure shows Black and Gray negotiating over a two-dimensional policy. Black will accept any points inside the black circle, since these are all closer to her most preferred point (marked with a black dot). Gray will accept any points inside the gray circle. Absent a ratification constraint, the bargaining space is the intersection of these two circles, with Gray favoring points to the northeast, and Black points to the southwest. Which point gets selected in this set depends on the bargaining strength of the actors. In the second figure, the introduction of Red provides a constraint on acceptable sets; now points are acceptable only if they lie inside all *three* circles. Red is more radical than Black on the dimension of disagreement between Black and Gray. The constraint she imposes rules out outcomes that are especially bad for Black and so may benefit Black, especially if she is a weak negotiator. In the third figure, Red has preferences that disagree with both Black and Gray. The implied constraint is so severe that it prevents Black and Gray from reaching *any* deal.

30 | Changing Fortunes Threaten Negotiations (The Commitment Problem)

In July 2015 the United States and Iran announced that they had reached a deal on Iran's nuclear capabilities development and the lifting of sanctions. The deal followed months of intense diplomacy and years of failed attempts. Why was it so hard?

One reason was worries about what would happen *after* the deal if Iran grew in economic and military strength. There was a lot of worry about Iran's "breakout time" (the time it would take it to make nuclear weapons if the deal fell apart or if Iran reneged) and particularly about the likelihood that that breakout time would become shorter and shorter over time.

Why does that matter? You might think that the fact that Iran will get stronger might alter the terms of the deal, but not challenge the possibility of a deal in the first place. The reason commitment is a problem is that when bargaining strength is likely to change over time there may be no deal today that can satisfy all sides.

Here's the logic. It's Monday and Jack and Jill set out to battle over Jill's goose. Eggs are worth $1 each. Say that the goose will lay one egg on Monday and two on Tuesday. Say the cost of battle to each is 10¢, and the probability that each will win is 50%. If there is a battle, the winner gets the goose and the loser loses it for good.

So if there is a battle, they could each expect to get the full $3 with 50% probability, for a total value (net of battle costs) of $1.40 ($3 x 50% − 10¢ = $1.40) each. That means that if they could bargain on Monday over how to divide the $3 profits from both Monday and Tuesday, then any deal that gave both at least $1.40 would be acceptable to both parties. Since two times $1.40 is less than $3 there exist deals that will work. For example, Jill might keep the goose but give Jack 50¢ today and $1 tomorrow.

Say though that Monday's deal is good for Monday but they know that, come Tuesday, they will face the same options to fight or to negotiate. Say moreover that Jack is growing in strength day by day and that if it came to a fight on Tuesday, he would win for sure. How do the prospects of Tuesday's actions affect Monday's negotiations?

The fact that Jack is growing in strength turns out to be bad news for *both* of them. As before, both know that if they went to battle, their expected gain would be $1.40. How does this compare with what Jill can really expect to get from bargaining? If she bargains today, then tomorrow she will be facing a much more formidable Jack; when she tries bargaining with Jack tomorrow she knows she will not be able to get more than 10¢ worth of tomorrow's production. More than that and Jack would go to battle. So the *best* outcome for her would be for Jack to let her have the entire $1 today plus an additional 10¢ tomorrow for a total value of $1.10.

But that deal, which involves full capitulation by Jack today, is just not enough for Jill. She's better off fighting.

Prospects of changing fortunes spell trouble for peace negotiations and provide a rationale for preemptive war. The problem arises if it is not possible to write contracts that bind far into the future or that prevent sides from changing in relative strength; in that case expectations of future shifts in relative strengths can make deal making impossible even in the short run.

Principle: It's impossible to reach a deal today if everyone expects big changes in bargaining power tomorrow.

Puzzle: So how was a deal possible in the Iran negotiations case even with the prospect of a vanishing breakout time?

Reference: Powell, R. (2004). The inefficient use of power: Costly conflict with complete information. *American Political Science Review, 98*(2), 231–241.

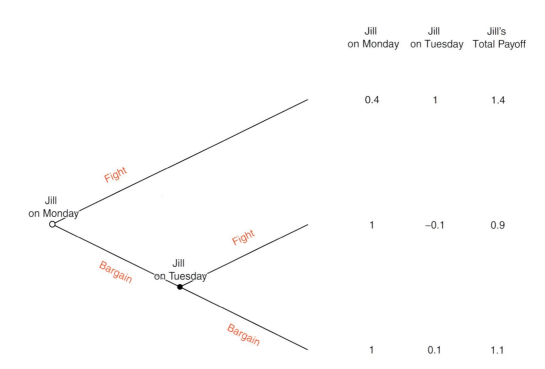

FIGURE 30 CREDIBLE COMMITMENTS

There is $1 to bargain over on Monday and $2 on Tuesday. If bargaining fails, there will be war with each winning with 50% probability on Monday, but Jack winning for sure on Tuesday. War costs each 10¢ (and runs the risk of losing everything). It's Monday: Should Jill bargain or fight? Under the most optimistic bargaining scenario, Jill would get to keep the entire $1 on Monday and gets to keep an additional 10¢ on Tuesday. Any suggestion to receive a better deal on Tuesday would not be **credible**. This is because with Jack sure to win a war on Tuesday, it would not be in his interests to surrender more than the expected costs of battle, 10¢. Compare this with the expected gains of going to war right away: with a 50% win probability today, the violent option would give Jill an expected payoff of $1.40, which is considerably more attractive than even the best outcome from negotiations.

PART 10
SELLING

There are many striking results on how markets operate but four stand out, all with implications for politics and policies.

The first is the Coase Theorem [§31]. The theorem is really more of a reflex than a theorem. It suggests that a large array of political problems can be, or maybe should be, reconceptualized as market problems. We worry a lot about what policies to implement but really many of these can be left to markets to solve. If there are inefficiencies, rather than asking how the politics produced them, the Coase Theorem suggests trying to figure out why markets failed.

The Coase Theorem assumes that markets operate efficiently. A second result—the Revenue Equivalence Theorem [§32]—that also assumes efficiency, shows that there is an amazing consistency in the outcomes you can expect to see under different types of auction-style market mechanisms. When auctions work they often produce the exact same gains for auctioneers no matter what clever systems auctioneers use to try to increase profits. This is a very positive result in that it suggests a high level of predictability over outcomes given efficient markets.

But auctions might not always work and markets might sometimes fail. Much of the most interesting work on strategy in the marketplace suggests that markets oftentimes do not work well. The parable of the Missing Market for Lemons [§33] shows how differences in the informational advantages of different sides of a market can prevent any trades from happening at all. Problems persist, however, even when information is symmetric: Grossman and Stiglitz's analysis of how markets gather and aggregate information [§34] suggests a surprising conflict between two functions attributed to markets: at least for speculative trade, the more efficient markets are at conveying information about the quality of goods, the weaker are the incentives to gather any good information about goods in the first place.

31 | Let the Market Decide (The Coase Theorem) ≈

Senator Mitch McConnell said he was distressed by Obama's 2014 climate deal: "[I]t requires the Chinese to do nothing at all for 16 years, while these carbon emission regulations are creating havoc in my state and other states across the country."

Climate action was described as a collective action problem in §1—a kind of Prisoner's Dilemma—but here it looks like it is really a kind of bargaining problem.

That's no coincidence. With a striking and extraordinarily influential argument, Ronald Coase claimed that all Prisoner's Dilemmas and in fact all collective action problems can be seen as bargaining problems. What's more, because of this you can solve all these problems by allocating property rights. What's even more, under some conditions, it does not even matter *what* property rights you establish (as long as you establish some). In other words, if what you care about is climate change as well as optimal economic production, then it's irrelevant how many years China is off the hook for; what matters is that there's a deal.

Here's the logic. You could imagine solving the Prisoner's Dilemma in a simple way if both parties could sign a contract saying that they would cut emissions. They should be willing to sign this contract and this would solve the dilemma. Coase's argument, though, is that you would get equally good outcomes even if only some people had the right to pollute in the first place. Or even if all of them did, as long as their rights were *tradable*. The reason is that if the allocation is bad, then the parties will just negotiate their way to better outcomes. If it's inefficient for McConnell's state to pollute so little while China pollutes so much, then McConnell should pay China for some of their pollution rights. If everyone is polluting too much, then they could pay one another to pollute less.

In all cases, thanks to the ability to contract, there would be the right amount of pollution. Who has the rights to pollute doesn't have any effect on the amount of pollution, it only affects who has to pay what to whom.

Apply that logic to the larger class of social dilemmas and the implications are enormous.

You might think that getting to good outcomes depends on who gets to make decisions: who is in government, who controls capital, who sets the agenda. But Coase's argument suggests that that is the wrong way to think about it. It doesn't matter so much who has the right to choose what, who is in government, or even who gets to vote: If people can simply bargain with one another, then all decision makers should do the same thing—choose whatever action maximizes the size of the pie and settle any differences with side payments. (Of course holding power does matter for getting side payments, just not for policy choices.)

Unfortunately, the logic breaks down at a few critical points. First, if people are really strategic, then bargaining might fail (see §30, the Commitment Problem, and §37, the Myerson-Satterthwaite Theorem). The result stated here also depends on a particular assumption about preferences: that all voters have **quasilinear utility** in cash. This technical assumption could be hard to defend, particularly for important decisions involving large transfers. It could also be that writing contracts is just too costly, or perhaps there are legal prohibitions on the sale of rights. Enforcing the contract might also be hard unless you have clear evidence of cheating by others. The deepest problem, however, might be that this solution to **public goods** dilemmas requires the existence of a third-party enforcer—the government—that both parties trust. But the existence of such a body itself depends on the resolution of strategic problems that are similar in form to the social dilemmas they are meant to resolve.

Principle (The Coase Theorem): It does not matter how property rights or other rights are distributed: if people can sign contracts costlessly with each other, that is sufficient to ensure that the social good is served.

Puzzle: Consider the Prisoner's Dilemma in Figure 31. Say that the value to China from playing D, while the United States plays C, was 5 rather than 3. What bargaining outcomes would you expect in this situation if both had rights to pollute? If China had rights to pollute? And if the United States had rights to pollute?

Reference: Coase, R. H. (1960). The problem of social cost. *Journal of Law & Economics, 3,* 1–44.

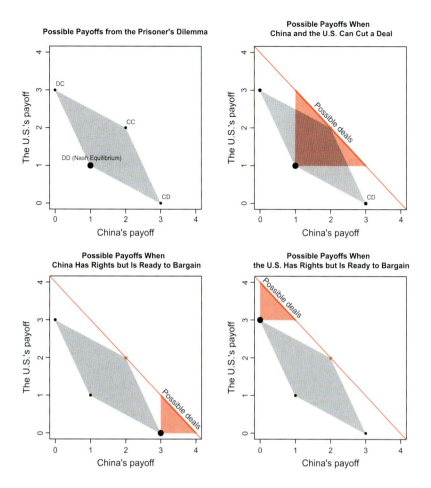

FIGURE 31 THE COASE THEOREM

The top left figure shows possible payoffs for the United States and China from their decisions to pollute. Here each of the four points corresponds to the payoffs from a cell in the Prisoner's Dilemma (see §1) **payoff matrix** ("CD" denotes the payoffs when the United States plays "cooperate" and China plays "defect"). Note these are exactly the numbers from the matrix but plotted in a two-dimensional space. Many more payoff possibilities open up if they can sign contracts. In fact, any of the payoff combinations marked in the shaded area can be achieved with deals such as "Let's toss a coin; if it comes up heads, I will stop polluting and you carry on; otherwise vice versa." The reason for this is that all these shaded outcomes are *averages* of outcomes that can be achieved by particular strategies implemented by the two sides and so different lotteries the sides agree on can pick out different averages. Even more possibilities open up if the two sides can make side payments. The red downward-sloping line in the top-right figure shows outcomes that can be achieved through deals of the form "Let's both stop polluting but let's have China pass $1 to the United States." These points all lie on a straight line under the assumption that a dollar transfer from you to me increases my payoff by a fixed amount but decreases yours by a fixed amount. Many (but not all) of these are better for both China and the United States than "all pollute." All the deals that are better for both than all pollute are marked in a shaded triangle and all the **efficient** ones are highlighted with a thick red line. These all involve no pollution: they are achieved by implementing CC and then possibly making side payments. Say now that China has managed to secure rights to pollute while the United States is legally required to go green. In that case in the absence of trade, you might expect China to pollute on her own for a payoff of 3 while the United States gets 0. But if they can trade, then they can both do better with deals of the form "the United States pays $2.50 to China for her to stop polluting"—all these deals are marked with the thick red line (bottom-left figure) and all involve no pollution. Exactly the same thing would happen if the United States were the one with rights to pollute (bottom-right figure); you would again expect no pollution but this time it would be China paying the United States not to pollute.

32 | Auctions (The Revenue Equivalence Theorem) ◁⊘⊙

Former governor of Illinois Rod Blagojevich, it seems, was in the business of selling the vacant Illinois Senate seat. Selling a political office can be a hard thing to do if you don't know how much people value it. Say he wanted to find out how much two candidates value his vote. He could use the following approach: Ask both candidates to write down their bids and then give his vote to the highest bidder but only charge the bid of the second-highest bidder. So if candidate 1 bids $100 and 2 bids $80, then 1 wins but only pays $80, not $100.

The clever thing about this design is that it gets Candidates 1 and 2 to tell the truth. Since your bid affects the chances you win but not the price you pay, you should make your bid exactly equal to your true valuation of the item being sold. If you bid less than the true value, you are just limiting your chances of winning at a good price, but if you bid more, you run the risk of winning at too high a price.

In the end, Blagojevich can sell his vote for the amount it is valued by the second-highest bidder. Curiously, this is the same as he would have gotten in the typical "ascending" auction, since there the second-highest bidder drops out once the price hits her valuation. More curiously, a first-price sealed-bid auction (in which the highest bidder wins the good but has to pay their own bid) would yield the same return. In this case the two candidates have an incentive to bid less than their true valuation (but not too much less) and it turns out again that the winner bids the expected valuation of the second-highest bidder.

It is not a coincidence that these auctions yield the same revenues: These equivalencies are implied by the "revenue equivalence theorem," which states that, subject to a small set of conditions (the valuations of bidders has a continuous and strictly increasing distribution; the bidder with the highest valuation wins **in equilibrium**; the bidder who values the good the least gains nothing; bidders are **risk neutral**), an auctioneer's expected revenue is the same no matter how cunningly she designs the auction.

The result has implications for a particularly interesting type of auction that gets used in politics: the "all-pay" auction. In the all-pay auction everyone makes a payment and the person with the highest payment wins, but the losers still pay their bid. Odd as it sounds, it makes sense for everyone to pay something since if only the winner were to pay she should not pay much, in which case any non-paying player would have been better off paying a little. . . . From the theorem you know that if Blagojevich simply asked the candidates to write him private checks, then when he adds up all the checks they will come to exactly what he would have gotten from any other auction.

Principle (The Revenue Equivalence Theorem): Potential buyers have to adjust their strategies depending on the type of auction but the revenues to the auctioneer stay the same.

Puzzle: If bidders are risk neutral, the revenues from the first- and second-price sealed-bid auctions would be the same. But say bidders were **risk averse**, would the revenues from each of these auctions go up or down?

Reference: Vickrey, W. (1961). Counterspeculation, auctions, and competitive sealed tenders. *The Journal of Finance, 16*(1), 8–37.

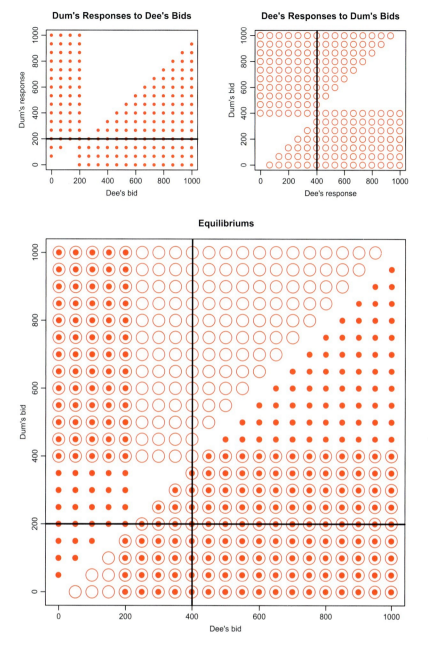

FIGURE 32 ILLUSTRATION OF STRATEGIES IN THE SECOND-PRICE SEALED-BID AUCTION
Say Dum values an item at $200 and Dee at $400. Then the top-left panel shows the actions that would be best for Dum given any possible bid by Dee. If Dee were to bid $1,000, then it wouldn't matter what Dum bid because he would never get the object; if Dee bid 0, then it again wouldn't matter what Dum bid as Dum would always win and pay nothing. In intermediate areas he has to be more careful, however, to avoid either not getting it when it was available at a good price (when Dee bids below 200) or getting it but paying too much (when Dee bids above 200). The top-right panel shows Dee's best responses to Dum. For both players, truth telling is optimal *no matter what the other does*. That is, it always make sense for Dum to bid $200 and for Dee to bid $400. The lower panel shows the intersection of best responses (the dotted circles at top left and bottom right of the lower figure). All these points are **Nash equilibriums**—best responses to the best responses of others. The fact that the point (400, 200) lies right inside this set means that all telling the truth is an equilibrium. But there are many more, including ones in which the seller does very well (and very badly!).

33 The Missing Market for Lemons (Asymmetric Information and Market Failure)

Despite winning elections, politicians are an unpopular bunch. In the United States, Gallup polls often place the approval ratings of Congress in the teens and sometimes in single digits. In global trust indicators, survey firms report that most people wouldn't trust a politician to return £10, and claim they have much greater trust in industry or in NGOs. Scholars at one recent academic conference tried to figure out just why it is that more good people don't go into politics.

One answer from the study of information economics is that high-quality candidates don't enter politics because everyone will assume they are low-quality candidates and treat them as such.

The logic is traditionally illustrated by thinking about the market for secondhand cars. It goes like this. Say there are lots of sellers of used cars (many of which may be "lemons") and lots of buyers. And let's say that any car worth x to a seller is worth $1.5x$ to a potential buyer. So there is a lot of scope for trade. But say that all the lemons have all sorts of different values and that the real value of each car is known only to the seller and not to the buyer.

Then, it turns out, we have a big problem.

The problem is this. Imagine a car of some type sells on the market for $1,600. Then only sellers with cars worth $1,600 or less to the sellers will be willing to put their cars on the market. Buyers can then figure out that the only cars that are for sale are those worth between $0 and $1,600 to the sellers. So they can use this fact to work out an estimate of the value of the actual cars for sale. Say they reckoned then that the average value of the cars (to sellers) that are put on the market is $800; then the expected value to them (the buyers) is $1,200, not $1,600. But say then the price dropped to $1,200. Then all the sellers with cars worth (to them) between $1,200 and $1,600 would drop out of the market. Buyers might then expect that the average value of a car (to sellers) is really $600 and so they would only be willing to pay $900, not $1,200. And so on. No positive price works since for any positive price the high-quality sellers think the price is too low and leave the market, while the buyers expect the price is likely too high given that only low-quality sellers are still selling. In the end the only cars on the market are worth nothing and go for nothing.

Now apply the logic to the market for politicians.

Principle: Markets can collapse if only one side has good information on the true value of offerings.

Puzzle: Is the lemons problem solved by the right to return low-quality goods for a cash refund?

Reference: Akerlof, G. A. (1970). The market for "lemons": Quality uncertainty and the market mechanism. *Quarterly Journal of Economics, 84*(3), 488–500.

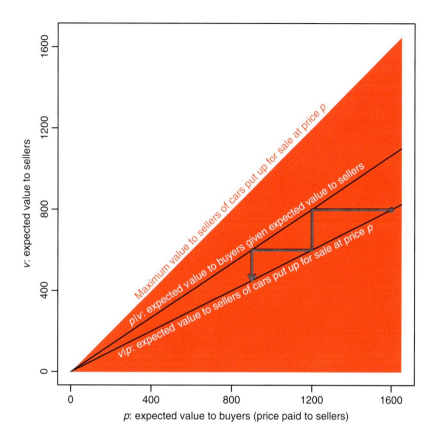

FIGURE 33 THE COLLAPSING MARKET FOR LEMONS

The figure shows how the value to sellers of cars on the market reacts to price and how the price in turn reacts to the values of sellers. Follow the arrow in the figure to trace the collapse. In the first instance assume that the price of a typical car of some type is $1,600. Then only sellers who value the car at less than $1,600 will sell. With an even distribution of car qualities, the average car on the market will be worth $800 to the seller (marked with a dot). Say then that a car worth $800 to a seller is worth $1,200 to a buyer. Then for a sale, and given the cars on the market, the car would have to be sold for $1,200, not $1,600 (leftward shift). But then sellers valuing the car between $1,200 and $1,600 will take their cars off the market, and so buyers will again revise down their estimate of the quality of the car (downward shift) from $800 to $600. But then the value to buyers (price) shifts left from $1,200 to $900, and the value to sellers drops (down) again to $450. And so on.

34 | The Impossibility of Informationally Efficient Markets (The Grossman-Stiglitz Paradox) ◁

When states intervene in economies, setting minimum wages, regulating products, or licensing producers, they make allocational decisions that are only as good as the information they have about the economy. Critics of state intervention have argued that markets are much more **efficient** than states at aggregating information about the economy. Part of the miracle of the market is its ability to figure out what things are really worth. Von Mises made the point in 1920, warning that a socialist economic order would flounder "in the ocean of possible and conceivable economic combinations without the compass of economic calculation."

Unfortunately, when you start taking account of strategic logics, it turns out that markets might not be so great at aggregating information either. In fact, perversely, it may be that the better markets are at communicating, the less informative they will be.

Here's the logic. The Queen of Hearts is coming to town and is planning to buy Cox's Apples. Dum has two apples but has no idea whether they are Cox's or not. If they are, they'll fetch $1 each; if not, they are worth nothing. He is unhappy about not knowing whether he will be able to make any sales to the queen. Dee has no apples but has cash. She starts to think. Could she turn Dum's uncertainty to her profit? Perhaps Dum would be pleased to reduce his risk by selling Dee one of the apples at a knockoff price? The trade seems risky for both sides: Dee is worried about buying worthless apples and Dum is worried about inadvertently selling good apples too cheaply. But maybe they can find a price to make it worthwhile for both.

While Dum and Dee puzzle about whether to trade in apples of dubious value, along comes Rabbit. Rabbit looks at the apples and says: "I can tell you *exactly* what sort of apples these are. In fact, if either of you pays me 1¢, I will tell you *both*."

What happens? Will either of them pay to find out whether the apples are worth anything? Or will they go ahead and trade the apples without trying to figure out first what they are worth?

Grossman and Stiglitz provide a surprising answer to this problem. In situations like this, people prefer to trade possibly worthless assets than to find out what the assets are really worth.

There are three critical elements to the insight. The first is that this kind of speculative trading (buying in order to sell at a profit) can make sense when there is uncertainty on both sides. Dum might think: There is a chance these apples are worthless, in which case I should get rid of them, but it is also possible that they are valuable, in which case I should keep them. Best thing might be to hedge my bets and sell some and keep some. Dee is thinking similarly. If they both prefer cash in hand to holding risky assets, then they should be able to find some price that will make them both happy. The second is that with *no* uncertainty there is no reason to engage in speculative trading. If both knew the apples were worth $0, then Dum wouldn't be able to sell them to Dee at all. But if they had a resale price of $1, then Dum would not want to sell them for less than $1, which would give Dee no incentive to buy them. The third is that when you find out the true value of the assets (and if as a result everyone else also learns its value) then you lose the uncertainty and so you lose the gains from trade but you are still stuck with the bill for figuring out the worth of the assets. So, better not to know.

Principle: If markets are good at communicating information, then no good information will be gathered in the first place.

Puzzle: Here Rabbit proposed to make the information about the value of the assets **common knowledge**. Would things be different if either party could privately figure out the value of the assets before engaging in trade?

Reference: Grossman, S., & Stiglitz, J. (1980). On the impossibility of informationally efficient markets. *The American Economic Review, 70*(3), 393–408.

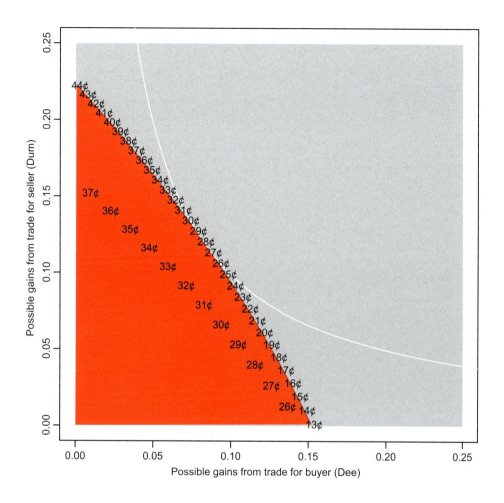

FIGURE 34 THE GROSSMAN-STIGLITZ PARADOX

The figure shows possible bargaining outcomes available to Dum and Dee when they are both uncertain about the value of the apples (see notes on page 158 for technical details). The outer curve shows the value of deals in which Dum sells one apple to Dee (for the price indicated by the numbers on the graph). This reduces Dum's exposure and gives him cash for sure, whereas previously he had no guarantee of cash. Dee's exposure is increased but she gets an apple that has an expected value of 50¢ for less than 50¢. The inner curve shows the deals if two apples are sold (again, at various unit prices). In these deals Dee takes on all the risk rather than sharing it with Dum. The fact that this two-apple line is inside the one-apple trade line indicates that these two apple trades are not **efficient**. The one-apple trades are efficient, however, and you might expect bargaining to settle on one of these deals. For example, the white curve to the northeast picks out the Nash Bargaining Solution [§27], which is to sell one apple for about 27¢. The key point here is that many deals are possible when there is uncertainty. However, all these deals disappear when players figure out the true value of the assets. If the value is known, then it will be sold at its value and there is no gain to either the buyer or the seller. In that case there are no benefits from the research. All that remains is the bill for whomever was generous enough to fund it.

PART 11
INSTITUTIONAL DESIGN

Game theorists often think of institutions as being the rules of the game. Once you have a handle on how to solve a game, you can start thinking about how behavior changes as the rules change in particular ways. But more subtly, you can turn the problem around and ask: What rules might be *needed* if your goal is to get people to act in a particular way?

Things really become interesting when you think about designing the rules of the game *without knowing who is going to play it*—and what they value. For example, your goal might be to set up rules so that people will choose whatever is collectively the best thing given whatever preferences they have: if all-cooperate is the best thing, the rules should steer them to select that; if all-defect is the best thing, then that's where they should end up, in equilibrium. This is the business of institutional design, or to use the term of art, mechanism design.

Back in §19 (the Gibbard–Satterthwaite Theorem) there already was an important result from the study of mechanism design. The Gibbard-Satterthwaite theorem showed that as a general matter there is no mechanism that selects a desirable outcome based on people's reported preferences that can make it always worthwhile to tell the truth about your preferences. This section has three more big results on mechanism design in contexts where there is more constraint on people's preferences. All three are depressingly negative and deceptively general.

The first result, due to Maskin [§35], shows that in general there is no possible institutional design that can produce desired outcomes for a large class of problems. The second, on the Clarke-Groves Mechanism [§36], is more positive, showing that under some conditions there is a mechanism for figuring out the optimal amount of public goods to produce. Even in that case, though, it turns out that the cost of the institutions that arise from the need to counter strategic impulses can be so large as to make them not worthwhile. The third result, the Myerson-Satterthwaite Theorem [§37], uses the tools of mechanism design to show that even the craftiest designers can never create mechanisms that will guarantee good outcomes from bargaining.

35 | Solomon's Dilemma (Maskin Monotonicity)

In the story from the Book of Kings, two women are claiming rights over a baby. Good King Solomon wants the baby to go to its mother. But which is the real mother?

Solomon comes up with a clever plan. "Let me divide the baby in two and give you each one half." Solomon correctly figures that the true mother (unlike the imposter) loves the baby so much that she would rather give up the fight than see it killed.

Of course, once the true mother revealed herself, Solomon awarded her the child.

But things might not have worked out so well for Solomon. Say both women were to cry out that the other should have the baby. Then where would Solomon be?

Here Solomon faces a fundamental problem that every benevolent dictator has to deal with. He wants a particular outcome, but the outcome he wants depends upon something he does not know: Who values what and how much? He needs a scheme to figure out people's values so that he can select the best outcome. Any such scheme is really a set of rules that say what happens when different people do different things.

The scheme he came up with worked, but only because the imposter was not smart enough to see through it. Is there another scheme that he could have come up with that would work even with cunning imposters?

Eric Maskin showed that for this type of problem the answer is no. There is no mechanism that will align incentives so that the right outcome emerges as a **Nash equilibrium** of the resulting game. The reason is that what Solomon wants is in a way too out of sync with what the women want. Technically, the problem is that Solomon's preferred outcome is not *monotonic* in the women's preferences. Monotonicity is a tricky idea, but in essence it means that if Solomon wants to see outcome *a* in situation *A* but outcome *b* in situation *B*—then, for at least one woman, *a* is ranked more highly than some other alternative in situation *A* compared with situation *B*. If he wants Jane to have the baby when it's hers but not when it isn't, then if having the baby is what Jane most wants if it is her baby, it should not be what she most wants if it is not. Here the key thing is that Solomon's preferred outcome (who should have the baby) is different depending on who the true mother is but the *women's preferences* over these outcomes are the same in both cases. Solomon wants different outcomes in different cases but he cannot induce them to act in different ways in different cases because they don't see the cases as sufficiently different.

Principle: Unless you have full information, you can only set things up to get the outcomes you want if there is minimal alignment between your goals and the preferences of others.

Puzzle: Would things be different if the women could *pay* Solomon as a way to communicate the value they place on the baby?

Reference: Maskin, E. (1999). Nash equilibrium and welfare optimality. *Review of Economic Studies, 66*(1), 23–38.

FIGURE 35 THE IMPORTANCE OF MONOTONICITY FOR TRUTH REVELATION

Jane	Joan	Solomon
To Jane	To Joan	To Jane
To Joan	Split	To Joan
Split	To Jane	Split

(i)
Preferences if Jane is the true mother

Jane	Joan	Solomon
To Jane	To Joan	To Joan
Split	To Jane	To Jane
To Joan	Split	Split

(ii)
Preferences if Joan is the true mother

A. Either the baby goes to Jane or to Joan, or it is split. The tables show Jane's and Joan's preferences in the case in which Jane is the true mother and the case in which Joan is. The tables also show Solomon's preferences. You can see the violation of monotonicity: as you go from the left panel to the right panel the rankings of the "To Jane" and "To Joan" outcomes stay constant for Jane and Joan, but they switch for Solomon.

Jane	Joan	Solomon
To Jane	To Joan	To Joan
To Joan	Split	To Jane
Split	To Jane	Split

(i)
Preferences if Jane is the true mother

Jane	Joan	Solomon
To Jane	To Joan	Split
Split	To Jane	To Joan
To Joan	Split	To Jane

(ii)
Preferences if Joan is the true mother

B. Solomon could figure out who is who if he had much less benign preferences. Say in particular that if the baby were Jane's, he would get great pleasure in giving it to Joan; if it were Joan's he would want to split it. Cruel as these preferences are, they are monotonic relative to Jane's preferences. In this case Solomon can figure out who is who fairly easily. If he simply asks Jane who is the true owner, Jane will tell him the truth. If it is Jane, Jane would admit to it as she would prefer the baby to go to Joan than to be split; if it were Joan, then Jane would say it was Joan since she would prefer to see it split than for it to go to Joan. Truth telling becomes possible here because monotonicity is satisfied; as you move from the left to the right table the relative ranking of "Split" and "To Joan" move in the same direction for Jane and for Solomon.

36 | How to Choose a Policy (The Clarke-Groves Mechanism)

When countries decide on joint actions they often have to make two separate decisions: What will they do and who is going to pay for it? These decisions are intimately related in a subtle way: if two states enjoy a **public good** to the same extent but they contribute different shares to the production of the good, then the one that contributes less might have incentives to insist on bigger public goods. In the UN, for example, the decision to implement a peacekeeping mission is decided by the UN security council, with all permanent members having equal say. But the costs are paid by individual members based on "assessed contributions," with richer states paying more than poorer states. The United States pays 28% of costs, France and China just 7%. The United States faces greater marginal costs for every additional blue helmet.

Let's assume that the secretary general was a powerful and benevolent decision maker, who would identify the socially optimal action and would be able to have it selected. That would all be fine if indeed the secretary general knew how all the parties valued the option. But what if he didn't?

A lot of work in the study of mechanism design has focused on figuring out whether there are institutional arrangements that can provide actors the incentives to declare their valuations honestly, thus allowing for the selection of **efficient** actions. A seminal, remarkable, but ultimately disheartening result due to Edward Clarke and Theodore Groves (building on work by William Vickery) suggests that under some conditions one can set up an institution (really: devise a **game**) that encourages all players to truthfully report their preferences *no matter what the other players' preferences are*. You can make them, in effect, all want to be unconditionally honest in order to get the outcome that's best for everyone, despite acting unrelentingly in their own self-interest.

The basic insight is fairly simple: say for any pair of "declared preferences" for two players you implement the policy that would be best if in fact those were the true preferences. But then you charge each one the difference between the total cost of the project and the gains that accrue to the *other* person (based on their declared preferences). Then when any person is choosing what sort of preferences to declare, their calculation forces them to choose the preferences that would maximize both their and the other person's preferences, less the costs. In other words, they will be driven to maximize social welfare. But of course, this is just what the institution does when it has the correct information and so the best thing to do is to give the correct information to the institution.

It's an extraordinary result. But on closer look it has some awkward features. First, the payments that players need to make to stay honest might be more than is needed to pay for the public good. This means that to get the most efficient project you need to remove cash from the system, making people worse off, and possibly worse off than they would be if they didn't use the mechanism. Later, more disappointing results show that as a general matter, finding mechanisms that get people to tell the truth, have balanced budgets, and are worth using is impossible.

Principle: When information about the value of collective projects is private, then institutions can help ensure that true valuations are revealed and the best projects are selected. But figuring out which projects are efficient produces costs of its own that may make it not worthwhile.

Puzzle: Could the Clarke-Groves scheme be made ex post efficient if all excess transfers were divided back equally among the members?

Reference: Groves, T. (1973). Incentives in teams. *Econometrica: Journal of the Econometric Society, 41*(4), 617–631.

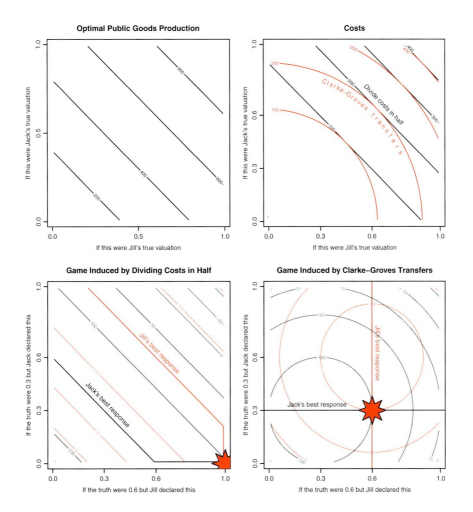

FIGURE 36 CLARKE-GROVES

Jack and Jill have possibly different valuations (weights) they place on gains from a **public good**. For example, if there were 1,000 units of a public good produced and Jack had a valuation of 0.5, the public good would be worth 500 to him. Public goods are costly to produce, so how much should be produced depends on how large these valuations are. In this example, Jack has a true valuation of a public good of 0.3 but could report valuing it at anywhere between 0 and 1. Jill has a true valuation of 0.6 but is also free to report different valuations. The first figure (top left) shows the optimal amount of the public good given any possible combination of true valuations. The black lines in the top right figure show what the costs would be for each under optimal production with costs divided in half. The red lines show a set of Clarke-Groves payments, which again charge both players the same amount but charge more the more different the valuations are of the two players. The bottom two figures show the games that are induced by these two sets of payments. In each case the pink/red lines represent Jill's **utilities**, which are conditional on the reports of both players, and the gray/black lines show Jack's (utilities have been normalized so that the utility is 100 at the Clarke-Groves **equilibrium**). From these one can figure out the best responses of each—that is, the actions that produce the highest utility given the actions of the other—and calculate the **Nash equilibrium** as the intersection of the best responses, marked here with a star. In the first game (in which costs are divided in half), players do not report the truth in equilibrium but they each end up with a utility greater than 100. Amazingly, with the Clarke-Groves payments each player has a **dominant strategy** to tell the truth. This means the Clarke-Groves mechanism makes sure the ideal amount of the public good gets produced. But because of the high payments that the mechanism requires, it also has the depressing property that both players are *worse* off in the equilibrium of this game (getting 100 each) than in the original equilibrium.

37. Not Getting to Yes (The Myerson-Satterthwaite Theorem)

Just before the United States began air strikes against Afghanistan, CIA official Robert Grenier delivered a message from the White House to the Taliban: hand over bin Laden unconditionally and we won't attack. The Taliban responded with a counteroffer: if there is evidence of his involvement, we will try him domestically. The offer was rejected and the bombing started. A week later the Taliban made a second offer, this time to send bin Laden to a third country for trial. This offer too was rejected and the war escalated.

The bargaining failed. Maybe it failed because both sides wanted a war. Although if that were the case, you might not expect the Taliban to improve its offer at all. They did improve their offer, but not enough.

Perhaps it failed because the two sides misjudged each other. A result due to Roger Myerson and Mark Satterthwaite shows that if there is sufficient *ex ante* uncertainty, then there is no conceivable (or inconceivable) budget-balancing mechanism that can be used to get parties to an agreement: everyone's desire to do as well as possible pushes them to take positions that result in bargaining failure with positive probability.

To get a flavor for why, consider a seller who thinks a buyer values some good somewhere between $1 and $3. The buyer is also uncertain and thinks the seller values it at something between $0 and $2, but is not sure how much exactly. The analogue to the good being sold in this case is noninvasion by the United States and the "price" is the manner in which bin Laden is to be handed over. An important feature of the assumption on the beliefs is that there is no guarantee that there is a deal to be made: it is possible that the minimum price the United States would accept is more than the Taliban would even be willing to pay.

With so much uncertainty, both sides might waste time trying to bluff. But imagine, more optimistically, that both sides can call on the good offices of a third party that they both trust. They can tell the third party in confidence how they really value the good and ask the third party to propose some mutually acceptable deal.

For example, the third party might say: "Each of you tell me how much you think the good is worth. If the buyer values the good more than the seller does, then the seller should sell at a price halfway between the two valuations." Say the seller valued the good at 1 and thought the buyer would tell the truth to the third party, then should the seller do likewise? By telling the truth she can expect to make a profit of 1. But by exaggerating a little (and saying it's worth 4/3) she can expect a small (1/6) chance of no trade but also a chance of a larger profit *conditional* on trade for a higher total expected gain. In that case, better to lie a bit and take the risk of a bargaining failure.

The third party could try other mechanisms, but as long as they are voluntary (so there is no point in the third party coming up with a mechanism that one of them can see right away is going to make them worse off) they will run into problems. Both sides will try to game *any* system the third party comes up with and their gaming always means risks of bargaining failure.

Principle (The Myerson-Satterthwaite Theorem): With enough uncertainty there is always a chance of bargaining failure. Institutions cannot fix this problem short of forcing people to accept systems that they expect will make them worse off.

Puzzle: Say the buyer knew the good was worth less than $1 to the seller (rather than less than $2). Then does there exist a mechanism that can guarantee a trade? Would both prefer this mechanism to no third-party involvement?

Reference: Myerson, R., & Satterthwaite, M. (1983). Efficient mechanisms for bilateral trading. *Journal of Economic Theory, 29*(2), 265–281.

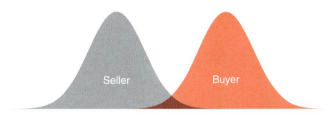

Valuations I: Uncertainty is a Continuous Distribution Over Types

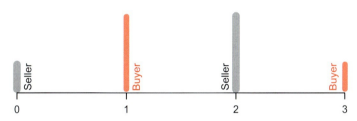

Possible Valuations II: Uncertainty is a Discrete Distribution Over Types

FIGURE 37 THE MYERSON-SATTERTHWAITE THEOREM

Say two bargainers have beliefs about each other's valuations of a good and their beliefs overlap, as in the top figure. Here gray gives the beliefs about the valuation of the seller and red the valuation of the buyer. In that case it is possible (though perhaps not likely) that there are no gains from trade to be made. Note that in this figure the distributions are *continuous*. In such cases, the Myerson-Satterthwaite theorem says that there is no mechanism that the two bargainers would both want to adopt that ensures that they trade **efficiently**.

Things are different if beliefs are not continuous. To see why, say we were in the world of the lower panel and the seller thought there was a 3/4 chance that the buyer thought the good was worth just $1 and a 1/4 chance she thought it was worth $3; say, similarly, the buyer thought there was a 1/4 chance the seller thought it was worth $0 and a 3/4 chance he thought it was worth $2. In that case there is a reasonable chance (9/16) that there is no deal to be made (this arises if the seller thinks it's worth $2 and the buyer thinks it's worth $1). Say a third party proposed the following scheme: "Both tell me what you think it's worth. If there is a trade to be made, I will set a price to split the profits equally." In that case if the seller thought it was worth 0 and said 0, then (assuming the buyer tells the truth) the seller would have a 3/4 chance of a sale at $0.50 and a 1/4 chance of a sale at $1.50 for an expected value of $3/4. If instead he said $2, then there would be a 3/4 chance of no sale and a 1/4 chance that it would go for $2.50, for an expected value of $5/8. So if the good is worth 0 to the seller, he would want to say that. The risks from exaggerating the worth of the good are too great. And if in fact he valued it at $2, then he would certainly want to say that. The buyer is in a similar situation and has incentives to tell the truth no matter what. The key difference between the continuous and the discrete distributions is that with continuous distributions you can always lie a *little* bit; with discrete distributions you might only be able to lie a lot, and perhaps too much for your own good.

PART 12
POLITICAL ECONOMY

Most of the principles in this book operate at a high level of abstraction. But the approaches also have implications for applied problems that many polities face.

A multitude of models seek to explain how elections can, or cannot, be used to keep politicians in check. An early model of retrospective voting developed by John Ferejohn [§38] gives an interesting argument for why elections might be associated with reasonably good policies when politics is not about distribution and for why this might not be the case if distributive concerns play a large role.

The Selectorate Model [§39], by Bruce Bueno de Mesquita and colleagues, provides a more fully developed framework that characterizes political accountability under different institutional procedures, providing insights into why different types of governments choose different types of policies.

The Meltzer-Richard Model [§40] focuses on the choice of tax rates in competitive democracies and uses the Median Voter Theorem [§12] to generate insights linking economic structures and distributive politics. It provides an argument for when and why political competition in democracies should lead to higher or lower tax rates.

Other applied models try to explain how political calculations give rise to inefficient economic outcomes. One of these, by Avinash Dixit and John Londregan [§41], focuses on the pernicious effects of political favoritism in the context of distributive politics.

None of these models seeks to truly capture the complexities of decision making in any particular polity—and in every case, basic assumptions of the model are obviously questionable—but they all succeed in clarifying subtle political logics regarding how political systems and institutions operate.

38 | Throw the Rascals Out (The Logic of Political Accountability)

Let's assume the worst about politicians for a moment. Imagine that the only thing that politicians—and all prospective politicians—wanted to do in office is implement the worst policies possible and get paid for doing it.

Say the only power that voters had over politicians is the threat to remove them from office and replace them with someone else. You might think that the threat of punishment would be pretty ineffective if voters could only replace politicians with others who are just as bad. In fact, though, voters might draw power precisely from the fact that they do not see much difference between all the politicians. It is precisely because one politician is as bad as another that voters can **credibly** commit to removing the politician if she performs badly, and keeping her in office if she performs well. How well voters can make politicians behave depends, in this model, not on how much voters care about good policy but on how much politicians care about being in office and how much they are willing to trade off the gains from misuse of office against the benefits of a longer political career.

But things look very different if voters can't agree on what to demand from politicians. This happens especially when politics is largely about distribution. In this case, the ability of voters to control politicians gets compromised.

For the intuition, imagine a politician auctioning $1 to two voters. In principle, one of two voters could make $1 profit. But because they are competing to win, the price will rise to $1 and neither will get any profit. For the electoral case, imagine all voters declaring the minimum amount of benefits they have to receive in order to support the politician. The politician then chooses the cheapest majority of supporters. If any voter is demanding as much as the median voter then they run the risk of being excluded from the politician's coalition and getting nothing. So, someone will always have an incentive to lower their demands if they can and so it goes until everyone demands nothing. The politician ends up capturing all the benefits and the threat of dismissal is of no help to voters.

Principle: If voters can agree on policy priorities, elections can be used to make bad politicians perform well even when there are only bad alternatives.

Puzzle: Say one of the candidates is your uncle and, all else equal, you would prefer to see him elected. Does this affect your ability to hold him to account?

Reference: Ferejohn, J. (1986). Incumbent performance and electoral control. *Public Choice, 50*(1), 5–25.

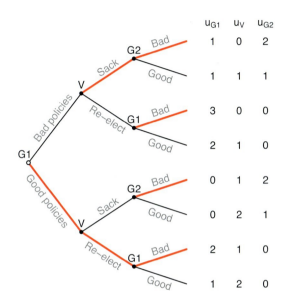

FIGURE 38 THE LOGIC OF POLITICAL ACCOUNTABILITY

This **game tree** shows a government G1 deciding what policies to implement in time 1. Voters (V) then decide whether to re-elect or sack them. In time 2 the next government (G1 or G2) chooses policies afresh. I assume pessimistically that governments prefer bad policies but that they value being in office. In this case in the last period they are sure to implement bad policies. But because of this, voters are strictly indifferent between re-electing incumbents and throwing them out. This indifference allows voters to threaten credibly to re-elect if and only if incumbents perform well. In the **equilibrium** shown in red, the incumbent government will prefer to perform well early on, get re-elected and then underperform, rather than being evicted in time 1. As I show in the notes, the logic extends very naturally to longer-run interactions.

39 | Why More Inclusive Governments Produce More Public Goods (The Selectorate Model)

Hissène Habré ruled Chad for eight years with almost no popular support, fending off threats as they arose with military help from France and overseeing a regime charged with countless atrocities. In 1990 France changed tack ("the times have passed when France would pick governments . . . ," Foreign Minister Dumas explained later). Taking the cue, rebel leader Idriss Déby marched on the capital to oust his former boss only to find he had already fled. Like Habrè, Déby has a very small core support base. But he still gets by. He has been there ever since, withstanding a half-dozen rebellions and coup attempts, dispensing benefits from sales of oil, and presiding over what is now the seventh poorest country in the world. How do governments survive with so little support and why do they govern the way they do?

The selectorate model—developed by Bueno de Mesquita, Smith, Siverson, and Morrow—was designed to answer this kind of question. Start off assuming that a government is in place. Now ask what does the government have to do to make sure it doesn't get dislodged?

A key insight of the selectorate mode is that a government does not have to make a lot of people happy, it just needs to make sure that enough of the right kind of people won't be tempted to take the risk of supporting a would-be challenger.

Simple though that structure is, a formalization of the choices available to different actors can shed a lot of light on features that might account for why some governments act better than others, who they choose to support them in seizing power, and who they purge once its members are in. The moving parts can include the types of budgets available, the ease of converting revenues into **public goods**, and the types of affinities between incumbents and challengers.

Perhaps the most important feature that Bueno de Mesquita and colleagues focus on is the size of the decision-making class in a polity (the "selectorate," s), and the number of members of the selectorate you need to control to be able to guarantee that you will be around tomorrow (the "winning coalition," w). Dictatorships might have small selectorates and among these the winning coalition might also be small in size. One battalion could get you far, as long as they are well-placed and loyal. Democracies could have both large selectorates and large winning coalitions inside these. The sizes, and relative sizes, of w and s can have big implications for the campaigns that challengers can mount and the strategies leaders take to avert them.

A critical insight relates to how institutional structure affects the quality of government. In the core model, a government's ability to retain its supporters depends on what it can offer them. The leader can choose mixes of two strategies—she can dole out privileges (land, offices, cash), or she can invest some share of her budgets in public goods that benefit everyone in society. The more people you have to please, the harder it is to do it with special privileges, and the easier it is to do it with public goods. So if w rises, the logic of political survival pushes leaders to be better rulers. But in becoming better rulers they also get punished: better governments mean more benefits for nonsupporters, but that means that the *specific* gains powerful players get from being a supporter start to vanish, which means weaker bargaining power for the boss, which all adds up to making governing a much less rewarding affair.

Principle: When leaders have to please larger coalitions to ensure their survival they do better by investing more in public goods.

Puzzle: Compare a situation in which a leader has to maintain support from the 25% richest citizens to survive and one in which she has to maintain support from any 50% of the richest 50% of the population. Which situation is better for the leader? Which is better for the richest 25%?

Reference: Bueno de Mesquita, B., Smith, A., Randolph, S., & Morrow, J. (2005). *The logic of political survival.* Cambridge, MA: MIT Press.

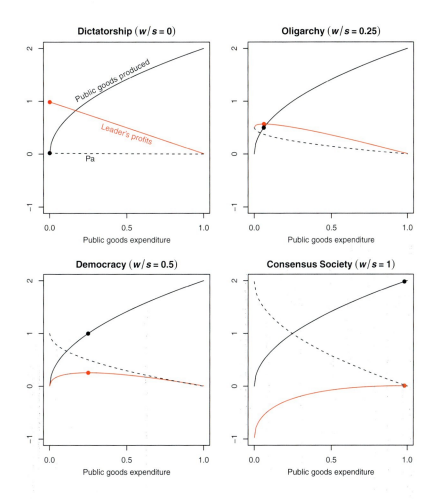

FIGURE 39 THE SELECTORATE MODEL

A leader has to decide on a mix of public and private goods in order to ensure that at least w out of s citizens have payoffs that they value at at least $2. Citizens value private goods in a simple way: every x pennies given to them (*personally*) is worth x to them. Resources allocated to public goods are more complicated: x pennies invested in public goods creates $2\sqrt{x}$ of value to *all* citizens. Given these values, a leader decides the optimal allocation of $1 of state resources between public goods that benefit everyone and private transfers to her coalition. We assume that citizens form a "unit mass," which means that if $1 is divided among 50% of people, they get $1/.5 = $2 each (it seems odd, but it works out mathematically). In this case, a coalition of 50% could be satisfied either by allocating $1 to public goods or by allocating $1 to private goods split among them. In both cases, their **utility** is 2. Let's now see what works best for the leader. The solid black line shows the benefits from public goods, the dotted line is the value of resources the leader has to provide to keep her constituency happy, *in addition to the gains they have from public goods*. The red line is her utility from each possible strategy. The optimal expenditure (picked out with a red point at the maximum of the red curve) depends on the size of the coalition she has to satisfy to stay in office. In the first figure (the dictatorship) the tiny constituency is easily satisfied without any public goods and the government retains a large share of rents. In the last case the government has to satisfy everyone and the best way to do this is to invest entirely in public goods, with no private retention of rents. An alternative interpretation of the consensus society is that the opposition has to get everyone on board to displace the government. In that case the dynamics would be the same as in the dictatorship, with the government making sure that a tiny minority stayed loyal.

40 Redistribution and Inequality (The Meltzer-Richard Model)

In January 2015 the chairman of the Senate Finance Committee, Orrin Hatch, criticized Obama's tax reform plans as being "about redistribution . . . and class warfare, directed at job-creating small businesses." The warfare account of tax policy resonates broadly in the Republican party. High taxes use the power of the state to take from the rich and redistribute to the poor. But the decision on the *level* of taxes is made with votes not violence. With such fundamental disagreement on the right tax levels, and voting as the way to select policies, what kind of taxes can you expect?

Let's get more specific. Imagine there were three groups: the poor, the middle class, and the rich. Say these groups are of size 40%, 30%, and 30%, respectively. Say they have to decide over a simple tax policy: set a marginal tax rate, and use what is raised for the production of **public goods**. How high their optimal tax policy would be depends on various things such as the value to them of public goods, and the extent to which higher taxes will reduce production. The poorest groups might not want 100% taxation, for example, because this might mean that the rich in fact produce less and then nothing gets transferred.

So, given all these considerations all voters probably have different ideal tax rates. Say, moreover, that when comparing two tax rates that are both above or both below their ideal they prefer the one that is closer to their ideal. To keep things simple say that the poor want a 60% rate, the middle class want 20%, and the wealthy want no taxes at all.

What tax rates do you expect to see if the decision is made by majority rule? Note that this means we are assuming no false consciousness, no coercion, no undue influence of the rich.

You probably wouldn't expect to see either a zero tax rate or a 60% rate, but something in between. But what? The average preferred tax rate is 30% (.4 × 60 + .3 × 20 + .3 × 0 = 30), and that seems like a reasonable guess. Or you might think that guessing is a waste of time since Condorcet [§8] showed that democratic majorities are prone to preference cycling. Both conclusions would be wrong. As shown by Duncan Black [§12], what matters is what the *median* (middle) voter cares about. So 20% in this case. The unique thing about the median (assuming odd numbers of voters) is that there are no majorities to the left or the right of it and so nothing can beat it.

The attractive and retentive power of the median leads to a key insight on two-party competition. Say two parties were competing for office and both wanted to choose the policy that would get them to win. Then the only positions they could adopt (such that neither would want to switch positions) is at the median. Both end up at the same place, dividing the vote between them. Moreover, the draw of the median does not depend on the polarization of society. No matter how distant the typical Democrat from the typical Republican, the battle for office will be fought over the middle.

More generally, this means that if voters vote on tax levels, then taxes will reflect the desires of the median earner. The more unequal the society, the bigger the difference between the average income and the income of the median voter, and the greater the median's gains from redistribution.

Principle: The median voter's preferences determine democratic tax rates. The more unequal the society, the higher the tax rate desired by the median voter.

Puzzle: Say that rather than producing a public good, taxes could be targeted at particular groups (for example, at the poor or the rich in different combinations). Does this affect what tax rates you might expect to see?

Reference: Meltzer, A. H., & Richard, S. F. (1981). A rational theory of the size of government. *The Journal of Political Economy, 89*(5), 914–927.

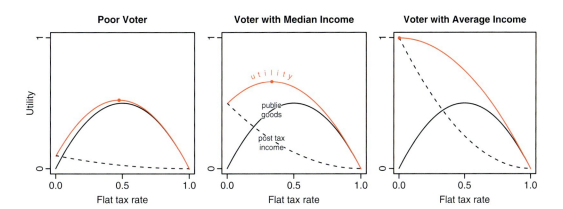

FIGURE 40 THE MELTZER-RICHARD MODEL
Each figure shows the costs and benefits to different voters associated with different possible tax rates. The benefits to voters from different tax rates is the same for all voters in this example (black curve). These are greatest at intermediate levels because when taxes are too high production goes down. But the income losses from higher tax rates are greater for wealthier voters than for poorer voters (dotted curve). The total **utility** is marked in red for different voters. The result here is that all voters with income below the mean prefer middling taxes but among these, poorer people prefer higher taxes. Voters with income above the mean want no redistribution. For most plausible income distributions, keeping total income fixed, the greater is the income inequality, the poorer is the median voter, and so the higher is the demanded tax rate. In this model, inequality in productivity imposes net costs on society.

41 | Redistribution and Inefficiency (The Dixit-Londregan Model)

Two politicians are competing for the votes of city and country voters. The groups are of equal size but city workers earn $100 a year and country workers earn $50 a year. Say that 60% of the country workers are undecided (the rest are staunch partisans of one or another party) and 30% of the city workers are undecided. These voters are more likely to support politicians who promise to do more for them, so the politicians need to choose tax-and-spend policies to win voters. Who should they tax? Where should they spend?

Let's put more flesh on the problem. Say that redistribution is economically **efficient** in the sense that there is no loss in economic value when money is transferred from one group to another; people don't adjust their labor supply in anticipation of taxation. So this is a setting where you might not expect taxes to produce inefficiencies.

In this setting the distributions that are possible are those that arise from taxing all groups as much as possible and then redistributing the total amount in the most effective way. The optimal policy for the politicians ignores whether one group has more supporters who are faithful to them or not. Instead politicians should target redistribution to the groups with more swing voters. But they also have to take account of the plans proposed by the other side—if one side is putting a lot of resources into one group, then the other side will be better off following suit. The net result is that, **in equilibrium**, both end up allocating resources to the same groups as a function of the extent to which they have more independent voters. The benefits that each sector receives are a function of a political attribute: how *non*partisan it is. Whether or not you are partisan, you do well being in a group with a lot of nonpartisans.

To figure out optimal policies we need to know how undecided voters respond to promises of transfers. Assume that the share of volatile votes that a party receives is equal to the share of all promised net transfers to the group that come from that party. So for example, if party 1 is the only one to promise benefits, then it gets all the votes; if the parties offer equal benefits, then they get equal shares; if party 1 promises $1 and party 2 promises $3, then party 1 could expect 1/4 of the votes (other mappings from promises to votes are of course possible). Then (see Figure 41) if you set up the policy choices as a **game**, the optimal platforms—for both parties—would involve taxing 100% of all income and setting the share returned to the country workers equal to the share of all volatile voters who are country workers (two-thirds). In practice, to do this, the parties would make return payments of $100 to each country worker and $50 to each city worker—effectively reversing the income distribution.

The effect of the transfers means that your net income depends more on your political characteristics than on your economic characteristics. This feature, however, can introduce inefficiencies of its own. Now, any country worker thinking of moving to a more productive city job would face an implicit tax to do so and would rather stay in the economically less productive (but politically more rewarding) sector. More depressingly, if moving between sectors is costly, even a move to a more productive sector that has the same political characteristics may not be optimal because the mover will only benefit from a small share of the increase in the size of the pie.

Principle: Political competition can drive politicians to redistribute national income toward undecided voters. If so, then voters might have little incentive to contribute to national income in the first place.

Puzzle: What kind of institutional or policy innovations could restore efficiency in a distributive environment like this?

Reference: Dixit, A., & Londregan, J. (1995). Redistributive politics and economic efficiency. *American Political Science Review, 89*(4), 856–866.

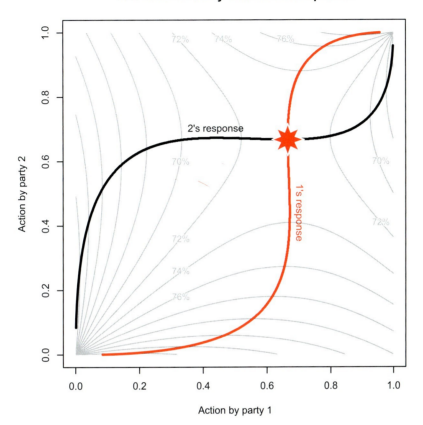

FIGURE 41 A GAME BETWEEN PARTIES USING TAX POLICY TO COMPETE FOR VOTES FROM TWO SECTORS

Assuming a fixed allocation to be split between two sectors, each party's choice can be summarized by their proposed allocation to the first sector. The figure shows the indifference curves for each party from the choice of strategies by both. You can think of each party's **utility** surface as shaped like a saddle: for any level of support for sector 1 provided by party 2, party 1's utility is maximized by a somewhat centrist allocation, however, her utility is lowest when the *other* party plays a more centrist allocation. Since this is a **zero-sum** game, party 2's utility is the inverse of this (and so the indifference curves are identical to each other!). The optimal action, given the action by the other, is given by the highest point on each person's surface given the other's action. These best responses are traced out in the figure (party 1's in red). Each has a broadly (though not everywhere) positive slope reflecting the need to spend resources in a way similar to your opponent; the intersection of these best response curves is at 66% and marks the **Nash equilibrium** of this game.

PART 13

REVOLTING

Seminal applications of game theoretic logic to politics focus on the problem of political protest. Some of these build on the original set of social dilemmas, characterizing the decision to revolt as a collective action problem. The question then becomes: What sort of groups will be more or less successful at solving different collective action problems? A powerful logic suggests that smaller groups will be more effective than larger groups, though when you really work through it, that result can be quite sensitive to details of the collective action problem [§42]. Threshold models [§43] highlight a feature observed by many revolution watchers: violent action, revolutions, riots, coups, often come as a surprise. A simple logic that focuses on the complementarities of collective action also sheds light on its unpredictability: when there are complementarities, small changes in fundamentals can have big implications for social outcomes. Psychological Games [§44] are based on a third logic that moves outside the collective action framework and shows how the decision to revolt can be explained by intrinsic valuation of revolt, but that this valuation may itself be the product of strategic actions. Reputation Models [§45] focus on the counterinsurgency side and describe a logic of resistance to revolt even when the costs of that resistance seem to outweigh any possible benefits.

42 | Small Is Beautiful (The Logic of Collective Action)

When people compete over political outcomes they often do it in packs. But once you start working with a pack you have to deal with politics at two levels—the politics of between-group competition and the politics of figuring out who does the work within your own group. Some groups do better than others at solving their within-group collective action problems and this makes them more effective in between-group competition. How does this effectiveness depend on the size of your pack?

You might expect that bigger groups generally do better. But things can look very different if people are strategic. A core principle of political economy is that even though small groups have a disadvantage in between-group competition, they can be so much better than big groups at solving the within-group problems that they sometimes get to punch well above their weight.

The Game of Chicken [§2] logic suggested one reason why small groups might do better than larger groups: when people's contributions substitute for each other, more potential contributors can mean greater incentives to free ride. There are other reasons why small is beautiful, however. Sometimes, as groups get bigger, coordination becomes exponentially more complex. It is also possible that as groups get bigger, any gains they make get diluted by having to be shared between group members. These effects can be so severe that not only do individual contributions decline as groups get larger but the combined effort of all members can also go down. This is the paradox of group size: *the more people you have working on a problem, the less likely it gets solved*.

But other more subtle details also matter and these can change the calculus. A critical detail is the individual pain of contributing. If contributing becomes increasingly onerous the more you put in, then it becomes easier for a lot of people to put in a little than for a few people to put in a lot. In that case even though per capita contributions decline, overall group contributions increase. Again, small details matter profoundly and determine whether for a given problem it makes sense to form tiny special interest groups or to band together to form broad coalitions.

Principle (The Group Size Paradox): Although larger groups have the potential to be more powerful than smaller groups, their power advantage can be entirely undone by the perverse effects of group size on the strategic behavior of individual members. Think twice before bandwagonning.

Puzzle: Say there are 3 people deciding whether to contribute to a **public good** or not. The public good is produced if at least one person contributes, and not otherwise. Say that the public good is worth $2 to everybody. But say that people differ in the costs to them of contributing. In particular, the cost to each person is a random amount somewhere between 0 and $1; each person knows their own cost but not the costs of others. In this case how should people play? How should they play if there were 10 people playing instead of 3?

Reference: Olson, M. (1965). *The logic of collective action: public goods and the theory of groups.* Cambridge, MA: Harvard University Press.

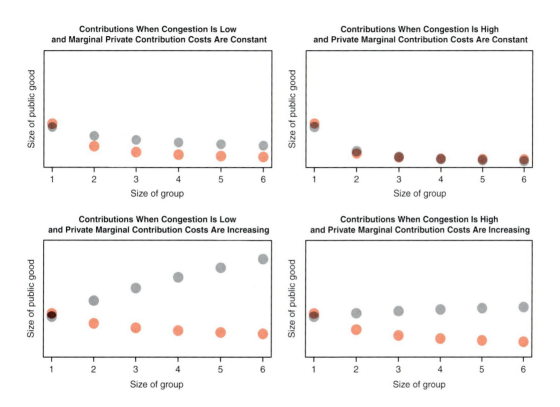

FIGURE 42 THE POWER OF SMALL GROUPS

The figure shows the contributions you might expect of groups of different sizes depending on the extent to which there are congestion problems (which happens when the more people there are in the group, the lower is the value to any one member of a public good of a given size) and the extent to which the costs of contributions are increasingly onerous for individuals. In each set of graphs the gray dots show the total amount of public goods produced by a group of a given size, the red dots show the per capita contributions. In all these cases the per capita contributions decline; in some—but not all—cases this decline is so steep that the total contributions of the groups fall. The full details of the underlying model are provided in the notes (see p. 165).

PART 13 | Revolting 109

43 | Surprised by Revolt (Threshold Models)

On December 21, 1989, Romanian dictator Nicolae Ceaușescu addressed tens of thousands of workers he had bused in for the occasion. Used to devotion from crowds, he was stunned to hear boos and hisses growing louder and louder as he spoke. Cutting short his speech he tried to flee but he was already too late. After the crowds turned the army turned on him too. He was apprehended, arrested, and executed live on national television.

A few things had changed for Ceaușescu. Four days before, he had his troops fire on crowds, further exposing the brutality of his regime. Revolutions were also taking place throughout the region. But while times were changing, Ceaușescu hadn't seen it coming. Perhaps he had misunderstood the politics of crowds.

Crowds are not like people. Occasionally, small changes in how individuals value outcomes can have a big effect on their decisions, but even if individual responses to small changes are always small, group responses to small changes can be very large. The reason is that a small change that has a moderate *direct* effect on each individual can have a large *indirect* effect on the calculations of all as a consequence of strategic responses to all those small effects.

The key idea is that sometimes a person's actions depend on the expected actions of others as well as the fundamental issues at stake. If a misstep by a regime changes attitudes in a way that increases the likelihood that each person takes an action against a regime by just 1%, that might translate into hundreds or perhaps thousands of people taking an action. Hundreds, or even thousands of protesters might not be a great threat. However, if thousands of people are willing to take an action, that might, indirectly, be enough to make many more willing to join them, leading to massive revolt. In theory the indirect effects can be so large as to create sharp discontinuities in crowd responses; whereas the propensities of individuals to vote might change a little in response to small actions of the state, the propensities of crowds to revolt might leap forward.

Complicated as that might sound, the basic logic can be seen way back in the social dilemmas described in §1 and §3. A tiny change in individual values can change a Prisoner's Dilemma into an Assurance Game, producing a large effect on what can be supported as an **equilibrium** outcome.

Principle: Strategic complementarities can make the actions of crowds much more sensitive to small changes in individual payoffs than the actions of individuals.

Puzzle: In the logic of Information Cascades [§22], the information that crowds have about one another's preferences can change rapidly in response to the actions of a few. Is imperfect information about the values of others an important feature of the threshold model described here?

Reference: Kuran, T. (1989). Sparks and prairie fires: A theory of unanticipated political revolution. *Public Choice, 61*(1), 41–74.

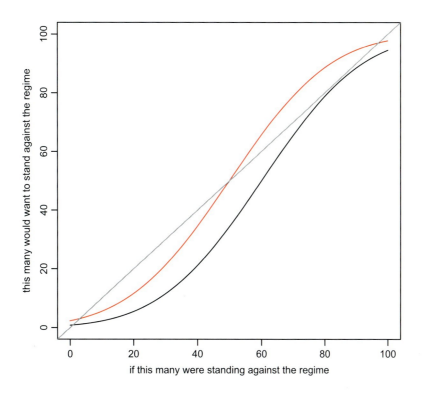

FIGURE 43 A THRESHOLD MODEL
Say that the value of joining a rebellion depends on how many others are also rebelling. For example, when others rebel, the risks that any individual who rebels will be targeted by the regime go down. Then, with information about everyone's preferences, you can figure out how many people would be willing to join given that they expect some particular number would join. That is shown here by the black line. The black line is generally below the gray 45-degree line. That means that if everyone thought that share n of people will join, then in fact less than share n of people will be willing to join. For example, if everyone expected 60% to turn up, then only 50% would be willing to turn up. The line intersects with the 45-degree line at one point, around the 1% mark. This means that if everyone expects that 1% will show up, then indeed 1% will show up. At that point peoples' actions are consistent with their beliefs and so the no-show revolution is in equilibrium. Imagine though that there is a small drop in the value of supporting the current regime. Conditional on any number of people rebelling, this increases the attractiveness of rebelling by only a small amount—as shown here by the small shift from the black to the red line. But the *strategic* effects of this change are dramatic. The response curve associated with this new situation is marked with the red line. Like the black line, the red line crosses the 45-degree line close to zero, which means there is still a no-show equilibrium. But unlike the black line the red line also crosses at the 50% mark and then again at close to 100%. This means that if, say, 60% of people are expected to rebel, then *more* than 60% of the people will want to; if 70% are expected to rebel, then even more will want to. In equilibrium if about 97% are expected to rebel, then indeed 97% will be willing to. The small shift in costs, coupled with the logic of strategic complementarities, creates a full participation equilibrium in which previously only a no-show equilibrium existed. (See the notes on page 166 for details on the assumptions behind these curves.)

PART 13 | Revolting

44 Dashed Expectations (Psychological Games)

Most formal models of participation in politics seek to explain actions in instrumental terms: What are the benefits to be achieved by joining a rebellion, by speaking out against a government, by voting? But people might also engage in politics for noninstrumental reasons. Perhaps because they think they should, or perhaps because they think it is intrinsically valuable.

If the motivation for taking an action is simply that the action is desirable, then formal models might not have much to say. Sometimes, however, they can shed light on how strategic interactions *render* particular actions particularly desirable. In research on rebellion, a long-standing literature has highlighted frustration, vengeance, or anger as motivations leading people to engage in risky behavior, even when the instrumental gains are not clear.

Though seemingly nonstrategic, a family of **games** called "psychological games" can shed light on such behavior and the strategic interactions that can give rise to it. In psychological games, players have preferences not just over outcomes but also over *expectations* around behavior. These expectations can themselves be formed as part of play or be given by the **equilibriums** of a game.

In a psychological game, someone who expects to receive benefits from a government may be frustrated not simply because they did not receive benefits but because they did not receive them *when they expected to*. In such situations the possibility of disappointment, grievances, or frustration may give rise to strategic play by other actors, and the failure to prevent disappointment may give rise to oppositional politics. If that logic is right, then the politics of counterinsurgency may lie as much in managing expectations as it does in managing information or favors.

Principle: To stay in power, managing citizen expectations may be just as important as satisfying demands.

Puzzle: Are psychological games analytically distinct from games of incomplete information?

Reference: Geanakoplos, J., Pearce, D., & Stacchetti, E. (1989). Psychological games and sequential rationality. *Games and Economic Behavior, 1*(1), 60–79.

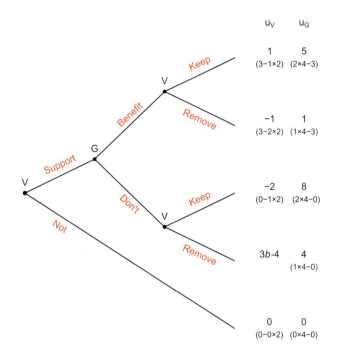

FIGURE 44 PSYCHOLOGICAL GAMES

This **game tree** shows voters (V) deciding whether to support a new government (G). The government in office gets income of $4 and can decide whether to transfer either $3 or $0 back to voters. Voters then decide whether to retain the government or not. Assume the cost of changing the government is $2. If the new government does not come to office, then everyone gets status quo payoffs of 0. In general, voters and government care just about their dollar returns. But there is a wrinkle: I allow here for the possibility that voter dissatisfaction with a government that fails to provide benefits depends on their *expectations* of what it was going to do. Dashed expectations provide them with a *vengeance* motivation to take action against a failing G. Formally, let b denote the expectations that a government will help the voters and let b be determined by the equilibrium strategies. Then the following is an equilibrium: the voters do not expect that the new government will do anything good for them ($b = 0$) and so do not bother electing it, preferring the status quo payoff of 0 to the −2 they get from putting in the new useless government. Importantly, the government if elected would in fact be useless since, as the voters expect nothing of the government ($b = 0$), they would not bother turning the government out of office if it fails to deliver. But there is another equilibrium here in which the voters are very optimistic about the government ($b = 1$), they support it in expectation of great things from it, and remove it from office if expectations are dashed—which of course, they will not be. (Bonus puzzle: Is there also a hidden **mixed strategy** equilibrium in which poorly performing governments sometimes face revolt?)

45 | Feigning Tough (Reputation Models)

In the 1990s Indonesia was facing secessionist claims from Aceh and Timor. The government reacted strongly and a bloody civil war ensued. Its reaction followed a pattern also seen in the response by Nigeria to the secessionist bid from Biafra, by Sudan against the South, Serbia against Kosovo, Sri Lanka against Tamil insurgents, and in many other cases. In some cases the costs of such conflicts seem higher than the value of retaining the territory. Why fight so hard?

One answer is that when states fight secessionists they are not thinking just about this war but about the next one also. By fighting hard, states try not just to win the war but also to signal their *willingness to fight*, and in doing so, hope to deter future secessionist bids. They are fighting a war to build a reputation.

Figuring out the conditions under which it makes sense to do this is a little tricky. Return to the hostage-taking example from Figure H. Here the government would have benefited from having a reputation for not negotiating with hostages. If would-be hostage takers believed the government, they would be better off. Say that instead of this one-shot game, the government expected that it might face hostage takers on two separate occasions. It's as if the game was played twice instead of once. Would it then have an incentive to refuse to negotiate the first time?

No. In this repeated game the hostage takers might be puzzled by the government's refusal to negotiate the first time, but still when they strike a second time they have no reason to expect that the government will not negotiate this time. The second time is after all just the same strategic environment as the original one in which hostages only act once. Just because the government played one way once does not mean that it will play the same way every time. Knowing this, the government would fold the first time, and the second time. No point in trying to build a reputation when the other side can see right through you.

But what if the other side cannot see right through you? That changes everything. Then by fighting today you might convince would-be secessionists that you are the type of hard-line government that will fight every time. In fact even if a would-be secessionist is *not* sufficiently convinced that you are a hard-liner, they might nevertheless be convinced that you are sufficiently determined to try to convince the world that you are hard-line and that you will fight anyhow, and that could be enough to keep them at bay. So even if you would rather give in every time, it can still make sense to fight early wars to prevent later ones from even starting.

In reputation **games**, your incentives to bluff are higher the more you are concerned with the future. For an Indonesia or a Serbia with many threats ahead that may be motivation enough.

Principle: It can be worth paying a heavy price to build a reputation, especially if you are an unknown quantity, are farsighted, and face many threats.

Puzzle: Are there conditions under which it makes sense to build a reputation for tough behavior even though there is no uncertainty about your preferences?

Reference: Kreps, D. M., & Wilson, R. (1982). Reputation and imperfect information. *Journal of Economic Theory, 27*(2), 253–279. Walter, B. F. (2009). *Reputation and civil war: Why separatist conflicts are so violent.* Cambridge, UK: Cambridge University Press.

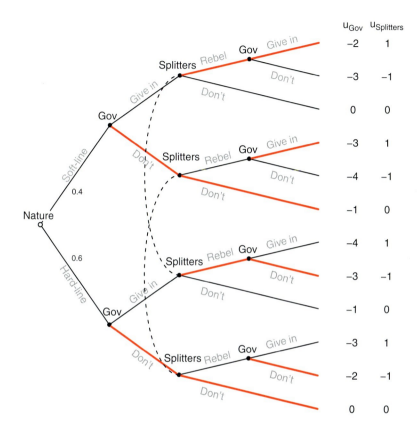

FIGURE 45 A REPUTATION MODEL

This game shows a two-period version of the "chainstore game." In the classic chainstore problem a monopolist decides whether to try to fight off new market entrants. The same logic has been used to understand the incentives of governments to fight against secessionist threats. In the first stage the government is facing a threat from a seceding region and has to decide whether to give in or to fight. In the example, in the absence of any future threat, a soft-line government would prefer giving in to fighting. A hard-line government would prefer to fight, however. Similarly, if there is a second secessionist bid in the second period, a soft-line government would prefer giving in to fighting and a hard-line government would prefer to fight. Rebels believe that a government is hard-line with a 60% probability. If the government gives up in the first period, then they will infer that the government is soft-line and will launch a rebellion in the second period, expecting the government to fold. If the government fights in the first period, however, the rebels will continue believing that the government is hard-line, with a 60% probability, and will prefer not to start the second war. These logics give the soft-line government incentives to fight in the first stage.

PART 14

LIMITED RATIONALITY

I have described a wide range of results that suggest that social behavior is often likely to be unpredictable, uncoordinated, and inefficient. Amazingly, these messy results are generally generated under the assumption that people's *individual* decision making is not particularly messy. In fact, although formal methods can handle many different models of how people think and make decisions, most of the work in this area assumes that humans are extremely sophisticated, and much, much more sophisticated than we know ourselves to be.

In recent years, an entire branch of game theory dispenses with rationality assumptions entirely and assumes instead that strategies are selected through evolutionary pressures rather than through the foresight of strategists. Surprisingly, this very different approach often produces the exact same predictions. As shown in a canonical result on evolutionary games [§46], any strategies that are "evolutionarily stable" have to be Nash equilibrium strategies. Evolutionary processes can, however, not just justify Nash equilibriums, they can also help select among them in cases in which there are several equilibriums. If people play *adaptively* and select strategies in response to the past actions of others [§47], then in noisy environments the kinds of equilibriums that get selected are often the ones that are the least risky, even if they are not necessarily the best ones for players.

Two last items examine mixed situations when strategic players play with others who are not thinking too much. The first, §48, shows that strategists can do well playing against people who are only somewhat strategic but can be exposed if they overestimate how strategic others are. The second, §49, shows how hard things can be for strategists when nonstrategists use a particularly simple strategy: imitation. Imitators often do very well when playing with strategists and sometimes their nonstrategic behavior can force strategists to take a hit for the common good.

46 | Strategy without Strategizing (Evolutionary Stability)

The core prediction from **game** theoretic accounts of human behavior—**Nash equilibrium**—seems to depend heavily on people being very strategic, willing to think through what everyone else is doing and finding the best responses to all possibilities.

Here is a completely different approach. Let's drop the idea that people give any consideration to the strategies of others. Assume instead that people play random strategies, watch how things go over time, and then switch to try out any strategies that seem to be doing better than theirs. At any point in time, random strategies might be introduced into the mix (technically there can be "mutants") but those mutant strategies will only gain ground if they are seen to do well. If that's how people operated, how might they end up playing?

One reasonable prediction is that if their behavior ever settles down, it will settle down on strategies that are "evolutionarily stable"—that is, strategies that have the property that if everyone were playing them, then if a mutant started playing another strategy, that mutant would do badly against all the other strategies and would get forced out. In evolutionary language, a strategy is evolutionarily stable if small invasions of mutants always fail.

The condition for a strategy to be evolutionarily stable is that (a) when played against any alternative strategy the candidate evolutionarily stable strategy does strictly better than the alternative strategy or (b) the candidate evolutionarily stable strategy does just as well as the alternative strategy when they play against each other and does strictly better than the alternative strategy when they are each playing against the alternative strategy.

This method for identifying strategies assumes that people are not in any way strategic in any given interaction.

The amazing thing is that if people are playing evolutionarily stable strategies, then they must be playing Nash equilibrium strategies (although the converse of that claim is not true—a strategy can be a Nash equilibrium but not evolutionarily stable). The reason is simple: if everyone is playing some strategies that do *not* form a Nash equilibrium, then, by definition, some person would do better by adopting a different strategy; but that means that that different strategy could invade the pool of existing strategies and so these are not evolutionarily stable.

Principle: If people select their strategies nonstrategically, based on what seems to work over time, then, *if* the strategies stabilize (in the sense of not being vulnerable to infiltration by other strategies), the strategies must be the kind of strategies you would expect strategic people would have chosen anyway.

Puzzle: Can you think of a game with no evolutionarily stable strategies?

Reference: Dawkins, R. (2006). *The selfish gene.* Oxford, UK: Oxford University Press.

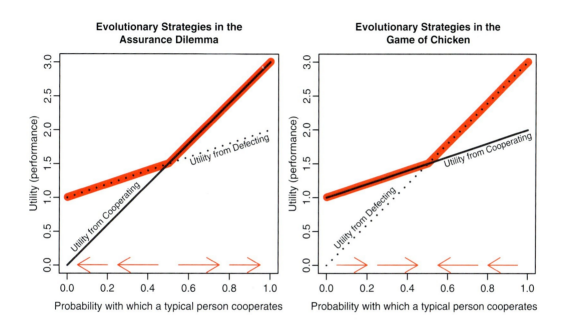

FIGURE 46 EVOLUTIONARY STABILITY

Payoffs from different strategies given different candidate evolutionarily stable strategies in populations playing the Assurance Dilemma [§3] and the Game of Chicken [§2]. In the Assurance Dilemma you see that if population cooperation rates are below 50% then a strategy that puts more weight on defecting would do well. If cooperation rates are above 50%, then strategies putting more weight on cooperation would do well. The stable points are at the extremes where all cooperate or all defect (strategies that correspond to two of the Nash equilibriums of the game). A similar logic holds in the Game of Chicken but here evolution pushes people to the position where they use **mixed strategies**, cooperating with a 50% probability. In this game a strategy that puts too much weight on cooperation or defection would be beaten ("invaded by") by the mixed strategy.

47 | Adaptive Play and the Dominance of Fear (Stochastic Stability)

Rival clans live in close quarters. When they encounter each other they can fight, or let each other go about their business. If you are in the world of Assurance Dilemmas [§3], what to do can depend a lot on what you expect others to do. You could all end up in a good place or be stuck in a very bad place. Fear that others will not cooperate can push toward bad outcomes, but gains from cooperation push in the opposite direction. So what to expect?

You might be hopeful that in these **games** everyone will end up doing the right thing. An extraordinary leader, for example, might shift society to a good place, leading everyone to expect good behavior, and there they will stay, with actions reflecting expectations. Or perhaps if rational people are also *reasonable*, they should simply expect to coordinate on good outcomes.

But say, more pessimistically, that expectations are formed from seeing how people behaved in the past and actions are taken based not on enlightened notions of how people *ought* to play but on how they have played. This is called "adaptive play." Say everyone played adaptively: Where would things end up?

You could imagine a world in which at first everyone is cooperating, and so everyone expects everyone to cooperate and so everyone keeps on cooperating. Then cooperation would be a stable outcome. Say though that people sometimes make mistakes. Perhaps there is a bad apple or just a bad day, and some person cheats (defects). In response, it might be rational for others to start cheating and then more, and there could soon be a whole cascade of cheating. Similar mistakes might also turn bad situations around and bring societies to a point in which everyone is cooperating again. Over time, when people play adaptively, small errors and shocks can shift everyone's behavior in and out of good **equilibriums**.

This way of thinking treats social dynamics as a kind of *process* or more specifically a "Markov process" in which you move from state to state randomly as a function of where you were in the previous period. In these processes, where you end up in the long run can depend on the number of mistakes that need to cumulate before everyone switches from one set of strategies to another.

In the assurance game, the cheating equilibrium can be more robust than the cooperation equilibrium in the sense that fewer errors are needed to push you into it and overall you stay there for longer periods. This happens whenever the cheating equilibrium is less risky than the cooperation equilibrium (which means that you would be better off cheating if you thought it equally likely the other side would or wouldn't cheat). In that case if people are playing adaptively, then *even though everyone prefers cooperation, they will all end up cheating in the long run*. In contrast if fewer errors are needed to produce a shift to cooperation, good outcomes can emerge over time from the play of shortsighted agents even if they start off in a bad place.

Principle: When people play adaptively rather than thinking through future scenarios, then less risky actions get selected whether or not they are more **efficient**.

Puzzle: Agents that play adaptively in noisy environments sometimes manage to cooperate in assurance-type dilemmas. Might they also succeed in cooperating in Prisoner's Dilemmas [§1]?

Reference: Young, H. (2001). *Individual strategy and social structure: An evolutionary theory of institutions.* Princeton, NJ: Princeton University Press.

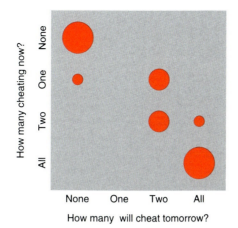

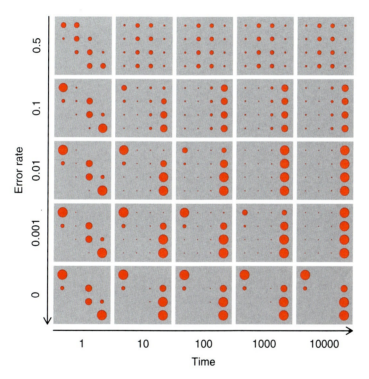

FIGURE 47 STOCHASTIC STABILITY

The top figure shows a "transition matrix," depicting how strategies evolve in a three-person society: the larger the circle, the more likely it is that society will move from the state marked in the row to the state marked in the column. If none cheat today, none will tomorrow, but if one does today, maybe two will tomorrow, and so on. The lower figures show how behavior looks after some length of time when people make small errors each period. The matrices in the rows are estimated by multiplying the first matrix in each row by itself a given number of times—these tell you where you will be after 1, 10, or 10,000 periods depending on where you are today. When error rates are small (but not 0), you see that in the long run everyone cheats no matter how many are cheating at the beginning.

48 | Too Clever by Half (The *k*-level Model)

Jack and Jill are competing for office and have to propose tax policies. They would both love to keep taxes at the present high rate of 64%. But they also know that voters want taxes as low as possible and they are ready to compromise to win. Say now they are simultaneously asked to propose policies. Jack and Jill, putting career before policy, reckon that their optimal strategy to maximize the chances of winning while still maintaining *some* revenue would be to declare a rate about 50% below what their competitor declares. So what should they declare?

Jill might figure as follows. If Jack writes 64%, she should write 32%. But if Jack thinks that Jill is thinking like that, then he will write 16%. In that case she should really write 8%. And so on. If she thinks through any chain of reasoning long enough, then she will figure that the only consistent outcome is for all to write 0.

So Jill reckons it is a race to the bottom and declares 0. Jack meanwhile does indeed declare 64%, not having given the question any serious thought whatsoever. Jill wins the election, but she is broke in office. She would have done a lot better if she hadn't overestimated Jack's reasoning skills.

Jill could instead have based her strategy on her beliefs about Jack's reasoning capacity. Say she thought that there was some chance that Jack wouldn't reason at all and declare 64% and some chance that Jack would reason just a bit and declare 32% (on the assumption that *Jill* doesn't reason at all). Then she might be better off choosing some number between 16% and 32%; how low she should go depends not on how much she reasons, but how much she thinks Jack reasons (and her beliefs about how much she thinks Jack thinks she reasons).

How many steps of reasoning like this do real people actually take? Colin Camerer and colleagues tried to answer that question by looking at actual behavior in **games** of this form ("beauty contest games") and assessing how many levels of reasoning people engage in given that someone who engages in k levels of reasoning assumes others engage in less than k levels. From their analysis, people do not seem so sophisticated: in the typical game people reason on average between just one and two steps.

Principle: Never overestimate the rationality of your opponents.

Puzzle: Say everyone is a strategist and everyone knows that everyone is a strategist, but they don't all know that everyone knows that everyone is a strategist. Might they still choose taxes above 0?

Reference: Camerer, C., Ho, T., & Chong, J. (2004). A cognitive hierarchy model of games. *Quarterly Journal of Economics, 119*(3), 861–898.

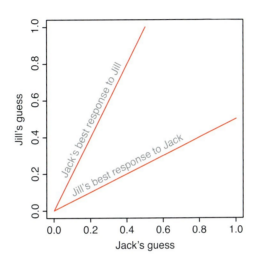

FIGURE 48 BEST RESPONSES IN THE GUESSING GAME
Assume that Jack and Jill each want to guess half each other's guess. The players' best responses are then straight lines that intersect at 0, making 0 the only **Nash equilibrium** of the game. If there were **common knowledge** of players' rationality, they could reach this equilibrium by reasoning in the following way: "If I want my number to be half of their number, then there is no point in me ever writing down more than 50. But if they know that, then they would never write down more than 25…" and so on down to 0. Writing down positive numbers might make sense though if you think that the other players are not as calculating as you.

49 | The Irrationality of Others (A Theorem on Imitation)

In some interpretations, when Kennedy set up the blockade on Cuba he was engaging in *brinkmanship*: he pushed Khrushchev to a point where the risks were so great that any further escalation would be too costly. The strategically rational thing for Khrushchev was to back down and so back down he did.

Perhaps. But if so, the strategy depended critically on Khrushchev's thinking through things strategically. What if rather than calculating all the risks and thinking through all the possible actions and counteractions, Khrushchev opted for the simpler copycat policy of just doing whatever the United States does? Then where would we be?

While most of **game** theory has focused on what happens when strategic players play with other strategic players, there are also lessons for what happens when a strategic player plays with *non*strategic players. Curiously, in these settings strategic players sometimes lose.

Here's the logic. Say Dee and Dum play the same game with each other over and over. Dee puts a lot of time into thinking through the best possible strategies to play against Dum. But Dum doesn't. Dum just looks to see whether Dee is doing better than him and if she is, then he copies whatever she is doing.

How does Dum do? Can Dee take advantage of the fact that Dum is just copying her in order to do well? Collectively, does Dum's failure to act strategically make them all better or worse off?

For some games, copying the past actions of others is about the worst you can do. If Dum and Dee play a penalty shootout, then whenever Dee is shooting, she just swaps from left to right to left, while Dum trailing behind jumps the wrong way every time. Similarly, when they play a rock-paper-scissors game (in which each chooses one of the three objects and scissors beats paper, which beats rock, which beats scissors), Dee just cycles through the three objects and beats Dum every time.

But in some games Dum is not exploited by Dee. Say they play a Prisoner's Dilemma. Then if Dee were to cooperate every time so would Dum, and collectively they would do better than if Dee simply defected every time. In this case Dum's failure to strategize helps both players.

In fact, for a very large class of games, imitation performs quite well. For every two person symmetric game that is not like rock-paper-scissors (which means that there is no triple of actions for which the "A beats B" ordering is cyclical), the imitator is sure to do almost as well as the strategic player. This includes all games with two options—the Assurance Dilemma [§3], the Prisoner's Dilemma [§1], and the Game of Chicken [§2]—as well as all symmetric **public goods** games with more players.

Principle: Nonstrategic players can do very well when playing against strategic rivals, and can sometimes do even better than if they were strategic.

Puzzle: Describe a two-person game in which a nonstrategic player does even better than the strategic player she is playing against.

Reference: Duersch, P., Oechssler, J., & Schipper, B. C. (2012). Unbeatable imitation. *Games and Economic Behavior, 76*(1), 88–96.

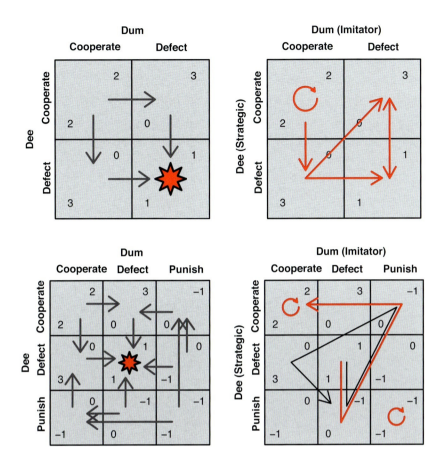

FIGURE 49 A THEOREM ON IMITATION

The two upper figures show a Prisoner's Dilemma. The arrows on the left show the optimal actions for two strategic players. The arrows on the right show some of the possible movements that can be orchestrated by a strategic player playing against a player that simply copies the last action of the strategic player if the strategic player did better than him last time.

Critically, you can see in the upper-right figure that if both players start cooperating, they could cooperate forever (indicated by the circular arrow in the all-cooperate cell). The strategic player would stay cooperating because if she defected, then the copier would defect in the following round *and never cooperate again*. The copier keeps cooperating because he does as well as the strategic player. This outcome is fragile, however, since if one player ever played defect, then the copier would play defect forever and the best outcome the strategic player could orchestrate would be all defect forever.

In the lower figures, the players have one extra strategy at their disposal: they can punish the other player, at a cost to themselves. This strategy is one that *no strategic actor would normally ever play*—no matter what the other person does there is always something better than punishment. But it has the virtue that when you punish a defector, your payoff is higher than theirs. This introduces a rock-paper-scissors component that opens up the possibility that punishment can be used strategically to get imitators back from defection and on the road (marked in red in the lower-right figure) to cooperation. This makes the all-cooperate outcome more stable. But it also opens up a risk for the imitator: by letting the strategic player lead him by the nose there is a risk of *indefinite exploitation* (black path in lower-right figure). Note finally that if *both* players were nonstrategic, then they could get stuck in the *worst* place—all punish.

APPENDIX A: FOUNDATIONAL RESULTS IN THE THEORY OF GAMES

A1 | Reasoning Backward (Zermelo's Theorem)

At its best, game theory makes simple and unique predictions for complex problems. In principle, especially sharp predictions can be made for chess-like situations in which players are engaged in a game with a finite sequence of moves; at each point in time one player moves, and all players have full information—about both the preferences of other players and what actions everyone takes during the course of play.

For this type of game there is a very natural way to think about how rational actors might behave. Ultimately what they care about is where things end up. So to figure out what to do at any point in time they need to figure out how their choices affect future play. To answer that question they have to think right to the end of the **game tree** and work out what people will be doing down the road (or really, down all possible roads) and then start reasoning backward.

This thinking suggests a simple logic for solving games. First think about all the last moves that could be taken by any player at each possible ending of the game. Figure out what would be the best action (or actions) for whomever is the last mover at that point—ignoring everything that came before. Once you figure that out then assume that that is what's going to happen if you end up in that place. Then move one branch up the game tree and ask: say a *penultimate* choice has to be made, what is the best choice for the person choosing at that penultimate point, *assuming that the next person is going to make the ensuing (last) move in the manner just specified*. Then move up the game tree again and figure out what the optimal third last choice is, *assuming that the final and penultimate choices will be as just specified*. Continue in this way until you reach the very first decision to be made by the first mover. At this point this first mover can predict optimal actions for all players at every point in the future and can use this to determine what's the best first move to make.

The solutions you get when you do this are "sequential" equilibriums. They are **Nash equilibriums** but have the advantage of being particularly **credible** equilibriums in the sense that if people are playing by these strategies, no one has the incentive to deviate from their actions even if other people also deviate. Things work out particularly nicely if each player values all the different possible outcomes differently. In that case there is never any ambiguity about what is the best action to take at any point, which means, working up the tree, that there will be a unique prediction to the game.

In one sense this result is good news. It tells us, for example, that there is a solution to the game of chess and other seemingly complex games. What's more it gives a simple procedure for solving these games. But there's a catch: there is no guarantee that any human could actually implement this method or find the solution since the number of computations required could be well beyond our capacity (as it is for chess).

Principle (Zermelo's Theorem): For finite games played over time in which everyone has full information, there is at least one "sequential equilibrium" that can be worked out by reasoning backward. If each player values all outcomes differently, then there is exactly one such solution.

Reference: Myerson, R. (1997). *Game theory: Analysis of conflict.* Cambridge, MA: Harvard University Press.

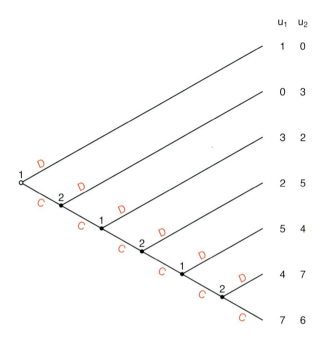

FIGURE i ZERMELO'S THEOREM

The "centipede game" shown above illustrates the logic of backward induction and how sufficient variation in payoffs at the end of the game can induce a unique solution. This game is especially easy: there is only one choice at the end of the **game tree,** in which player 2 decides whether to take action *D* or *C*. Since she does better choosing *D* we assume that that is what will happen. At the second last stage, player 1 decides whether to choose *D* (for a payoff of 5) or *C*—knowing that in choosing *C* she is going to induce a choice for player 2 in which player 2 will choose *D*—for a payoff of 4 for player 1. In that case, from reasoning backward, if she got there she would choose *D*. By a similar logic if 2 got to the previous choice, she would choose *D* and so on. Going the whole way back up the game tree you can see that players will choose *D* every time they have a chance, and so in the equilibrium, 2 will never get the chance to choose at all. The equilibrium outcome in this case gives all players about the lowest pair of payoffs that can be achieved.

A2 | Solving Zero-Sum Games (The Minimax Theorem)

Early game theory focused a lot on the problem of two-person **zero-sum games:** games in which one person's gain was another person's loss. Many distinct games have this form. Many classic games, like chess or soccer, are often thought of as zero-sum games also. Military contests are often framed as two-person zero-sum games. Electoral competition and competition for scarce resources can also sometimes be represented as zero-sum games.

One of the greatest achievements of the early study of games was the identification of a solution for these games: the minimax solution.

Here's an example to see how minimax works.

Jack is awarded a penalty kick and Jill is the goalie. If Jill jumps the same way as the ball, she stops the goal. Jack wants to maximize the chances he scores a goal and Jill wants to minimize it. Say now that Jack has a funny right foot. When he shoots left it goes left, but when he shoots right it veers left about a quarter of the time. How should they play? Will Jack aim left or right? Will Jill jump left or right?

In some sense, jumping left is a safer bet for Jill. If Jack aims left Jill stops the goal for sure, and even if Jack aims right Jill still stops it a quarter of the time, so left seems like a good option. But that kind of thinking breaks down since if she were *predictably* to go left, Jack would do very well by aiming right even though he often makes a mess of it.

There is a solution to this game, however. Say Jack aims right with a 2 in 3 probability. Then there is a 1 in 2 chance the ball will actually go right and so Jill has a 1 in 2 chance of stopping the ball whichever way she jumps. Say now Jill jumps left with a 1 in 2 probability. Then Jack would be indifferent between shooting left and right. If he went left he would have a 1 in 2 chance of scoring on the left; but he would also have a 1 in 2 chance of scoring if he aimed right, even if it goes the wrong way. So if both play these strategies, then neither can improve on them and the expected outcome is a 1 in 2 chance of a goal.

John von Neumann showed in 1928 that for all zero-sum games like this (games in which one person's loss is the other's gain) you can get to this result in two ways. In attack mode, Jill focuses on Jack's payoffs and does all she can to make sure Jack suffers as much as possible given that Jack will try to respond optimally to any action she takes. To do so she plays left with probability 1 in 2 since anything else would give Jack a chance at doing better. In doing so she minimizes Jack's maximum payoff (aka minimax). Alternatively, you can think of Jack in defense mode, focused on his own payoffs, and trying to do as well as possible for himself given that Jill is on the attack. This would push him to choose left with probability 1/3. In doing so he is maximizing his minimum payoff (aka maximin). These two approaches yield identical outcomes (as do the cases with Jill defensive and Jack aggressive).

Principle (The Minimax Theorem): In zero-sum games, maximizing the minimum payoff your opponent can impose on you yields the same payoff as you get when your opponent minimizes the maximum payoff you can guarantee yourself.

Reference: Von Neumann, J. (1928). Zur Theorie der Gesellschaftsspiele. *Mathematische Annalen, 100*(1), 295–320.

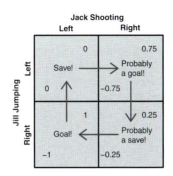

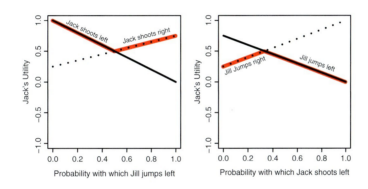

FIGURE ii ILLUSTRATION OF THE MINIMAX THEOREM

The top figure shows the **payoff matrix**. The other two figures show different payoffs for Jack given different strategies by Jack and Jill. The highlighted "V" shape in the lower left panel marks the best that Jack can do given any strategy by Jill. The lowest point of the V is the lowest **utility** that Jill can force Jack to have and it corresponds to a 50% chance of a goal (see the y axis). The highlighted inverse V(Λ) on the right panel is the *lowest* utility Jill can force Jack to have in response to any Jack strategy. The *highest* point on this curve is the most Jack can guarantee himself given Jill is trying to make life hard for him. This also yields a 50% chance of a goal. If p represents the weights Jack places on going left or right and q represents the weights that Jill places, then in this case what you have is $\min_q \max_p u_{Jack}(p, q) = \max_p \min_q u_{Jack}(p, q) = .5$. It is interesting to note that Jack's choice of random strategy is what's needed to ensure that there is exactly a 50% chance the ball goes left, taking account of his funny foot.

A3 | A Beautiful World? (Nash's Theorem)

Game theory is all about making predictions about what people will do in strategic environments. Classically the focus has been on cases in which all players think hard about what everyone else is likely to do and respond optimally. Are such predictions always possible? Does the world happen to be organized in such a way that predictions of reasonable behavior can always be made?

Clearly not. Say Dum and Dee each had to write down a number and whoever writes the highest number wins. Then you can't guess what they would write because anything Dum does could be beaten by something else that Dee could do, which could in turn be beaten by something else that Dum could do. So "in general" you cannot make predictions. John Nash showed, however, that for all games in which each player has a *finite* set of strategies there exists a set of strategies such that each person's strategy is the best they can do given what the others are doing. We call such a collection of strategies a **Nash equilibrium**. The fact that Nash equilibriums so often exist suggests there is some rationality to outcomes when people are rational. This is a fundamentally positive result.

The concept is trickier than it seems at first, however. The film *A Beautiful Mind* tried to illustrate it with an odd scene in which four men each choose whether to go for the blonde or for one of a group of brunettes. Each wants the blonde but would prefer a brunette to nothing. This is a game of chicken of sorts and it is deceptively hard to play. The film got the solution wrong, but thanks to Nash we know at least that there *is* a solution.

Principle (Nash's Theorem): In every game in which people have a finite set of options to choose from there is some set of strategies such that if everyone uses those strategies, then no one will have an incentive to change their strategy unilaterally.

Reference: Nash, J. F. (1950b). Equilibrium points in n-person games. *Proceedings of the National Academy of Sciences, 36*(1), 48–49.

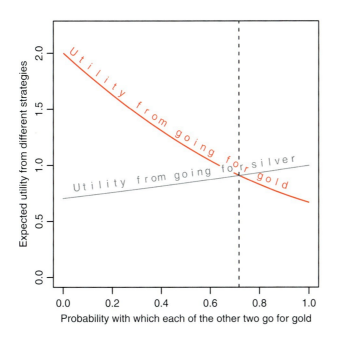

FIGURE iii ILLUSTRATION OF NASH EQUILIBRIUM

Dum, Dee, and Doe are each debating whether to go for gold (worth $2) or for one of three silvers (worth $1 each). Say you get what you go for with probability $1/n$ where n is the total number of people going for it. What should they go for? Is there a **Nash equilibrium**? Clearly all going for gold is not an equilibrium, since in that case each can expect $2/3, and could do better going for silver and getting $1 for sure. The film made that point. But all going for silver is also not an equilibrium, since then switching to gold gives $2 for sure (since all others are going for silver). The film missed that point. So is there an equilibrium? Yes, and you can know that from Nash's theorem. In fact there are many equilibriums. First, there are equilibriums in which one goes for gold and others settle for different silvers. There is also a symmetric equilibrium (illustrated above) in which each goes for gold with some probability between 0 and 1. This probability is calculated by figuring out which probability, p makes each person indifferent between going for gold and going for silver. The p has to be calculated carefully: if anyone expects that the others will play for gold with too low a probability, they'd be better off going for gold; if they expect others will play for gold with too high a probability, they'd be better off going for silver. The key mathematical insight is that the value of going for gold is *decreasing* in the probability with which each other goes for gold; the value of going for silver is *increasing* in that probability; if at any point these two values are the same, then the person is indifferent and so should be willing to play with these same probabilities. In the graph this corresponds to the point at which the lines showing the value of going for gold and silver intersect. The particular solution here is to play for gold with probability $p = 0.717$ and for each of the silvers with probability $\frac{1-p}{3} = 0.094$.

APPENDIX B: GLOSSARY

Bayes' Rule A formula for updating your beliefs about the probability of some event given new information.

Formally the rule tells you how to work out the probability of event A after observing X, written $\Pr(A|X)$, given prior probabilities about event A, $\Pr(A)$, and knowledge about the probability of observing X in event A:

$$\Pr(A|X) = \frac{\Pr(X|A)\Pr(A)}{\Pr(X|A)\Pr(A) + \Pr(X|\neg A)\Pr(\neg A)}$$

where $\neg A$ means "not A."

For example, if you roll a die and ask what the probability is of scoring above 3, I would guess 50%. But if you gave me a hint and told me that you had scored an even number, then I would shift my belief from 50% to two thirds. I update based on what events are consistent with the information you provided.

Bayes' Rule is in the background of many of the results discussed in this book and used in all cases when people want to make inferences of the form "What are the chances he is really willing to go to war given that he just did this crazy thing?" (see Costly Signaling [§23]).

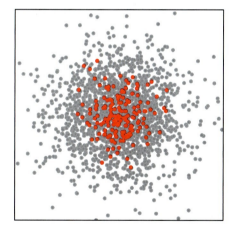
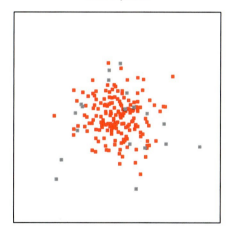

FIGURE iv ILLUSTRATION OF BAYES' RULE
Say circles represent healthy people and squares sick people. Say that red indicates testing positive for a sickness. You should see from these figures that the test is pretty accurate: 90% of healthy people test negative and 90% of sick people test positive. With such an accurate test what are the chances that you are sick given that you test positive? This is the same as asking what are the chances of being a square given that you are red? The answer is just 50%. You still have a good chance of being healthy even though you test positive on an accurate test simply because there are so many healthy people in the population: even though they are healthy and the test is accurate, they still make up a sizable share of the group that tests positive.

While Bayes' Rule gets the statistics right, it seems that humans do not use it very accurately. Say, for example, that a disease affects 1 in 10 people and that a test correctly says that afflicted people are afflicted 90% of the time (and says, 90% of the time, that unafflicted people are unafflicted). Then you could use Bayes' Rule to figure out the chances you are afflicted if you test positive. For questions like this people (and medical professionals) often answer 90% or something close, when the right answer is 50% (see Figure iv). This calls into question the usefulness of basing game theoretic models on the assumption that people use the rule.

common knowledge A situation in which a set of individuals all know something and in addition they all know they know it, they all know they know they know it, and so on.

For example, it is possible that I know you know I like you, but you don't know I know you know I like you. Then we both know I like you, but it is not *common knowledge* between us that I like you.

Two people having common knowledge about something is very different from both people simply knowing it and this difference can matter for strategic purposes. For example, say you and I are in a feud and either would back down if we knew the other was crazy. Say now we both know that I am not crazy but that I don't know that you know I am not crazy. Then it might make sense for me to do a crazy thing to get you to think I am crazy so that you will back down. For more on this see Aumann's Agreement Theorem [§26].

credible A future action that people will in fact have the incentives to implement when the time comes to do it.

I may say that I will never negotiate with terrorists. Whether or not that is credible depends not on how much I don't want to talk to terrorists now but on what I will want to do if in fact they take my cabinet hostage.

discounted utility An approach to modelling people's preferences over benefits that arise over time, in which rewards delivered in the future are considered less valuable than rewards delivered today.

Say that outcomes $x_0, x_1, ..., x_T$ arise in periods 0, 1, ..., T. Then in the discounted utility model you assume that there is a utility function u and a "discount factor" δ such that the utility for the stream of outcomes can be written $u(x_0) + \delta u(x_1) + \delta^2 u(x_2) + ... + \delta^T u(x_T)$.

This captures the idea that things are valued the same way in each period but that it is better to have things sooner rather than later. Interestingly, built into this model is the idea that the *relative* gains from two future outcomes look the same when evaluated now and when evaluated in the future. Alternative approaches that do not have this feature—such as the hyperbolic discounting model—allow for the possibility that players may choose rationally at any point in time but still be "dynamically inconsistent" and end up playing games against themselves.

dominant strategy A strategy that is optimal *no matter what other people do*.

Games with dominant strategies are easily solved and require very weak assumptions about player rationality: in these games players do not have to be strategic to choose the best outcome. In the Prisoner's Dilemma [§1] both players have dominant strategies to defect. In mechanism design problems the goal is sometimes to create games that have dominant strategies and for which players don't have to figure out what preferences other players have. There is an example of this in the Clarke-Groves Mechanism [§36].

efficiency An outcome that is as good as possible for everyone, in the sense that there is no other outcome that would make someone better off without making anyone else worse off.

This definition uses the notion of "Pareto efficiency," which has the advantage of being applicable if all one knows is how people rank different outcomes (but not how much they prefer one thing over another). The problem with this notion is that it is often hard to say that an outcome is inefficient under this definition, even if nearly everyone does badly under the outcome. For example, if people care only about how much cash they have, then every possible division of a sum of money among a set of people is efficient no matter how inequitable it is. This is true even if people have "diminishing marginal income" from cash and so an extra penny means more to someone when they have nothing than when they have a lot. There are other notions of efficiency that are sometimes used, however. For example, you could assess efficiency with respect to people's expectations over outcomes rather than over the outcomes themselves. Say we were considering two ways to divide a dollar. In one I split it 50/50. In the other I toss a coin and if it comes up heads I give the dollar to you, and if it comes up tails I keep it. Even though both possible outcomes from the lottery are efficient, we might still both prefer the even split to the risky lottery. In that case the second scheme is not *ex ante* efficient. Sometimes it might be that an outcome is Pareto efficient but that one could imagine implementing another outcome and then arranging transfers between people so that after the transfers everyone is better off. If that can be done, then you would say that the outcome is not "Kaldor-Hicks efficient," even though it is Pareto efficient. Thus if Dum had two pairs of shoes and Dee none, but (hypothetically) both would prefer a situation in which they each have one pair of shoes and Dee gives Dum $1, then the original situation was not Kaldor-Hicks efficient. The tricky thing about Kaldor-Hicks is that because the transfers don't actually happen, the criteria can favor some outcomes over others even though they leave some people worse off.

equilibrium See **Nash equilibrium**.

expected utility hypothesis The hypothesis that people's preferences over uncertain outcomes can be represented as weighted averages of the utility they would get from certain outcomes.

Say there exists a set of possible outcomes X, then under the expected utility hypothesis there exists a set of utility numbers u_j associated with each outcome $x_j \in X$ such that the value of a "lottery" over elements in X that assigns each element with probability p_j is given by the expected utility, $\Sigma_j p_j u_j$. Lottery p is then considered at least as good as lottery q if $\Sigma_j p_j u_j \geq \Sigma_j q_j u_j$.

Say I think that one banana is worth $2, three bananas are worth $5 and five bananas are worth $6, then under the expected utility hypothesis I think that a lottery that gives me an equal chance of having one banana or five bananas is worth $4 (0.5 × 2 + 0.5 × 6). That's my *expected utility* of this lottery. It is not the same as the *expected number of bananas* I would get from the lottery, which is three (0.5 × 1 + 0.5 × 5) and which is worth $5 to me (more than the value of the lottery). The expected utility hypothesis is assumed throughout game theory, but many results from experimental work suggest that it does not describe people's preferences very well. In fact people place much greater weight on small probabilities than one would expect if the hypothesis were true.

extensive form game A game played out over time.

More formally, an extensive form game comprises a set of players, a set of possible sequences of actions ("histories"), some of which are "terminal" in the sense of there being no other histories that include them, a function saying who plays after each nonterminal history, and a set of preferences over terminal histories.

For example, a_1, b_1 might be a history in which A takes action a_1 and B then takes action b_1. Then a_1, b_1, a_2 might be another history that contains the first history, with A moving again after B. In this case the first history is not a terminal history, but the second one might be if the game ends at that point. The preferences are defined over the terminal histories—or the different ways that games get played out and end. The set of histories themselves are constrained to have tree-like properties—all histories start at the same place (the null history) and then separate over time, which formally means that if a history is in a game, so are all truncations of the history. Representing a game in extensive form is a natural way to take account of time. See also the discussion of extensive form games in the introduction and the entries under **game tree** and **subgame perfection**.

game A situation in which a set of players have a set of strategies they can deploy and everyone has preferences over the outcomes that arise once everyone plays their strategies.

Technically a (normal form) game consists of (1) a set of players, (2) a set of possible actions that each player can take, and (3) a set of preferences, or **utilities**, for each player for all the different combinations of actions that all the players might choose.

Thus, for example, chess is a game consisting of two players, actions of the form "if I am white, move my king's pawn first; then if black does a, I do x; if she does b, then I do y; if she then does ... I do ..."; the combinations of these actions either lead to a win, a loss, or a draw, which might be valued at say, 1, –1, and 0, respectively. A "solution" to a game is a statement about what combinations of strategies you expect to observe. Note that in the definition of the game there are no assumptions of any form about how people behave. It is just a description of the problem they face. Different solution concepts, like **Nash equilibrium**, generally do make behavioral assumptions at least implicitly.

games of incomplete information Games in which individuals are uncertain about some features of the game, such as the preferences of players or the strategies available to them.

Formally these are set up as games in which a new actor, "Nature," takes a first move and chooses the actual state of the world (such as the actual preferences of players) from among the possible states of the world. Some players know what Nature has chosen; others do not. Solutions to these games generally involve people taking optimal actions given the range of possible responses they might face depending on how the world really is. To solve these games you generally have to specify what each possible type of player would choose, if Nature were to select them, and specify beliefs that all actors have that are themselves consistent with the strategies they choose. See the discussion and illustrations in the introduction.

game tree A graphical representation of a game played over time.

Game trees start with a single node (often marked with a white dot) followed by subsequent branches that link to more nodes (generally marked with black dots). Each node indicates the actor that chooses among the successive branches. At the end of the tree are "terminal nodes" that indicate the various possible endings of the game. The payoffs to each actor are normally provided beside the terminal nodes.

In games with incomplete information it may be that when a given actor makes a decision she does not know which of some set of nodes she is at. In this case the set of nodes over which there is uncertainty is connected by dotted lines (or placed within dotted shapes).

in expectation Calculated as the average outcome of some random event if it were to happen many times.

Note that something might take a value "in expectation" but never actually take it in practice (i.e., "in realization"). If I roll a standard six-sided die, the result will be 3.5 in expectation, but I would never expect to get 3.5.

mixed strategies Strategies in which players choose to take an action probabilistically. Instead of just shooting left or shooting right, my strategy is to toss a coin and shoot left if it comes up heads and shoot right if it comes up tails.

Formally, if a player has a set of actions A that she can take, then the set of "mixed strategies" available to her is the set of probability distributions over A.

Say that a player can choose to do one of two things (for example, in soccer to "shoot left" or "shoot right"). Then you can also think of all the strategies in which the player chooses one of these two "pure strategies" with a given probability. Thus a player may select the strategy "shoot right with probability 0.3." The set of all strategies like this is the set of numbers between 0 and 1. The ability to "mix" in this way is sometimes critical for the existence of a **Nash equilibrium**. Mixed-strategy equilibriums exist for the games studied in §2, 3, 18, 20, 21, 46, A2, and A3 (and more). While it may seem strange that people would choose strategies randomly, in general when mixed-strategy equilibriums exist there also exist strategies that look the same to an observer but which involve people playing deterministically as a function of unobservable features such as slight differences in how much they really care about one option or another.

Nash equilibrium A situation in which no player has an incentive to change their strategy given what everyone else is doing.

A little more formally, a set of strategies is a Nash equilibrium if everyone's best responses to everyone else's strategies includes sticking with their own strategy.

In the Prisoner's Dilemma [§1], for example, "all defect" is a Nash equilibrium because even though everyone would be better off if everyone cooperated, each is individually better off defecting given that the other is defecting. See §A3 for a discussion of Nash's theorem. There are many other related notions of equilibrium that may be more or less appropriate depending on how you think people choose their strategies. For example, a "strong equilibrium" is a Nash equilibrium in which no *group* of people has an incentive to change their strategy jointly given the actions of others. In the Prisoner's Dilemma there is no strong equilibrium in this sense. The term "in equilibrium" is used to describe actions people take given everyone is taking actions consistent with a Nash (or some other) equilibrium.

payoff matrix A graphical summary of a (normal form) **game**.

A payoff matrix needs to show the three key components of a game: the players, the possible actions, and the players' preferences over outcomes.

In a matrix representing a two-person game, one player "controls" the rows while another player controls the columns. See Figure v for an illustration. Thus, given the row choice of the row player, the column player can effectively determine which cell will be selected (by selecting the column); likewise given the column choice of

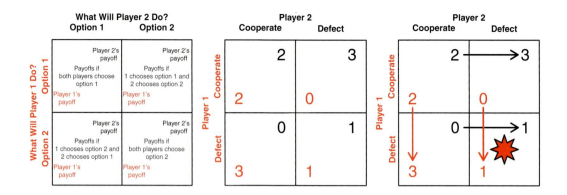

FIGURE v A PAYOFF MATRIX
The first figure shows how the payoffs for two players are indicated for each combination of strategies (options) that everyone chooses. The second figure shows an example of particular payoffs, in this case for a Prisoner's Dilemma [§1]. The third shows the same payoff matrix but adds in arrows to indicate which shifts in strategy are good responses for each player; the star in the figure highlights that no arrow is leading *out* of a particular cell, which means that that particular combination of strategies is a **Nash equilibrium**.

the column player the row player can determine which cell is selected (by selecting the row). In the matrices used in this book I normally include arrows to show the movements that you might expect to see between cells. An arrow shows a movement from one column to another (within a row) if the "'to" cell gives a higher payoff to the column player than the "from" cell. Similarly for vertical movements. Thus a cell with no arrows pointing out of it is one in which the row player cannot do better by changing rows and the column player cannot do better by changing columns; in this case if no one can do better given the actions by the others, then the cell corresponds to a **Nash equilibrium** (and is then often marked with a star).

Critically, the "payoffs," or **utilities**, represent how much people *value* particular outcomes, not how much they gain in any objective sense. It is possible, for example, that I value a situation in which we both receive $50 more than a situation in which I receive $100 and you get nothing. In that case, even though I get more money in the second situation, my payoff is higher in the first. In that sense any altruism is *already* factored into the payoff matrix and it does not make sense to say that someone might prefer a cell that gives them a lower payoff because they are altruistic; by definition they prefer the cells with the higher payoffs.

public goods Goods that everyone gets to enjoy whether or not they contributed to producing them.

Technically, public goods are nonexcludable (meaning that you cannot easily prevent people from benefiting from them) and nonrival (meaning that one person benefiting does not prevent another from benefiting).

National security, for example, has the feature of a public good: everyone in a state benefits from it and one person enjoying it does not decrease its value for another. Many goods have public goods-like characteristics even if they don't meet the definition strictly; for example, it may be possible to exclude some people but not others, or to exclude only at some cost; or it might be that when others benefit there is some loss to everyone (for example, through congestion). The key difficulty with public goods is that if individuals, when deciding how much to invest in them, only take account of their private benefits from the goods, then they will produce less than is socially optimal. All of the collective action dilemmas described in Part 1 can be thought of as problems associated with producing different types of public goods.

quasilinear utility Preferences with the feature that the gains you get from an extra unit of some good do not depend on how many units you already have.

More formally, individuals have "quasilinear utility" if their **utility** is linear in one component.

Generally, the component in question is a transferable good, such as money. In such situations it is common to treat the good as a "numeraire" and so count the utility from other goods in terms of the marginal utility of that good. For example, an individual might have preferences represented by the utility function $u(\pi, y) = \alpha v(\pi) + \beta y$. In that example, utility is linear in y. In that case, if the **expected utility hypothesis** is maintained, the preferences can also be represented by $u(\pi, y) = \alpha' v(\pi) + y$ where $\alpha' = \alpha/\beta$.

rational preferences Preferences that make it possible to say which item from a set of items an individual likes the most.

More formally, we say that individuals have "rational preferences" if their preferences are "complete" (for any two items they can tell you which they prefer) and "transitive" (for any three items if they like x at least as much as y and y at least as much as z, then they like x at least as much as z).

Note that this definition of rationality says nothing about whether people are self-interested, knowledgeable, or clever. It's really just about how "consistent" their preferences are. Transitivity rules out preference cycling. However, it is possible to have nontransitive preferences that do not cycle. For example, I might strictly prefer A to B and be indifferent between B and C and between A and C. Can you see why these preferences are not transitive?

revelation principle The idea that in situations in which the choice of strategies communicates information about people's preferences you should be able to set things up so that people just tell you their preferences truthfully.

More formally, the revelation principle says that if it is possible to design a game that gets you a given desired outcome (where what you desire as an outcome depends on the players' preferences), then it is possible to get your desired outcomes from a simple game in which everyone simply has to state what their preferences are and the outcome is chosen based on these and in which everyone has an incentive to tell the truth (see also the section on "Institutional Design").

Note that the converse is very important: if you cannot devise a simple game like this in which people have incentives to tell the truth, then from the revelation principle you know that you cannot devise *any* game (technically: any game *form*) that does the trick.

risk averse, risk neutral, risk seeking Descriptions of how and when people prefer to take a risk rather than choosing a safe—but possibly second rate—outcome.

Formally, we say you are "risk neutral" over outcomes $x = (x_1, x_2, ..., x_n)$ when, for all probability distributions, $p = (p_1, p_2, ..., p_n)$, you are indifferent between a lottery that gives $(x_1, x_2, ..., x_n)$ with probability $(p_1, p_2, ..., p_n)$ and getting outcome $px = (p_1 x_1, p_2 x_2, ..., p_n x_n)$ for sure. That is, if for **utility** function u, $u(\Sigma_i p_i x_i) = \Sigma_i p_i u(x_i)$. We say you are "risk averse" if you prefer the sure thing and "risk seeking" (or "risk acceptant") if you prefer the lottery.

Note that this idea is normally defined over a one-dimensional set of outcomes (generally money). From the expected utility theorem, risk neutrality over X

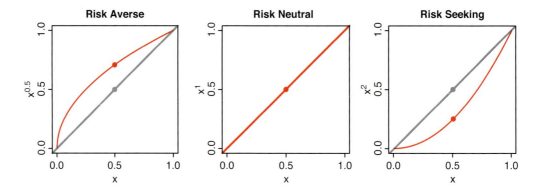

FIGURE vi THREE UTILITY FUNCTIONS OF THE FORM $u(x) = x^\alpha$
In each case the red line marks the utility for different levels of x and the red dot shows the value $u(0.5)$—that is, the utility gotten from getting $x = 0.5$ for sure. The gray dot is the halfway point between $u(1)$ and $u(0)$ and shows, under the conditions of the **expected utility hypothesis**, the value of a gamble between 0 and 1. You can see in the first case—with a concave function, or diminishing marginal returns—the red dot is above the gray dot, which means you prefer the sure thing to the gamble. You are indifferent between them in the middle case (risk neutral, or constant marginal returns). In the third case with increasing marginal returns (convex function), the gamble is preferred to the sure thing.

corresponds to a linear function over X; risk aversion corresponds to a concave utility function and risk seekingness corresponds to a convex utility function. For some of the applied examples in this book I assume utility of the form $u(x) = x^\alpha$ for $\alpha > 0$. Here $\alpha = 1$ implies risk-neutral preferences, $\alpha < 1$ implies risk aversion, and $\alpha > 1$ implies risk seekingness. See Figure vi for an illustration.

 social choice A problem in which you seek to find a method to determine what groups want, or to understand the properties of such methods.

The challenge is generally to find a way to aggregate individual preferences into a group's preferences in a way that, hopefully, makes it possible to say what a society would or should choose. Unlike game theorists, many social choice theorists do not try to predict what people will do, and they often do not impose assumptions about how individuals behave.

The Gibbard–Satterthwaite Theorem [§19] provides a link between game theory and social choice theory: the difficulty of finding a nondictatorial rule to aggregate people's preferences in desirable ways means that it is difficult to generate a game that gives people incentives to choose strategies that produce desirable outcomes.

subgame, subgame perfect Nash equilibrium Tools for thinking about how people play games after the game has started. A subgame is the part of a game that's left after you have started, and being subgame perfect is a property of strategies that the strategies continue to make sense to players after the game has started and not just at the beginning.

More formally a "subgame" of an **extensive form game** is a subset of the game that starts at a single node and contains all histories that include that node (and only those histories) along with the following technical constraint: if in the original game a player is uncertain over whether she is at one or another node, then if one of those nodes is in the subgame, both are in the subgame. A **Nash equilibrium** is "subgame perfect" if it is a Nash equilibrium, not just of the game, but also of all subgames of the game.

utility How much people value different outcomes, described in numbers.

Formally, utility numbers $u_1, u_2, \ldots, u_k$ represent someone's preferences over options $x_1, x_2, \ldots, x_k$ if it is the case that $u_i \geq u_j$ if and only if the person likes option x_i at least as much as option x_j. For continuous outcome spaces these utility numbers can be usefully summarized with a "utility function" that assigns a utility number to each outcome.

Game theoretic work often invokes the idea of a player's "utility" for a given outcome—for example, my value (utility) is 5 if this outcome arises, but 2 if that outcome arises. But no game theorist literally believes in the existence of such utilities. What matters for them is whether numbers can effectively *represent* preferences. Note that if a set of numbers represents preferences over a set of outcomes, then so too does any increasing monotonic transformation of those numbers. Note also that if preferences can be represented by a utility function, then those preferences are **rational** (but the converse is not true: not all **rational preferences** can be represented by a utility function). The **expected utility hypothesis** places some further constraints on what numbers can be used so that utility over probabilistic events can be expressed in a simple way; but even then the numbers that can be used are not unique, and any set of utilities can be replaced by a "positive affine transformation" of those utilities—which in essence means you can always change the units.

zero-sum games Games in which one person's loss is another person's gain.

More formally we say that a game is "zero sum" if the sum of utilities adds up to zero (or more generally if there is a "positive affine transformation" of utilities—that is, a rescaling of utilities—such that they add up to zero).

The earliest studies of games focused on zero-sum games since classic games such as poker or soccer are zero sum (von Neumann mentioned roulette, chess, baccarat, and bridge). War games were often thought of as zero sum also. Work in political economy almost always assumes that games are not really zero sum. Even if two people are at war, there could be joint gains from them negotiating a settlement.

APPENDIX C: NOTES

§1 (THE PRISONER'S DILEMMA)

To illustrate the prisoner's dilemma we used a "bimatrix"; this bimatrix fully describes the strategic problem facing the players. If you want to illustrate a bimatrix like this in **R**, simply type:

```
payoffs <-  matrix(c(2,3,0,1),2)
gt_bimatrix(payoffs, labels1=c("C","D"))
```

This code solves the game and graphs the result. If you want to graph the matrix without solving the game you can turn off the arrows and stars using:

```
gt_bimatrix(payoffs, labels1=c("C","D"), nash=F, arrow1=F)
```

Note that the statement in the summary principle might seem to imply a kind of comparability of **utility** since it involved a comparison of private costs and social gains. In fact this is not necessary. The key thing is that each individual prefers the situation where all cooperate to the one where all defect, even if they prefer defecting individually no matter what others do. That condition does not require any comparison of utilities across individuals.

Sources: David Nakamura and Steven Mufson, "China, U.S. agree to limit greenhouse gas emissions," *The Washington Post*, November 12, 2014; Kelly Riddell, "Tales from the abyss: The final hour of CNN's marathon GOP debate," *Washington Times,* September 18, 2015.

§2 (THE GAME OF CHICKEN)

One strategy in the chicken game might be to rip the steering wheel out of the car to demonstrate that you are unable to swerve and thereby force the other person to swerve. But that's not as clever as it sounds at first because the decision to rip out the wheel is itself a chicken game with the possibility that both players simultaneously rip out their wheels and speed to their deaths.

To replicate the Chicken matrix, type:

```
payoffs <- matrix(c(2,3,1,0),2)
gt_bimatrix(payoffs, labels1=c("C","D"))
```

§3 (THE ASSURANCE DILEMMA)

This stag and hare story was originally described by Jean-Jacques Rousseau in *A Discourse on Inequality* (see Rousseau, 2000), and in many applications the game is described as the stag hunt game, or sometimes a "trust dilemma."

To replicate the Assurance matrix, type:

```
payoffs <- matrix(c(3,2,0,1),2)
gt _ bimatrix(payoffs, labels1=c("C","D"))
```

§4 (THE FOLK THEOREMS)

There are a few versions of the folk theorem. The simplest one states that "Any payoff profile that is 'feasible' and 'individually rational' can be sustained as part of a **Nash equilibrium** provided people are sufficiently patient." Here is the heart of the proof. Say that $\underline{v}_i$ is the largest (average per period) payoff that an individual can be sure of getting even if everyone else gangs up against them. Assume that time preferences are captured by $\delta \in [0, 1]$ in the sense that payoff x delivered tomorrow is worth δx today. Getting x from today on into the future is worth $x + \delta x + \delta^2 x + \cdots = x/(1 - \delta)$. Now consider a candidate equilibrium that gave i **utility** $v_i \geq \underline{v}_i$. Let $\bar{v}_i$ be the very best that i could possibly do in a single period by deviating from whatever strategies are needed to sustain the candidate equilibrium payoffs. Player i will not want to deviate if the gains from deviation today ($\bar{v}_i$), plus punishment payoffs every period from next period onward (valued at $\frac{\delta \underline{v}_i}{1-\delta}$), do not exceed the equilibrium payoffs now and into the future (valued at $\frac{v_i}{1-\delta}$). Then we need:

$$\bar{v}_i + \frac{\delta \underline{v}_i}{1-\delta} \leq \frac{v_i}{1-\delta} \leftrightarrow \delta \geq \frac{\bar{v}_i - v_i}{\bar{v}_i - \underline{v}_i}$$

which can clearly be achieved with δ close enough to 1. Essentially the same proof can be used to establish a version that replaces "Nash equilibrium" with "**subgame perfect Nash equilibrium**" and "individually rational" payoffs with "minimal payoffs that can be obtained in a Nash equilibrium of the single period game."

To replicate the set of supportable payoffs from the Prisoner's Dilemma type:

```
payoffs <- matrix(c(2,3,0,1),2)
gt _ folk(payoffs)
```

Use the same code to examine any other two-person game. For example for the Assurance Dilemma, try:

```
payoffs <- matrix(c(3,2,0,1),2)
gt _ folk(payoffs)
```

§5 (OVERLAPPING GENERATIONS)

Alesina and Spear (1988) apply the overlapping generations insight to address the problem of explaining the credibility of party platforms when individual politicians have political preferences that differ from what's most effective for getting them elected. In such cases there is a risk that a politician will say one thing to get into office and do another once elected. Embedded within a party with overlapping generations, however, the problem becomes solvable. In the equilibrium examined, the younger party member ("the vice president") makes a transfer to the older party member ("the president"), for him to choose a policy that will get the party elected.

§6 (THE EVOLUTION OF PREFERENCES)

For a treatment of the closely related idea that self-interest is self-defeating see Parfit (1984). For the idea that greater freedom of choice can be harmful, see The Schelling Conjecture [§29]. For the related idea that strategizing can be self-defeating see A Theorem on Imitation [§49].

§7 (THE ROBBINS CRITIQUE)

There are thought experiments that might make the kind of comparisons Robbins rules out perfectly imaginable. It might be that I cannot meaningfully compare the happiness you and I would receive from two different options; but I might be able to assess how I would feel in conditions like mine and conditions like yours. This is one interpretation of the kind of thought experiment that Rawls (1971) invites in his book *A Theory of Justice*. See also the rich development of this idea in Binmore (1998). To some extent, however, the usefulness of this thought experiment on evaluating social arrangements depends on thinking that others think broadly like oneself. See the discussion on this by John Roemer (2001).

§8 (CONDORCET'S PARADOX)

The example from the Danish elections comes from Kurrild-Klitgaard (2001). Broadly, there has been strikingly little evidence for Condorcet cycles (understood as cycling of preferences, not necessarily cycling of policy) in real voting situations even though theory suggests (see Plott's Theorem [§14]) that they should be very common. The theory of course focuses on all possible policies (or candidates), not just those under consideration at a given point in time.

§9 (ARROW'S THEOREM)

The contribution of Arrow's theorem is often misunderstood.

In one respect the theorem is deeper than sometimes thought. The theorem does not simply make the ontological point that there is no general will, in the sense understood by Rousseau (1968). You don't need the theorem to argue that the idea of group preferences is a construct. Rather, the theorem says that you can't even have a meaningful construct, at least not without violating the axioms. This goes not just for aggregating preferences but also for aggregating moral principles and judgments.

But in two respects the result is less profound than it might seem. First, the theorem only says that every rule that satisfies the axioms *might* run into problems of nontransitivities for various configurations of preferences, but it does not say whether this is likely or not (such a claim would require empirical information on the distribution of preferences). Second, and more importantly, the requirement of transitivity might be too strong, at least if the goal is to make statements about what is preferred to what. Readers of the theorem sometimes assume that a violation of transitivity means the possibility of preference cycles, but that is not right. The difference between intransitivities and cycles is subtle but critical. Say I strictly prefer A to B but I am indifferent between B and C and between A and C. Then my preferences are not transitive (since under transitivity if I strictly prefer A to B and am indifferent between *B* and *C*, I should really prefer *A* to *C*) but my preferences do not cycle. I have some top preferences, in particular, I can't do better than *A* or *C*. If the absence of cycles is really all we seek in order to feel comfortable about making claims about society's preferences, then there are rules that can achieve this alongside Arrow's other conditions. The rule that says "*A* is preferred to *B* if and only if everyone prefers *A* to *B*" will do the trick, for example. This won't produce transitive social preferences but it doesn't produce gibberish either. See Gibbard (1969) and Brown (1975) for more. Later results for particular rules (see The McKelvey-Schofield Chaos Theorem [§15] and Nakamura's Theorem [§16]) show, however, that many common rules actually produce gibberish and not just intransitivities.

§10 (CONDORCET'S JURY THEOREM)

Surowiecki's (2005) popular book on the wisdom of crowds largely draws on a logic similar to that employed by Condorcet. Though for a less sanguine view see Mackay's (2012) classic collection of how bad things can go when groups act as one.

Condorcet's jury theorem sometimes seems to be unconnected with the cycling problem that is also associated with Condorcet [§8]. One seems to assume two options and fundamentally consistent preferences, the second more than two options and irreconcilable preferences. There is, however, a deep connection. One can think of the multi-choice problem as being one in which there is a true ranking of best outcomes but individuals make mistakes in their assessments. The aim then is to figure out what is really the best choice given different evaluations. For a discussion of these connections and links to the Borda approach and the "Kemeny" method, or maximum likelihood method, see Young (1988).

You can replicate the plots by typing variations of:

```
gt_jury(n_voters=7, probability_correct=.6)
```

§11 (MAY'S THEOREM)

You might expect that an implication of Arrow's Thorem [§9] is that any attempt to generalize May's Theorem to multiple options will quickly run into problems. In fact, however, a generalization is possible. Goodin and List (2006) show that in situations with many options in which voters reveal only their most-preferred option (rather than their full ranking of options), plurality rule (and only plurality rule) satisfies May's principles. This result, though positive, requires mechanisms that employ very limited information, thus effectively masking the kinds of disagreements that produce cycles. To see why note that it is possible that both of the following are true for some polity: (a) more voters have *A* as a first choice than have *B* as a first choice, and (b) *most* voters prefer *B* to *A*.

Source: Aristotle, *Politics*, Book VI, Part II.

§12 (MEDIAN VOTER THEOREM)

Note that single peakedness is a condition on *all* voters' preferences and not something that can be checked independently on each. There must be some single ordering of options such that for *all* individuals there is a preferred point and people like options less and less as you move away (defined in terms of the ordering) from their ideal. Over two dimensions, people might have a **utility** function that *looks* single peaked in the sense that they like one point the most and then utility declines by distance; but this does not mean that the preferences of a *set* of voters over two dimensions is single peaked. To check single peakedness you'd have to see if you can collapse the two dimensions into one dimension in some way so that over that one dimension all players have preferences with the desired properties. Give it a go.

The key idea of parties converging to the median can be traced back to Hotelling (1929), who noted that politicians could have an incentive to converge on policies just as businesses on a street might have incentives to locate their businesses close to one another or to make their products similar. Note that one can think of the logic of convergence as operating even if parties do not choose the median. If for whatever reason one party shifts to the left of the median, then a vote-maximizing second party would have an incentive to move to the left also, to gain a larger share of the votes lying between their positions, rather than symmetrically adopting a more rightward, polarizing position. Can you think of logics for why a left party would respond to a rightward shift (by the right party) by moving left rather than by moving right?

§13 (POWER INDICES)

To replicate the Banzhaf figure for the simple majority case, type:

```
gt_plot_banzhaf(weights = c(1,1,3,7,9,9), q_rule = .5)
```

The same function can be used to explore different weights and decision rules; for example, try:

```
gt_plot_banzhaf(weights = c(1,1,3,7,9,10), q_rule = .6)
```

A lot of work has been done to justify these different indices on axiomatic grounds. This work asks which principles *imply* these indices. For a discussion of various different axiomatizations, see, for example, Feltkamp (1995).

Note that these indices seek to capture a notion of *a priori* power. In practice it might be that there are three equal-sized groups, yet a coalition is only likely between two of these and the third never gets to be pivotal. For a discussion of empirical considerations see Gelman, Katz, and Tuerlinckx (2002).

§14 (PLOTT'S THEOREM)

To create a version of the vector field plot type:

```
ideals <- matrix(c(0, 0, .5, 1, 1, 0), 2)
gt_majority_phase(ideals)
```

The code allows you to examine what sort of movements of different lengths are possible from any point. For example, try:

```
ideals <- matrix(c(.2, .2, .5, .9, 1, 0), 2)
gt_majority_phase(ideals, raylengths=c(.5, .2))
```

§15 (THE MCKELVEY-SCHOFIELD CHAOS THEOREMS)

The included **R** code produces random paths like this for any number of people and any number of motions. Here is code to produce a random path like this:

```
gt_cycles(n_voters = 3, n_motions = 25)
```

§16 (NAKAMURA'S THEOREM)

Nakamura's theorem says how sticky sticky rules have to be to guarantee that there will be some unbeatable outcome. What many rules do is determine which collections of individuals count as "decisive coalitions" (in the sense that if members of a decisive coalition all think A is better than B, then A will get chosen). A rule is very sticky if these different decisive coalitions generally include the same people. For example, if someone holds a veto (and so can always prevent one option being ranked above another), then that person will be in *every* decisive coalition and so the rule is very sticky. Under unanimity everyone has a veto and so unanimity is very sticky. Under majority rule, however, although every two decisive coalitions have at least one person in common, you can always find three decisive coalitions for which there is not a single person that is in all three of them (for example, none of A, B or C is in $\{A, B\}$ and $\{A, C\}$ and $\{B, C\}$), so majority rule is not so sticky. (To be a bit more precise, that is true if there are either three voters or more than four voters.) A rule that says you need four out of five people to make a decisive coalition is stickier since for that rule, every four decisive coalitions have one person in all of them, but no one person is in all five four-person decisive coalitions. More generally, for any rule you can define the "*Nakamura number*" as the smallest number of coalitions that have no one person in all of them. For majority rule that is generally three, for the 4/5 person rule that is five, for unanimity rule (or any other rule with veto players) we say it is infinity. Nakamura's theorem then says that for any rule, if the number of choices available is as large or larger than the Nakamura number, then you cannot be sure of an unbeatable option. Nakamura's Corollary 2.4 shows that the Nakamura number can't be greater than the number of players (unless it is infinite) and so if you have as many options as people, then you know that an unbeatable point cannot be guaranteed. The basic insight is relatively straightforward. Say for some problem there are k options $(x_1, x_2, \ldots x_k)$ available and say the Nakamura number is also k. Then one can construct k winning coalitions $\{C_1, C_2, \ldots, C_k\}$ such that everyone in coalition $C_j, j \in \{1, 2, \ldots, k-1\}$ prefers x_j to x_{j+1} and everyone in C_k prefers x_k to x_1. This would not be possible if the Nakamura number were greater than k since in that case there would be at least one person in all these coalitions and this person would not be able to simultaneously prefer x_1 to x_k and x_k to x_1.

A much more negative result on general rules shows that in some environments, cycles are not just possible, but are to be expected. Say $n \geq 5$ people have smooth **utility** functions over points in a d dimensional Euclidean space, then there is almost never an equilibrium point if $d > \frac{3(n-3)}{2}$. This result is given as Corollary 6.2 in Austen-Smith and Banks (2000a); see also Saari (1997).

§17 (AGENDA MANIPULATION)

Some types of agenda rules can put meaningful constraints on agenda setters. Consider, for example, an "amendment rule" in which there is a set of items $x_1, x_2, \ldots$ and in which x_1 and x_2 are compared first, the winner is then compared against x_3, the winner of that against x_4, and so on. For this type of rule only Pareto optimal outcomes will be selected **in equilibrium** (in other words an item will not be selected if there is some other item that everyone prefers to that item). What's more, if the final item is the status quo, then the only possible winners are winners that not only beat the status quo but also beat anything else that beats the status quo. A key lesson from this is that the improvements in predictability come from constraints on the decision rule, not from a move to a noncooperative solution concept. For more on this, see Austen-Smith and Banks (1998).

§18 (LEGISLATIVE BARGAINING)

If you are not familiar with alternating offers bargaining, skip ahead to read The Ståhl-Rubinstein Solution [§28] (and notes to §28). The legislative bargaining problem is a type of alternating offers bargaining where instead of requiring the agreement of two people you require the agreement of some coalition of people. Another difference is that who gets to offer is determined by a random mechanism rather than through alternation. A last difference is that **discounted utility** does not play quite as essential a role (because the risks of exclusion that can arise from not being part of a future winning coalition can play a similar role as discounting in creating a risk of loss from delay).

In the division game we described equilibrium outcomes for different "recognition probabilities." These are calculated using the logic of alternating offers bargaining and assuming that **in equilibrium** each player, if asked to enter a coalition, has to be offered their "continuation value"—that is, at least as much as they would expect if they said no. We assume people are very patient and so we can calculate their continuation value as the sum of the probability of different coalitions that might arise times the expected benefit from membership in each. If we say that v_i is the valuation to i, p_i the probability that i gets to offer, and q_{ji} the probability with which j chooses i to be in her coalition, then, assuming people are offered their continuation values, we are typically dealing with equations that look like this:

$$v_i = p_i(1 - v_k) + p_j q_{ji} v_i + p_k q_{ki} v_i$$

The idea being that the continuation valuation to i is given by the probability that i gets to offer, times the share she gets to keep after paying off the cheapest person, plus the probabilities that the others get to offer, times the probabilities they choose i times what they have to offer i, v_i. For the three-person simple majority rule game there are some simple patterns. First, if all three players have recognition probabilities greater than 0 but less than $\frac{1}{2}$, then in equilibrium everyone receives one-third. To see why, assume first that one player receives less than the other two **in expectation**. Label the players based on their continuation values, so that player 1 does best and player 3 does worst. Then the top two players will want to select the bottom one as a partner. In this case the valuation of the worst-off player, person 3 is $v_3 = (p_1 + p_2)v_3 + p_3(1 - v_2)$, which can be satisfied only if $1 - v_2 = v_3$ (contrary to the assumption that $v_3 \leq v_1$) or $p_3 = 0$ (contrary to our assumption on positive recognition probabilities). Say instead that one player receives more than the others and that these others tie in expectation. Then this top player will never be offered benefits by the others and her valuation will be $v_1 = p_1(1 - v_3)$. Then, since 2 and 3 tie, we have $1 - 2v_3 = p_1(1 - v_3)$ and so $v_3 = \frac{1 - p_1}{2 - p_1}$. However, this can only be consistent with the requirement that $v_3 < \frac{1}{3}$ if $p_1 > .5$. With $0 < p_3 \leq p_2 \leq p_1 \leq \frac{1}{2}$, the equal division can be achieved in different ways; we can, for example, simply set $q_{12} = \frac{p_3}{p_1}$, $q_{13} = \frac{p_1 - p_3}{p_1}$, $q_{21} = 0$, $q_{23} = 1$, $q_{32} = \frac{p_1 - p_2}{p_3}$ and $q_{31} = \frac{1 - 2p_1}{p_3}$. (More generally we need to make sure that conditions of the form $q_{ij} = \frac{p_k}{p_i} - \frac{p_j}{p_i} q_{ji}$ are satisfied.)

Say, however, that one of the players has a recognition probability greater than $\frac{1}{2}$ or if one has a probability 0, then it becomes possible for different divisions to obtain and for one player to receive more than one-third of the pie. In the $p_3 = 0$ case, any division $v_1 \geq v_2 \geq v_3$ is possible for recognition probabilities $(\frac{v_1}{v_1 + v_2}, \frac{v_2}{v_1 + v_2}, 0)$; conversely, with recognition probabilities $(p_1, p_2, 0)$ any division is possible such that $\frac{v_1}{v_2} = \frac{p_1}{p_2}$ and $v_3 \leq v_1, v_2$.

In the $p_1 > \frac{1}{2}$, $p_3 > 0$ case from the reasoning above, the three players cannot receive different valuations in expectation. It is possible, however, for the highest-valuation player to have a valuation strictly higher than the other two, while these two tie. In that case: $v_1 = p_1(1 - v_3)$ and from the reasoning above, $v_2 = v_3 = \frac{1 - p_1}{2 - p_1}$ and $v_1 = \frac{p_1}{2 - p_1}$. Note that to ensure that the bottom two players do indeed tie, player 1 should select q_{12} such that: $v_2 = p_1 q_{12} v_2 + p_2(1 - v_3) + p_3 v_2$.

The importance of this result depends on whether there really is a random recognition mechanism or something like it. In multiparty democracies the problem of forming governing coalitions sometimes takes a bargaining form like this. In these cases there is often a third party that determines who will have the first chance to form the government and who will try next when they fail. Often there are no formal rules governing how these appointers should choose but there are reasons to suspect that they do not choose randomly in the manner assumed by this type of model (see Laver, Marchi, and Mutlu, 2011).

To see examples of different outcomes when one player has no bargaining power, run this line multiple times:

```
probabilities <- c(.8,.2,0)
gt_leg_barg(probabilities)
```

Each time you should see that the first player gets four times what the second player gets, but the third player could do well or badly.

§19 (THE GIBBARD-SATTERTHWAITE THEOREM)

The Gibbard-Satterthwaite theorem, as well as being an important result on voting systems, is also a fundamental result in the study of mechanism design (see Part 11). One way of thinking about the result is as an answer to the question: Is it possible to design a game in which people declare their preferences and then some nondictatorial outcome is implemented such that people will have a **dominant strategy** to tell the truth about their preferences? A little more formally, say you have a mapping f from preferences P to outcomes X and so you want to be able to choose $f(P)$ whenever people have preferences P; is it possible to design a game in which people will have an incentive to tell you their preferences, P, knowing that you will then implement $f(P)$? The answer is no. But then from the **revelation principle** it follows that there is no mechanism or game form of any kind that implements $f(P)$. For a generalization of the theorem to a broader class of rules see Duggan and Schwartz (2000).

§20 (THE RATIONAL VOTER PARADOX)

The conditions for an equilibrium of the form provided in the graph are quite exacting. It's worth walking through the logic for a simple case. Say there are two parties with three supporters each. Say all supporters of party 1 vote with probability p_1 and all supporters of party 2 vote with probability p_2. This probabilistic voting requires that given everyone else's strategy, each person is indifferent between voting and not. Then the probability that a member of party 1 is pivotal should be equal to her cost/benefit ratio, c_1:

$$(1-p_1)^2 \times (1-p_2)^3 + 2p_1(1-p_1) \times (3p_2(1-p_2)^2) + p_1^2 \times 3(p_2^2(1-p_2)) = c_1$$

The left-hand side sums up the probabilities of a tie with none voting, with one other voting on each side, and with two others voting on each side. Similarly, we need:

$$(1-p_2)^2 \times (1-p_1)^3 + 2p_2(1-p_2) \times (3p_1(1-p_1)^2) + p_2^2 \times 3(p_1^2(1-p_1)) = c_2$$

The challenge is to find just the right p_1 and p_2 to solve both of these equations given c_1 and c_2. As an illustration, if $c_1 = c_2 = 5/16$, then $p_1 = p_2 = 1/2$ would do the trick. If everyone plays with these probabilities we have a **Nash equilibrium** precisely because these probabilities induce the indifference needed to make everyone willing to play them.

There is some disagreement in the literature regarding the fragility of the kind of equilibrium described here. With fixed levels of uncertainty, participation becomes harder to sustain as the numbers increase. Nevertheless recent work by Kalandrakis (2009) suggests that there is no sharp distinction between situations with complete and incomplete information and that these equilibriums are robust to the introduction of mild levels of uncertainty.

Source: David Hill, "Blogging election night in London." *The Guardian*, May 6, 2010.

§21 (THE SWING VOTER'S CURSE)

The logic of the swing voter's curse dealt a small blow to arguments for the virtues of majority decision making by suggesting that even in completely costless two-party elections, some strategic voters might feel their interests are best served by abstaining. In a closely related study, however, Feddersen and Pesendorfer (1998) show that the problem may be even worse for nonmajoritarian decisions. For example, if unanimity is required, as in a jury case, a voter might be very reluctant to vote innocent since this will only matter if she is the only one of *all* the jurors to vote innocent, in which case, she might infer, she may have read the evidence wrongly. Voting guilty might be a safer bet. This worry could be even greater in larger panels precisely because being pivotal requires that you are at odds with more people. Given logics like this, Feddersen and Pesendorfer (1998) show that a unanimous decision may lead to a high probability (relative to majority rule, say) of convicting an innocent person (*and*, under some conditions, of failing to convict a guilty person). See also Coughlan (2000) and The Limits of Deliberation [§25] for different treatments of the related problem of sharing information prior to voting.

§22 (INFORMATION CASCADES)

In the code you can assess how likely you are to get the right answer for this problem over a large number of random orderings. Let x denote a sample of private beliefs, then `gt_declarations(sample(x))` returns play given some random ordering of players. You can then simulate many orderings as follows:

```
signals <- c(1,1,1,1,1,1,0,0,0)
D <- replicate(50000, gt_cascade(sample(signals))$Declarations)
mean(D[9,])
```

You should get an answer around 0.9. Using the same method you can check whether you are more or less likely to get the wrong answer with larger groups (for this, keep the share with the correct answer at 2/3 but vary the size of the groups by making the *x* vector longer). What do you expect to find?

Source: Brian Whitaker, "How a man setting fire to himself sparked an uprising in Tunisia," *The Guardian,* December 28, 2010.

§23 (COSTLY SIGNALING)

Note that in many treatments of costly signaling the key thing is not that the signal is costly for the person taking the action; it is that it *would* be costly for them if they were of a different type. For example, I can likely persuade you that I am Irish by speaking some Irish to you. That's easy for me, but it would be costly (if not impossible) for a non-Irish person trying to pass as Irish, even with a couple of days to prepare. What is striking about §23, however, is that the signaling comes from actually incurring a cost (technically, "burning money"). Types still matter here though; the signaling works because, given the strategic response to the signal, the cost is worth paying for one type and not for another.

Source: Reuters, "Merkel, Hollande meet Putin in Ukraine talks," February 7, 2015.

§24 (CHEAP TALK)

Cheap Talk [§24] shows that you can communicate effectively (if imperfectly) without bearing costs, or going to the lengths of burning money described in Costly Signaling [§23]. In fact there are some deeper relations between these two types of communication and the ability to burn money can sometimes lead to more effective cheap talk. See Austen-Smith and Banks (2000b).

Source: For a media discussion of Obama's vetoes see Tessa Bereuson, "Here are 8 bills Obama has threatened to veto," *Time Magazine,* January 23, 2015.

§25 (THE LIMITS OF DELIBERATION)

The logic of when it makes sense to tell the truth or not can be confusing in these problems because of the range of different types of other players you might be playing with. Figure vii shows the full set of possibilities you need to think through.

To figure out what sorts of equilibriums exist, you have to think through the probability with which each type expects to encounter different combinations of players of different types. Say p is the quality of information (which means that you are likely to get a correct signal with probability p) and q is the probability that a judge is a soft-liner. Say that prior to receiving any signal you think the probability the person is innocent is 0.5. The positive hard-liners would lie if the probability of facing two negative soft-liners exceeds the probability of facing two positive hard-liners. The first of these can be worked out as the probability that both are soft-liners, q^2, (easy), times the probability both think guilty $p(1-p)$ (not so easy, but try working it out, thinking through all the ways in which you could have opposite beliefs to the other two). The second is the probability that both are hard-liners, $(1-q)^2$, times the probability both think innocent, which is $((1-p)^3 + p^3)$. When these two are equal the positive hard-liner is indifferent between telling the truth and lying. A similar calculation can be done for the negative soft-liners. The values that create these indifferences are what produces the curves on the graph in Figure 25.

§26 (AUMANN'S AGREEMENT THEOREM)

For a nice discussion of the arguments for and against the assumption of common priors see Morris (1995).

Source: Rainer Buergin, Brigit Jennen, Brian Parkin, "Schaeuble 'agreed to disagree' with Greece's Varoufakis," *Bloomberg Business*, February 5, 2015.

FIGURE vii THE DECISION TO TELL THE TRUTH OR LIE IN PRE-VOTE DELIBERATIONS [§25]

In each of these panels the four columns represent the four types of player you might be. The rows show the nine different types of pairs of others you might be talking to. For each possible combination you can decide whether to tell the truth or to lie, *under the assumption that others are telling the truth*. A hollow circle indicates that given everyone's strategies the vote will result in the accused being acquitted; a solid circle means the accused is found guilty. Circles are marked red whenever the outcome is what you would want; gray if not. In most cases the color of the circle does not change depending on whether you lie or tell the truth—that is, most of the time it does not matter what you say. If your communication would be pivotal, however, then an arrow is used to highlight what action you should take (a black arrow means lying is a good strategy). In the upper panel with consensus we see that if you are a hard-liner who thinks the accused is innocent, then you never get a better outcome by telling the truth and *sometimes* you get a better outcome by lying. No one else benefits from lying. In the lower panel, under majority rule, we see that for the hard-liner who thinks the accused is innocent *and* for the soft-liner who thinks the accused is guilty there are some circumstances in which lying is best but others in which telling the truth is best.

§27 (THE NASH BARGAINING SOLUTION)

The tricky part of this proof is figuring out the slope of the possibility set at the NBS point. To figure this out note that the indifference curve that picks out the NBS can be written $u_2 = \text{NBS}/u_1$. At the NBS this has slope $-\text{NBS}/(u_1(\text{NBS})u_1(\text{NBS})) = -u_1(\text{NBS})u_2(\text{NBS})/(u_1(\text{NBS})u_1(\text{NBS})) = -u_2(\text{NBS})/u_1(\text{NBS})$.

The Nash bargaining solution is just one of a series of solutions derived from axiomatic reasoning. A powerful alternative is the Kalai-Smorodinsky solution that drops the independence of irrelevant alternatives axiom and replaces it with a monotonicity assumption: if the possible payoffs to a player increase, then the actual payoffs to the player should increase. Under this solution, and normalizing the bargaining failure utilities to 0, agents get payoffs that are proportionate to their greatest possible **utility**. For more see Kalai and Smorodinsky (1975).

Try plotting Nash solutions like this:

```
gt_nbs(u1 = function(x) x^.5, u2 = function(x) 1 - x)
```

§28 (THE STÅHL-RUBINSTEIN SOLUTION)

The solution to alternating offers bargaining is even more elegant in the infinite version of the game and interesting results emerge quickly from a very simple setup.

Say that each of two bargainers has **discounted utility** with a discount factor of δ_i (which means that \$1 given tomorrow is worth as much as δ_i given today) and that each person gets **utility** x^{α_i} from receiving x in any period. Here α_i captures attitudes toward risk (i is **risk neutral** for $\alpha_i = 1$, **risk averse** for $\alpha_i \in (0,1)$, and **risk seeking** for $\alpha_i > 1$). Let x_1^* denote the offer that 1 makes to 2 and x_2^* the offer 2 makes to 1, **in equilibrium**. Then, in equilibrium, each must be as happy to take the offer as to wait to have their own counteroffer accepted. In other words, the following two conditions should be satisfied:

$$(x_1^*)^{\alpha_2} = \delta_2(1 - x_2^*)^{\alpha_2}$$
$$(x_2^*)^{\alpha_1} = \delta_1(1 - x_1^*)^{\alpha_1}$$

Substituting gives:

$$x_1^* = \delta_2^{\frac{1}{\alpha_2}}(1 - \delta_1^{\frac{1}{\alpha_1}}(1 - x_1))$$

which lets us solve for x_1^* (or x_2^*):

$$x_1^* = \frac{1 - \delta_1^{\frac{1}{\alpha_1}}}{\delta_2^{-\frac{1}{\alpha_2}} - \delta_1^{\frac{1}{\alpha_1}}}$$

Note that 1's offer is increasing in both δ_2 and α_2 (the second follows from the fact that the δ terms are between 0 and 1; it's a bit less obvious, but for the intuition note that $0.5^{1/.5} = .25 < 0.5^{1/1} = .5$). Substantively that means that bargainers do better when they are patient, but also when they are not **risk averse**. Risk aversion acts a lot like impatience here, reducing further the *relative* value of a deal today and a deal tomorrow.

It is easy to expand this setup to include all sorts of features, such as multiple bargainers, different recognition rules, and so on.

For a discussion of the deeper connections between the alternating offers solution and the Nash bargaining solution see Binmore, Rubinstein, and Wolinsky (1986).

§29 (THE SCHELLING CONJECTURE)

The conjecture was brought to prominence in political science through Robert Putnam's (1988) work on "two-level games." Although it is easy to show cases where the Schelling principle is in operation, it is hard to make general statements about when constraints are good or bad as these depend on the nature of the problem and the bargaining protocol.

Sources: David E. Sanders. "Ex-advisers warn Obama that Iran nuclear deal 'may fall short' of standards," *The New York Times*, June 24, 2015; Peter Baker, "G.O.P. senators' letter to Iran about nuclear deal angers White House," *The New York Times,* March 9, 2015.

§30 (THE COMMITMENT PROBLEM)

The treatment of the commitment problem in Powell (2004) is much more general than what is provided above and considers a situation where deals have to be not just agreed upon but sustained in every period—there is, in a sense, a constant risk that the other side reneges. This feature is important since rather than assuming no credibility, the model derives the conditions under which deals can be rendered **credible** through repeated engagements. In the Powell model the commitment problem arises when there is a *risk* of large reversals of fortune, whether or not these in fact occur. The model thus allows for uncertainty but does not require asymmetric information.

Source: Josh Lederman, "Obama says Iran could cut nuke time to near zero in 13 years," *Washington Times,* April 7, 2015.

§31 (THE COASE THEOREM)

The main technical assumption needed for the strong result—that outcomes don't depend on the allocation of rights—is that people have **quasilinear** utility. That is what produces the flat utility possibility set in the figures. If, however, preferences change as you get richer, then what gets chosen could depend on who has the rights. Indeed in some cases there might be no deal that anyone can offer to a polluter to get her to stop and which makes everyone better off.

To replicate the graph of **efficient** outcomes from bargaining in a PD game type:

```
payoffs <- matrix(c(2,3,0,1),2)
gt_coase(payoffs, bargain = T, SQ = "minimax")
```

For a more general possibility set, try:

```
gt_coase(f=function(x) 1-x^2, bargain = T, SQ=c(0,1))
```

Source: Valerie Volcovici, David Lawder, "Republicans vow EPA fight as Obama touts China climate deal," *Reuters*, November 12, 2014.

§32 (THE REVENUE EQUIVALENCE THEOREM)

The revenue equivalence theorem is a remarkable result. The mathematics behind it are not all that difficult, however. To establish the result we make use of "**the revelation principle.**" I now show that in all games of this form in which people state their valuations truthfully and the good goes to the person with the highest valuation (though not necessarily at the same price), the revenue of the seller is the same. Here goes. Say you think some item is worth θ (where θ is distributed between $\underline{\theta}$ and $\bar{\theta}$ according to distribution function F). But say that if you *say* you think it's worth $\tilde{\theta}$, then you can expect to get it with probability $p(\tilde{\theta})$ and to pay $t(\tilde{\theta})$ for total gains of $u(\theta) = \theta p(\tilde{\theta}) - t(\tilde{\theta})$. How much should you say you think it's worth? The best $\tilde{\theta}$ to declare is whatever solves the first-order condition $\theta p'(\tilde{\theta}) - t'(\tilde{\theta}) = 0$. Note though that if everyone tells

the truth, then $u'(\theta) = \theta p'(\theta) + p(\theta) - t'(\theta)$, and so if people are telling the truth *and* playing optimally: $u'(\theta) = p(\theta)$. Integrating up: $u(\theta) - u(\underline{\theta}) = \int_{\underline{\theta}}^{\theta} p(x)dx$ and so $u(\underline{\theta}) + \int_{\underline{\theta}}^{\theta} p(x)dx = \theta p(\theta) - t(\theta)$. Say now that the person who values the good the least expects to gain nothing, so $u(\underline{\theta}) = 0$; recall that we are looking at games in which the good is to go to the person with the highest valuation, so $p(\theta) = (F(\theta))^{n-1}$. Then $t(\theta) = \theta(F(\theta))^{n-1} - \int_{\underline{\theta}}^{\theta}(F(x))^{n-1}dx$. All that is to say that **in equilibrium**, *expected transfers depend only on who all are bidding and have nothing to do with the auction design itself.*
Source: Emma Graves Fitzsimmons, "Prosecutors press Blagojevich," *The New York Times*, June 6, 2011.

§33 (ASYMMETRIC INFORMATION AND MARKET FAILURE)

This parable is most easily described as a dynamic process. Can you set it up as a simple game of incomplete information in which a single buyer names a price and a seller with a car of unknown quality decides to sell or not?
Sources: Gallup, "New Congress Has Slightly Higher Ratings, Still Unpopular," *Politics*, February 16, 2015; Edelman, "Edelman Trust Barometer—Global Results," 2015.

§34 (THE GROSSMAN-STIGLITZ PARADOX)

The graph is constructed assuming the following setup. Say both Dum and Dee think there is a 50% probability that the apples are worth $1 each. Say that Dee has $1 in cash and Dum has nothing. Say, moreover, that the value that Dum and Dee place on ultimate earnings of $y is $\sqrt{y}$. This captures the idea that they are "**risk averse**" in the sense that they would strictly prefer $1 for sure to an even chance of $0 and $2. Then the set of possible trades involves Dum transferring either 0, 1, or 2 apples to Dee in exchange for some amount of money. The expected **utility** to each person of each of these trades is then calculated in the following way: The expected gain for Dee of buying 1 apple for price p would be $.5 \times \sqrt{(1-p)} + .5 \times \sqrt{(1+1-p)} - 1$. Dum's expected gain would be $.5 \times \sqrt{p} + .5 \times \sqrt{(1+p)} - .5 \times \sqrt{2}$. Similar gains can be worked out for all possible trades. The figure then shows the gains in utility for the two players for all trades that give both gains from trade.

Note that in this example a lot seemed to depend on the feature that if you find out the true value of the assets, then the others will too: you can't secretly figure out what the apples are worth and keep that information to yourself. In this story it was Rabbit who made sure everyone had the same information. In fact that feature is not so important here. The key idea is that in real markets, the information gets conveyed by the markets themselves via the trades that people are willing to make. The logic is akin to that described in the Agreement Theorem [§26]. For example, if Dee were able to find out the value of the apples privately and then started to haggle over prices with Dum, then Dum should be able to figure right away that Dee must have learned that the apples were Coxes. Of course markets may vary in the extent to which prices communicate what everyone thinks things are worth. The general point then is that *the better markets are at communicating information, the less incentive anyone has to gather meaningful information in the first place* (von Mises 1990).

§35 (MASKIN MONOTONICITY)

The Maskin monotonicity result is a critical result in the study of "mechanism design" (which includes implementation theory). In standard game theory the game is given and the interest is in finding the solution to the game, and then the properties of that solution are analyzed. In implementation theory you are interested in an outcome with particular properties and you try to figure out if there is a game that will lead to an outcome with those properties. That becomes interesting only when you do not have full control over outcomes anyway. The focus in implementation theory is on situations where you do not know the preferences of different actors (that's Solomon's problem) and so you want the game that you design to produce the right outcome no matter what the preferences are. The Gibbard-Satterthwaite Theorem [§19] can be thought of as a negative result of this form: you cannot devise a game (electoral system) that induces all voters to tell you what their true preferences are. Note though that whereas the Gibbard-Satterthwaite Theorem assesses situations in which truth telling is a **dominant strategy**, Maskin's result focuses only on truth telling being a **Nash equilibrium**, which is a weaker condition. For a very useful review see Maskin and Sjöström (2002).

§36 (THE CLARKE-GROVES MECHANISM)

In the example in the figure I assumed that each of two players had **utility** of the form:

$$u_i(x|\theta) = \theta_i\sqrt{x} + t_i + k_i$$

Where θ_i is the player's "type," which is in general only known to the person herself, $\sqrt{x}$ (a non-negative number) is the amount of a **public good** produced, t_i is a transfer to player i, and k_i is a constant which is of no strategic importance. I assumed that public good of amount $\sqrt{x}$ is created at cost x. Note that this is a **quasilinear utility** function in the sense that the utility is linear in the transfers but not generally linear.

In that case, if a single person were choosing investments in the public good, x (and paying for it herself), she would select amount $\theta_i^2/4$. This is found by differentiating $\theta_i\sqrt{x} - x$ with respect to x and finding the value of x that satisfies the first-order condition. Note that (ignoring k_i) the utility for someone in that situation would be $\theta_i\theta_i/2 - \theta_i^2/4 = \theta_i^2/4$.

If you had to choose the investment, x, that is simultaneously optimal for two players you could get it by doing the same thing, but this time counting the gains for both when you optimize. This would yield solution $(\theta_1 + \theta_2)^2/4$ and i's utility (assuming costs are split evenly) would be $\theta_i(\theta_i + \theta_j)/2 - (\theta_i + \theta_j)^2/8$. Note that here we are using a utilitarian calculus after normalizing each person's utility by the value they put on transfers (cash).

Say now that the institutional procedure was for each person to declare their type (or equivalently, their valuation), then let the optimal amount of public goods be produced (assuming that the statements are true!) but with costs of implementation divided in half. Would players have an incentive to tell the truth about their type? Unfortunately not. To see why, note that each person i's best action is to choose a declaration, $\tilde{\theta}_i$, that maximizes:

$$\frac{\theta_i(\tilde{\theta}_i + \tilde{\theta}_j)}{2} - \frac{(\tilde{\theta}_i + \tilde{\theta}_j)^2}{8}$$

This has first-order condition:

$$\frac{\theta_i}{2} - \frac{\tilde{\theta}_i + \tilde{\theta}_j}{4} = 0;$$

which is solved by:

$$\tilde{\theta}_i = 2\theta_i - \tilde{\theta}_j$$

In equilibrium, the person who values the public good most states a marginal value twice as large as their true marginal value, while the person who values it the least claims it is worthless. In the end, the wrong amount of public goods would be produced.

(Note that for simplicity I am treating this as a game of complete information and finding a Nash solution, rather than a Bayes-Nash solution. This makes sense if, for example, the players knew each other's preferences even if the mechanism does not.)

However, things need not be so bad. The key idea of the Clarke-Groves mechanism is that it is possible to set things up so that the contributions associated with each declaration of value are just the right amount to make people want to declare their true valuations (no matter what other people do), and these prices can be set even when you don't know what the true values are.

The trick is to charge i the full cost of the action less the gains to j (which has to be done without the mechanism having any special information about valuations other than what it gets told by the players!).

So now, when i is deciding what to declare (and so ignoring the part of the transfers that do not depend on i's declarations), she is maximizing:

$$\frac{\theta_i(\tilde{\theta}_i + \tilde{\theta}_j)}{2} - \left[\frac{(\tilde{\theta}_i + \tilde{\theta}_j)^2}{4} - \frac{\tilde{\theta}_j(\tilde{\theta}_i + \tilde{\theta}_j)}{2}\right]$$

The first term here is i's benefit, the part in square brackets is her transfer, which is equal to the *full* cost less j's benefit (as inferred from the declarations).

First-order condition:

$$\theta_i - (\tilde{\theta}_i + \tilde{\theta}_j) + \tilde{\theta}_j = 0,$$

which is solved by $\tilde{\theta}_i = \theta_i$ regardless of $\tilde{\theta}_j$. So players have a **dominant strategy** to tell the truth: truth telling makes sense no matter what the other person is doing.

The prices charged could be increased or decreased by any amount without changing these incentives, as long as these additions do not depend on $\tilde{\theta}_i$. In the example in the text I add on the *net* benefit that j would receive if only her preferences were taken into account, but costs were still split in half. In this case, $\tilde{\theta}_j^2$ would be chosen and the net benefit to j would be $\tilde{\theta}_j^2/2$. In that case i's payment becomes:

$$\frac{(\tilde{\theta}_i + \tilde{\theta}_j)^2}{4} - \frac{\tilde{\theta}_j(\tilde{\theta}_i + \tilde{\theta}_j)}{2} + \frac{\tilde{\theta}_j^2}{2} = \frac{\tilde{\theta}_i^2 + \tilde{\theta}_j^2}{4}$$

which has both the advantage of being positive (no one actually has to get paid by the system) and being enough to cover costs, since $2 \times (\tilde{\theta}_i^2 + \tilde{\theta}_j^2)/4 \geq (\tilde{\theta}_i + \tilde{\theta}_j)^2/4$. (It might seem surprising that people end up paying the same amount even though they value the good differently, so take a second to check that with this charge, people still have an incentive to tell the truth!)

For intuition on how this works generally, note that the transfer forces each i to choose the declaration that maximizes the social value of the good (where this is itself selected as the social optimum, given the declarations). But then if there were an advantage to not being truthful, it would mean that it is possible to increase the social welfare beyond the optimum, a contradiction.

Note finally that the difference between payments made and actual project costs is positive (except in the case where $\tilde{\theta}_i = \tilde{\theta}_j$). Awkwardly, this means that unless players are in agreement anyway, some money generally has to be lost in equilibrium. Thus although the mechanism gets the best project selected, there are still inefficiencies generated by the need to figure out what the best project is.

For a version of Figure 36 try:

```
gt_cgm(theta1 = .2, theta2 = .4)
```

Source on UN financing: United Nations, *Financing Peacekeeping*.

§37 (THE MYERSON-SATTERTHWAITE THEOREM)

To get a feel for why the seller has an incentive to overstate her valuation of the good, note that a seller that values the good at $1 maximizes the expected price paid (when she declares $1 + x$) less her valuation ($1). If she told the truth, she would be guaranteed a sale (since the buyer values the good between $1 and $3); indeed she would be guaranteed a profit, though possibly a small one. When she states a higher price she trades off a gain in profits against an increased risk that the good won't get sold. Assuming that the true valuation of the (truth-telling) buyer is distributed uniformly over 1 and 3, the seller chooses an "exaggeration" quantity x to maximize:

$$\int_{1+x}^{3} \left(\frac{t+1+x}{2} - 1 \right) \frac{1}{2} dt = 4 + 4x - 3x^2$$

First-order conditions are:

$$4 - 6x = 0 \leftrightarrow x = \frac{2}{3}$$

She has, in short, an incentive to lie *a lot* in order to grab more profit. This basic incentive to exaggerate always holds and means that, in general, deals will not be made and the gains from trade will be left unrealized.

Source: Kathy Gannon, "Bush Rejects Taliban Bin Laden Offer," Associated Press, October 14, 2001.

§38 (THE LOGIC OF POLITICAL ACCOUNTABILITY)

The accountability logic extends elegantly to long-run interactions, and indeed the math becomes easier.

Say that a politician can choose effort level $e \in [0, 1]$ and that the benefits to a period in office are $1 - e^2$. If per period **utility** is **discounted** at rate δ, then a politician will prefer to perform effort level e^* rather than doing nothing as long as:

$$\frac{1 - e^{*2}}{1 - \delta} \geq 1 \leftrightarrow e^* \leq \sqrt{\delta}$$

You see right away that the extent to which you can hold politicians to account depends critically on how farsighted they are.

§39 (THE SELECTORATE MODEL)

Here is a very simple example of a selectorate model. There are two politicians, an incumbent and a challenger, and s citizens. The incumbent gets to choose how much of government revenue, R, to divide up (equally) among w supporters, how much to keep for herself, and how much, g, to spend on **public goods** subject to a budget constraint:

$$y + wt + g = R$$

where y is the revenue she keeps for herself, t are transfers made to w supporters, and g is an allocation toward public goods.

Citizens have **quasilinear utility** and get **utility** t_i from transfers plus $b\sqrt{g}$ from public goods:

$$u_i = t_i + b\sqrt{g}$$

You can think of the function on public goods as either capturing the voter valuation of the goods or as capturing some feature of the production of goods, or the costs of producing those goods. Note I assume symmetry here, which simplifies things. (In the full model there are also idiosyncratic benefits from having one or another leader in office, which are presumed to be known for incumbents, and unknown for challengers. This opens up the possibility that challengers seek to pick off *particular* members of the leader's coalition.)

Say the challenger can credibly commit to how she will use revenues if she takes office, that is, on how much of a public good she will produce and who she will give rents to. In order to defend the office, the incumbent needs to maintain the support of at least w citizens out of a "selectorate" of s citizens. (Note that in the standard model, leaders only need the support of $\min(w, s - w + 1)$, under the logic that controlling $s - w + 1$ is enough to stop a challenger getting control of w citizens.)

The basic production technology gives rise to some simple tradeoffs. Total social welfare of citizens is given by $wt + sb\sqrt{g}$ and so the best use of resources from a welfare point of view allocates nothing to politicians (set $y = 0$) and selects g to maximize $(R - g) + sb\sqrt{g}$. The optimal allocation (found by differentiating and solving the first-order condition) gives:

$$g^{**} = s^2 b^2/4$$

Thus public goods should always be produced but especially so for large polities and when citizens place a high value on public goods. For illustration if you normalize $s = 1$ and $R = 1$ and set $b = 2$, then welfare is maximized by investing entirely in public goods.

Say, however, that politicians, instead of trying to maximize welfare, sought to retain as much revenue as possible while ensuring that w citizens each get some minimum amount of benefits $\underline{u}$. Then they would maximize $R - g - wt$ subject to $t + b\sqrt{g} \geq \underline{u}$. Or, equivalently, maximize $R - g - w(\underline{u} - b\sqrt{g})$. This has the following solution (here, independent of $\underline{u}$):

$$g^* = w^2 b^2/4$$

To see why the level of $\underline{u}$ is irrelevant refer to The Coase Theorem [§31]; there too under the assumption of **quasilinear utility**, the optimal action was independent of who got what.

What are the implications? In effect, since $w < s$, less is spent on public goods than is socially optimal. Instead, incumbents seek to satisfy supporters using side payments, and pocket the surplus. The costs, meanwhile, are borne by those outside the coalition. These marginalized citizens get no private goods but also benefit less from public goods. The larger is w relative to s, the greater are the benefits in two ways: first, there are more citizens inside the coalition that get to enjoy different types of benefits; second, citizens outside the coalition also get to enjoy more benefits.

Note that this analysis is static and I assumed that there was a fixed amount by which coalition members had to be satisfied in order to support the government, independent of the institutions. Instead, though, this could be examined using a more dynamic approach where $\underline{u}$ is an output of the model that itself depends on the institutions.

Say instead that the game was played repeatedly with constant risks of new challengers. Assume then that the minimum utility from staying loyal has to match some temptation payment for disloyalty, k (in the selectorate model this is a one-time gain from payments from challengers that are not credibly providable in later periods; it might also be thought of as a share of the challenger's war chest) plus the value of a gamble of being an insider in the new regime (with probability w/s) or being an outsider (with probability $1 - w/s$). In an equilibrium in which incumbents are successful at keeping their coalitions together, the minimum utility must satisfy:

$$\frac{\underline{u}}{1-\delta} = k + \frac{(w/s)\,\underline{u} + (1 - w/s)(wb/2)}{1-\delta}$$

Note that the δ term here captures how people value benefits received over time, with something received tomorrow worth only the share δ of what it would be worth if received today (see **discounted utility**). The value of getting x in every period is then $x + \delta x + \delta^2 x \ldots$, which conveniently adds up to $x/(1-\delta)$. Note also that in this setup you get the policy payoff from the challenger starting right from the period of revolt.

Solving for $\underline{u}$ gives:

$$\underline{u} = \frac{k(1-\delta)}{1 - w/s} + \frac{wb}{2}$$

This suggests that leaders do worse when supporters are impatient (since the would-be supporters are more tempted by the flash-in-the-pan rewards of rebellion), and in more inclusive polities when w is large relative to s (since then exclusion is both less likely and less painful for a defecting supporter). Thus more inclusive polities hurt dictators twice—first in having to make more people happy and second in increasing how happy they have to be.

Note that Déby wins large majorities in Chad's elections though these are typically boycotted by opposition parties.

Source on Chad: Alan Riding, "Rebels in control of Chad's capital," *The New York Times*, December 3, 1990.

§40 (THE MELTZER-RICHARD MODEL)

For a fully worked-out version of the Meltzer-Richard model, imagine a situation with lots of voters and each voter having **utility** given by:

$$u_i = (1-t)y_i - x_i + r$$

where x_i is labor allocated to production, r are benefits provided by the government by redistributing taxes equally among everyone, y_i is pretax income, and t is the tax rate. Assume that income is produced according to the production function $y_i = \sqrt{e_i x_i}$ where e_i is the individual endowment of some factor of production (capital, land, talent, ...).

Assuming people take taxes, benefits, and endowments as given, the optimal production can be found by maximizing utility. This is equivalent to maximizing $(1-t)y_i - y_i^2/e_i + r$ (substituting y_i^2/e_i for x). The solution is $y_i^* = (1-t)e_i/2$. So people with bigger endowments have bigger incomes, but taxes reduce productivity for everyone. The total gains from production (excluding transfers) are then $(1-t)(1-t)e_i/2 - (1-t)^2 e_i/4$, which simplifies nicely to $(1-t)^2 e_i/4$.

Let's say that endowments are distributed according to a density function f, defined over the positive numbers and with a mean of 1 but possible right skew (a log normal density would be a good example of a distribution like this). We interpret skew as a measure of inequality, resulting in a median that is lower relative to the mean.

Total tax revenues depend on total production, which in turn can depend on the distribution of endowments. In this simple case, however, the *skew* in endowments does not affect average income. To see this, define $\bar{y} \equiv \int_0^\infty (1-t)e/2f(e)de$, and note: $\int_0^\infty (1-t)e/2f(e)de = \int_0^\infty ef(e)de(1-t)/2 = (1-t)/2$. Revenue is then $t(1-t)/2$ from which you can figure out that the revenue-maximizing tax rate is $t = 0.5$ or 50%.

Taking all this into account, each person's utility from a given tax rate, t, given their endowments, is given by:

$$(1-t)^2 e_i/4 + t(1-t)/2$$

And their *preferred* tax rate (calculated by differentiating with respect to tax and solving the first-order condition) is given by:

$$t = \frac{1 - e_i}{2 - e_i}$$

This means that people's preferences for taxes depend negatively on their initial endowments. Drawing on the logic of the Median Voter Theorem [§12] we care especially about the preferences of the median voter: What does the median voter want? In this case, if the median is equal to the mean, then she wants zero taxes. But if the median shifts closer to 0, she wants tax rates up to the revenue-maximizing amount of 50%.

The result here depends critically on the idea that the policy options are in some sense one dimensional—you can line them up such that everyone prefers things closer to their ideal than things far away. For tax policy that works if you only choose a very simple tax policy such as a single tax rate that applies to everyone. If you can impose different taxes on different groups arbitrarily, you are no longer in the world of the median voter theorem and are back to chaos [§15].

To replicate one of the graphs try:

```
gt_plot_mr(endowment = .5)
```

Source: *Reuters*, "Senior senate republican accuses Obama of 'class warfare,'" January 20, 2015.

§41 (THE DIXIT-LONDREGAN MODEL)

The Dixit-Londregan model describes optimal allocations of benefits across sectors (or groups or regions) that vary in the extent to which they harbor uncommitted voters.

Let β_j denote the share of the population that is an uncommitted voter working in sector j. If party i offers y_i to sector 1, then the expected vote share for party 1 is:

$$\alpha_1 = k_1 + \beta_1 \frac{y_1}{y_1 + y_2} + \beta_2 \frac{1 - y_1}{2 - y_1 - y_2}$$

where k_1 denotes the share of votes that is in the bag for party 1. This is a kind of "contest function" that says how well two players do given joint actions. In the original paper this is generated from a distribution of idiosyncratic preferences toward the candidates among voters in different sectors. If you maximize this vote share with respect to y_1, you get as first-order condition:

$$\beta_1 \frac{1}{y_1 + y_2} - \beta_1 \frac{y_1}{(y_1 + y_2)^2} - \beta_2 \frac{1}{2 - y_1 - y_2} + \beta_2 \frac{1 - y_1}{(2 - y_1 - y_2)^2} = 0$$

At the symmetric solution:

$$y_1 = y_2 = \frac{\beta_1}{\beta_1 + \beta_2}$$

Here this equilibrium transfer depends only on the relative share of voters in each group who are sensitive to tax policy. A given sector gets more from *both* parties the more undecided voters there are in that sector (and the fewer there are in other sectors).

This basic model can be extended easily to include features such as greater sensitivity to transfers from one or another party, or much more general preferences of voters and distributions of preferences within groups. Give it a go.

§42 (THE LOGIC OF COLLECTIVE ACTION)

Say that each person i can contribute some amount $x_i \in [0, 1]$ and that their **utility** is $\frac{1}{n^\gamma}(x_i + \Sigma_{-i} x_j)^\alpha - x_i^\beta$. The idea here is that your contributions (x_i) plus everyone else's contributions ($\Sigma_{-i} x_j$) pay for a **public good**. The α term captures the extent to which the public good exhibits decreasing returns to scale (decreasing returns arise if $0 < \alpha < 1$); the γ term captures the amount of "congestion" (if $\gamma = 0$, there is no congestion and the public good is enjoyed by all no matter how many are consuming it); the β term captures the extent to which the private costs to contribution become more onerous the more you contribute.

To figure out the solution note that the first-order conditions are:

$$\frac{1}{n^\gamma} \alpha (x_i + \Sigma_{-i} x_j)^{\alpha - 1} - \beta x_i^{\beta - 1} = 0$$

Second-order conditions are:

$$\frac{1}{n^\gamma} \alpha (\alpha - 1)(x_i + \Sigma_{-i} x_j)^{\alpha - 2} - \beta(\beta - 1) x_i^{\beta - 2} < 0$$

These are satisfied for $\alpha < 1$ and $\beta \geq 1$.

Then setting all the x_j's equal and solving for Σx_j gives

$$\Sigma x_j = \left(\frac{\alpha}{\beta}\right)^{\frac{1}{\beta - \alpha}} n^{\frac{\beta - 1 - \gamma}{\beta - \alpha}}$$

This means that in the symmetric **Nash equilibrium** the total amount contributed will be proportional to $n^{\frac{\beta - 1 - \gamma}{\beta - \alpha}}$. As shown in the figure in §42, this total can be increasing or decreasing in n but for $\beta > \alpha$ it is more likely to be increasing when β is high and γ is low. The effect of α depends on the size of γ. Note that I have deliberately made things simple by assuming that we (and all players) know the exact ways that contributions lead to individual benefits, but even in this simple case there is a striking sensitivity of conclusions to details of assumptions. For a discussion of this sensitivity and the role of β see Esteban and Ray (2002).

§43 (THRESHOLD MODELS)

For these graphs I assume that an individual i thinks that rebelling makes sense if $x_i + n > b$, where b is the value of remaining loyal to the regime, n is the share of others that take part, and x_i is an individual's personal dissatisfaction with the regime. I assume the individual dissatisfaction will be different for different people, and in particular that it is normally distributed around zero, with a standard deviation of 0.25. This is enough to calculate how many will rebel given the share of others rebelling: the share of people rebelling, $s(n, b)$, is the share with $x_i > b - n$, or $s(n, b) = 1 - F(b - n)$, where F is a cumulative normal distribution. In the figure in the text I compare two cases: one with $b = 0.6$ and one with $b = 0.5$. From the symmetry of the normal distribution around 0 we know that $F(0) = .5$, which means that $s(0.6, 0.6) = 0.5$, so in the first case if 60% rebel today, then 50% rebel tomorrow, a drop; if 50% rebel today, then less than 50% will rebel tomorrow. The second curve is generated by assuming a drop in the value of remaining loyal from $b = 0.6$ to $b = 0.5$. In that case if $n = .5$, then $n = b$ and so $s(n, b) = 0.5$.

§44 (PSYCHOLOGICAL GAMES)

Psychological games are in fact an *extension* of standard game theory. The standard model allows for very general preferences over all actions and all outcomes that are produced by those actions but it does not allow for preferences over expectations over those actions. That is the novel feature that is introduced in the study of psychological games.

In this example the preferences are given with respect to initial rather than updated expectations. Presumably once the population sees that the government is not sharing, they should no longer be in any doubt about the government's preferred strategy. A richer class of games allows for updated beliefs about the beliefs of others, for example, about the government's belief over the population's belief that it will act in the population's interest. Preferences over such updated beliefs provide a natural way to handle concern with norm following, or notions of guilt or betrayal. See Battigalli and Dufwenberg (2009) for more on this.

§45 (REPUTATION MODELS)

There are interesting connections between the reputation model and the problem of cooperation in a finitely repeated Prisoner's Dilemma (see §1 and §4). Recall that in a finitely repeated Prisoner's Dilemma the only rational thing to do is to defect in every period. But what should you infer if you see your opponent cooperating? One inference is that the other side is not rational and might continue to cooperate as long as you cooperate with her. Another possibility is that she *is* rational but wants you to think she is not rational—that is, she wants to do well by building a reputation for not being rational. For this to work you have to entertain the possibility that players are not rational, but once you do that, you open up the possibility for bluffing, which in this case might be to everyone's advantage (at least for a while). For more see Kreps, Milgrom, Roberts, and Wilson (1982).

§46 (EVOLUTIONARY STABILITY)

The fact that evolutionary stable strategies (ESS) form a subclass of **Nash equilibrium** means that if there is an ESS in a Prisoner's Dilemma [§1] it has to be all defect. Does that mean that it is impossible for cooperative behavior to evolve? Yes, at least if you limit the strategies to those that can be played in the single period game. But in the context of repeated interactions one can also consider strategies (similar to those discussed in The Folk Theorems [§4]) of the form "I cooperate with you if you have always cooperated with me, otherwise I defect" or "I cooperate every second time we play." The question then becomes one of finding an evolutionarily stable cooperative strategy for the repeated game. Unfortunately, though, with infinite games there are infinitely many such strategies so it can be hard to figure out if any of them are evolutionarily stable. Axelrod and Hamilton (1981) famously argued that a tit-for-tat strategy is evolutionarily stable in this sense. Later work shows, though, that that is not quite right. Other strategies, like an all-cooperate strategy, could survive well in a population playing tit-for-tat and so tit-for-tat does not drive out all invading strategies. In fact this kind of problem exists for every pure strategy. Even still, while getting what might be called "strongly stable strategies" (strategies that bounce back when invaded by others) seems to be impossible, tit-for-tat-like strategies do have some evolutionary advantages. For a detailed treatment of different notions of stability and what strategies do well by them, see Bendor and Swistak (1997).

§47 (STOCHASTIC STABILITY)

A focus on stochastic stability provides a rationale for selecting among multiple equilibriums. §47 illustrated the idea using an Assurance Game [§3], and found convergence to the Pareto dominated equilibrium. But that does not have to happen; whether the dynamics of an assurance game converge to the Pareto dominated outcome ("all defect") depends on the details of the **payoff matrix**. Say the other person is playing cooperate with a 50% probability of cooperation; if you would then be better

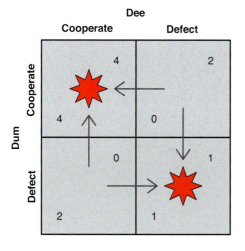 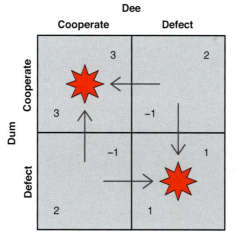

FIGURE viii TWO ASSURANCE GAMES
The Pareto optimal outcome (all cooperate) is risk dominant in the first but not the second game. Equivalently: say you thought the other person was going to play each strategy with a 50% probability, then in the first game you would be better off cooperating (cooperate would give you 2 **in expectation**, defecting would give 1.5), but in the second game you would be better off defecting (cooperation would give 1 in expectation and defecting 1.5). This means that in the left game the set of possible expectations about the actions of others for which cooperation is an optimal strategy is larger than in the right game.

off defecting, then defection is the "risk-dominant" action; if you would be better off cooperating, then cooperation would be the risk-dominant action. The stochastic dynamics studied by Young et al. (2001) select the risk-dominant action whether that be cooperation or defection. See Figure viii.

The key insight is that although the Pareto optimal outcome is better, the risk-dominant outcome has a larger "basin of attraction"—there is a larger set of possible actions that other people play that induce you to play the risk-dominant outcome, which means that more errors are needed to get out of it and fewer are needed to get into it.

Graph some transition dynamics by typing:

```
gt_sss(error = 0, periods = 2)
```

Or even better, try it out with different transition matrices.

§48 (THE *k*-LEVEL MODEL)

For more on the guessing game see Nagel (1995) "Unraveling in Guessing Games: An Experimental Study." Note that fully strategic players can still optimize in the usual way, taking account of the fact that they might face nonoptimizing partners. Say Jill thought there was a q chance Jack was fully strategic and a $1 - q$ chance that he wouldn't give any thought to the matter and just take some action z. Say, moreover, that she reckons that *if* Jack is sophisticated, then he would credit her with being sophisticated with the same probability. Then if her **utility** was based on how close she is to Jack's guess divided by two, she would try to maximize:

$$U_i = -q(x_i - x^s/2)^2 - (1-q)(x_i - z/2)^2$$

where x^s is the action a strategic player might take. Taking first-order conditions, setting x_i equal to x^s, gives $x_s = \frac{(1-q)}{2-q} z$. Thus she might play anything between half naive Jack's offer and 0 depending on how likely it is that Jack is really naive (and how likely he thinks that she is sophisticated).

§49 (A THEOREM ON IMITATION)

For a discussion of when mixed populations result in strategic actors mimicking non-strategic actors or vice versa, see also Camerer and Fehr (2006).

Source on Russell and the crisis: Bertrand W. Russell, (1959). *Common Sense and Nuclear Warfare.*

§A1 (ZERMELO'S THEOREM)

Zermelo's theorem gave conditions under which game theory can make sharp predictions, at least in principle. Two words of warning. First, the "in principle" is important here because the theorem only tells you that there will be a solution and how to work it out; that does not mean that you will actually have the computational capacity to work it out. Even a very simple game like naughts and crosses requires quite a bit of computation: in that game the first mover can take one of 9 actions, the second one of 8, and so on, which means that there are $9 \times 8 \times 7 \cdots \times 1 = 362{,}880$ ways the game could be played (assuming you play until the board is filled). Second, many of the problems you might care about in economic and political life are not like these games, since they involve people moving at the same time as well as uncertainty over people's preferences and their actions. For these games reasoning backward might still help a lot in ruling out some types of behavior, but there is no reason to expect that there will be unique predictions about how things will play out.

Note that it is not clear that this theorem is rightly called Zermelo's theorem since the claim does not appear in Zermelo's 1913 paper on the subject (see Zermelo 1913 and Schwalbe and Walker 2001). Note also that in some treatments "Zermelo's theorem" refers to a different result: that in chess either white should win, or black should win, or it should be a draw. This result has more recently been attributed to Kalmár (1928); see Ewerhart (2002). Ewerhart also points out that technically chess is not a finite game since the repetition of positions (which is inevitable if a game with finite positions goes on long enough) only gives a side a right to call a draw but does not automatically bring an end to the game.

§A2 (THE MINIMAX THEOREM)

It is easy to miss how striking the minimax result is. To appreciate it, it is useful to see when it does not hold. In non-**zero-sum games** it is not necessarily the case that the minimax strategies give a simple solution to the game. Return to the Game of Chicken from §2. In that game if I wanted to force you to as low a payoff as possible, I would go straight. Your best response would be to swerve and you would get a payoff of 1 and I would get 3. But if I wanted to do as well as possible knowing that you were trying to hurt me as much as possible, then I would swerve for a payoff of 1. Thus unlike in the zero-sum case I get different outcomes depending on whether I approach the problem aggressively or defensively. Minimaxing also might not always be **credible**: in some games you might each be able to minimize the other's payoff by producing situations that are terrible for everyone, but such actions would not be convincing solutions to the game if they were so costly that you would not actually want to play them. A strong attack is the best form of defense in zero-sum games but not in general.

§A3 (NASH'S THEOREM)

The mathematics behind Nash's theorem is simple and elegant. At the heart of the proof is a fixed-point theorem. Fixed-point theorems are theorems that say when you can be sure that some transformation of a set of points leaves at least one point unchanged. If the wind blows all the leaves around a courtyard in a continuous way (meaning that if two leaves started off beside each other, then they end up beside each other, though possibly both in a different part of the courtyard), then when you go check you can be sure that there will be at least one leaf sitting where it was before the wind came. Figure ix illustrates the logic in a simple case: if a function takes all the points between 0 and 1 and assigns them new values between 0 and 1 in a continuous way, then it has to leave at least one number unchanged. To check it try to draw a line that starts somewhere on the left-hand side of the square and goes rightward until it hits the right-hand side. As illustrated in the left panel you should find that if you don't lift your pen, you can't avoid crossing the 45-degree line. But when you cross that line your function is mapping a point onto itself. Not lifting your pen is important; as shown in the right panel you can avoid the 45-degree line by just jumping above or below it at critical moments.

Now back to Nash. Nash's theorem states that there exists a set of strategies such that no one wants to change their strategies given everyone else's strategies. The trick is to recognize that this claim is equivalent to the claim that there exists a particular type of fixed point. Define a "best-response correspondence" as a mapping that takes every possible combination of strategies of all players and for each one reports back what strategies would constitute best responses for all players to those strategies. For example, in the Prisoner's Dilemma [§1] the best-response correspondence simply says: "No matter what everyone does, everyone's best response should be to defect for sure." Now notice that a fixed point of the best-response correspondence is a collection of strategies with the feature that the best responses of all players include the strategies in question. In other words, no one has an incentive to change strategy and so it is a **Nash equilibrium**. The proof then requires showing that the best-response correspondence has features much like the function shown on the left panel of Figure ix. Note that this proof is not "constructive" in any way: it tells you that at least one equilibrium exists but it gives no guidance as to how many equilibriums there might be or what they might look like.

To get a feel for the best-response correspondence and why it has a continuity property, try graphing some:

```
goalie_payoff <- -matrix(c(0,1,.75,.25),2)

gt_brgraph(goalie_payoff, -goalie_payoff,
        labels1=c("Left", "Right"), P1="Goalie", P2="Shooter")
```

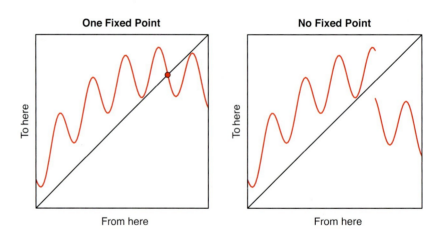

FIGURE ix FIXED POINTS

The graph on the left is continuous and so it has to pass through the 45-degree line, meaning it must map some point onto itself. The graph on the right is not continuous and so it can avoid the 45-degree line.

REFERENCES

Akerlof, G. A. (1970). The market for "lemons": Quality uncertainty and the market mechanism. *Quarterly Journal of Economics, 84*(3), 488–500.

Alesina, A., & Spear, S. E. (1988). An overlapping generations model of electoral competition. *Journal of Public Economics, 37*(3), 359–379.

Arrow, K. J. (1963). *Social choice and individual values.* New York, NY: John Wiley & Sons, Inc.

Aumann, R. (1976). Agreeing to disagree. *The Annals of Statistics, 4*(6), 1236–1239.

Austen-Smith, D., & Banks, J. (2000a). *Positive political theory I: Collective preference* (Vol. 1). Ann Arbor, MI: University of Michigan Press.

Austen-Smith, D., & Banks, J. (2005). *Positive political theory II: Strategy and structure* (Vol. 2). Ann Arbor, MI: University of Michigan Press.

Austen-Smith, D., & Banks, J. (1998). Social choice theory, game theory, and positive political theory. *Annual Review of Political Science, 1*(1), 259–287.

Austen-Smith, D., & Banks, J. (2000b). Cheap talk and burned money. *Journal of Economic Theory, 91*(1), 1–16.

Austen-Smith, D., & Feddersen, T. (2006). Deliberation, preference uncertainty, and voting rules. *American Political Science Review, 100*(2), 209.

Axelrod, R., & Hamilton, W. D. (1981). The evolution of cooperation. *Science, 211*(4489), 1390–1396.

Banzhaf, J., III (1964). Weighted voting doesn't work: A mathematical analysis. *Rutgers Law Review*, (19), 317.

Battigalli, P., & Dufwenberg, M. (2009). Dynamic psychological games. *Journal of Economic Theory, 144*(1), 1–35.

Bendor, J., & Swistak, P. (1997) The evolutionary stability of cooperation. *American Political Science Review, 91*(02), 290–307.

Bikhchandani, S., Hirshleifer, D., & Welch, I. (1992). A theory of fads, fashion, custom, and cultural change as informational cascades. *Journal of Political Economy, 100*(5), 992–1026.

Binmore, K., Rubinstein, A., & Wolinsky, A. (1986) The Nash bargaining solution in economic modeling. *RAND Journal of Economics, 17*(2), 176–188.

Binmore, K. G. (1998). *Game theory and the social contract: Just playing* (Vol. 2). Cambridge, MA: MIT Press.

Black, D. (1948). On the rationale of group decision-making. *Journal of Political Economy, 56*(1), 23–34.

Brown, D. (1975). Aggregation of preferences. *Quarterly Journal of Economics, 89*(3), 456–69.

Bueno de Mesquita, B., Smith, A., Randolph, S., & Morrow, J. (2005). *The logic of political survival.* Cambridge, MA: MIT Press.

Camerer, C., Ho, T., & Chong, J. (2004). A cognitive hierarchy model of games. *Quarterly Journal of Economics*, *119*(3), 861–898.

Camerer, C. F., & Fehr, E. (2006). When does "economic man" dominate social behavior? *Science, 311*(5757), 47–52.

Coase, R. H. (1960). The problem of social cost. *Journal of Law & Economics, 3*, 1–44.

Condorcet, M. J. A. N., Marquis de [1785] (1972). *Essai sur l'application de l'analyse à la probabilité des décisions rendues à la pluralité des voix.* New York, NY: Chelsea Publishing Co.

Coughlan, P. J. (2000). In defense of unanimous jury verdicts: Mistrials, communication, and strategic voting. *American Political Science Review, 94*(2), 375–393.

Crawford, V., & Sobel, J. (1982). Strategic information transmission. *Econometrica: Journal of the Econometric Society, 50*(6). 1431–1451.

Dawkins, R. (2006). *The selfish gene*. Oxford, UK: Oxford University Press.

Dixit, A., & Londregan, J. (1995). Redistributive politics and economic efficiency. *American Political Science Review, 89*(4), 856–866.

Duersch, P., Oechssler, J., & Schipper, B. C. (2012). Unbeatable imitation. *Games and Economic Behavior, 76*(1), 88–96.

Duggan, J., & Schwartz, T. (2000). Strategic manipulability without resoluteness or shared beliefs: Gibbard-Satterthwaite generalized. *Social Choice and Welfare, 17*(1), 85–93.

Esteban, J., & Ray, D. (2002). Collective action and the group size paradox. *American Political Science Review, 95*(3), 663–672.

Ewerhart, C. (2002). Backward induction and the game-theoretic analysis of chess. *Games and Economic Behavior, 39*(2), 206–214.

Fearon, J. (1997). Signaling foreign policy interests tying hands versus sinking costs. *Journal of Conflict Resolution, 41*(1), 68–90.

Feddersen, T., & Pesendorfer, W. (1996). The swing voter's curse. *The American Economic Review, 86*(3), 408–424.

Feddersen, T., & Pesendorfer, W. (1998). Convicting the innocent: The inferiority of unanimous jury verdicts under strategic voting. *The American Political Science Review, 92*(1), 23.

Feltkamp, V. (1995). Alternative axiomatic characterizations of the Shapley and Banzhaf values. *International Journal of Game Theory, 24*(2), 179–186.

Ferejohn, J. (1986). Incumbent performance and electoral control. *Public Choice, 50*(1), 5–25.

Fudenberg, D., & Maskin, E. (1986). The folk theorem in repeated games with discounting or with incomplete information. *Econometrica: Journal of the Econometric Society, 54*(3), 533–54.

Geanakoplos, J., Pearce, D., & Stacchetti, E. (1989). Psychological games and sequential rationality. *Games and Economic Behavior, 1*(1), 60–79.

Gelman, A., Katz, J. N., & Tuerlinckx, F. (2002). The mathematics and statistics of voting power. *Statistical Science, 17*(4), 420–435.

Gibbard, A. (2014). Social choice and the Arrow conditions. *Economics and Philosophy, 30*(3), 269–284.

Goodin, R. E., & List, C. (2006). A conditional defense of plurality rule: Generalizing May's theorem in a restricted informational environment. *American Journal of Political Science, 50*(4), 940–949.

Grossman, S., & Stiglitz, J. (1980). On the impossibility of informationally efficient markets. *The American Economic Review, 70*(3), 393–408.

Groves, T. (1973). Incentives in teams. *Econometrica: Journal of the Econometric Society, 41*(4), 617–631.

Hardin, G. (1968). The tragedy of the commons. *Science, 162*(3859), 1243–1248.

Heifetz, A., Shannon, C., & Spiegel, Y. (2007). What to maximize if you must. *Journal of Economic Theory, 133*(1), 31–57.

Hotelling, H. (1929). Stability in competition. *The Economic Journal, 39*(153), 41–57.

Kalai, E., & Smorodinsky, M. (1975). Other solutions to Nash's bargaining problem. *Econometrica: Journal of the Econometric Society, 43*(3), 513–518.

Kalandrakis, T. (2006). Proposal rights and political power. *American Journal of Political Science, 50*(2), 441–448.

Kalandrakis, T. (2009). Robust rational turnout. *Economic Theory, 41*(2), 317–343.

Kalmár, L. (1928). Zur Theorie der abstrakten Spiele. *Acta Scientiarum Mathematicarum, 4,* 65–68.

Kreps, D. M., Milgrom, P., Roberts, J., & Wilson, R. (1982). Rational cooperation in the finitely repeated prisoner's dilemma. *Journal of Economic Theory, 27*(2), 245–252.

Kreps, D. M., & Wilson, R. (1982). Reputation and imperfect information. *Journal of Economic Theory, 27*(2), 253–279.

Kuran, T. (1989). Sparks and prairie fires: A theory of unanticipated political revolution. *Public Choice, 61*(1), 41–74.

Kurrild-Klitgaard, P. (2001). An empirical example of the Condorcet paradox of voting in a large electorate. *Public Choice, 107*(1-2), 135–145.

Laver, M., Marchi, S., & Mutlu, H. (2011). Negotiation in legislatures over government formation. *Public Choice, 147*(3), 285–304.

Mackay, C. [1841] (2012). *Extraordinary popular delusions and the madness of crowds.* New York, NY: Start Publishing LLC.

Maskin, E. (1999). Nash equilibrium and welfare optimality. *Review of Economic Studies, 66*(1), 23–38.

Maskin, E., & Sjöström, T. (2002). Implementation theory. In K. J. Arrow, A. Sen, & K. Suzumura (Eds.), *Handbook of social choice and welfare* (pp. 237–288). Amsterdam, NL: Elsevier.

May, K. (1952). A set of independent necessary and sufficient conditions for simple majority decision. *Econometrica: Journal of the Econometric Society, 20*(4), 680–684.

McKelvey, R. D. (1976). Intransitivities in multidimensional voting models and some implications for agenda control. *Journal of Economic Theory, 12*(3), 472–482.

Meier, M., & Schipper, B. C. (2014). Bayesian games with unawareness and unawareness perfection. *Economic Theory, 56*(2), 219–249.

Meltzer, A. H., & Richard, S. F. (1981). A rational theory of the size of government. *The Journal of Political Economy, 89*(5), 914–927.

Morris, S. (1995). The common prior assumption in economic theory. *Economics and Philosophy, 11*(2), 227–253.

Myerson, R. (1997). *Game theory: Analysis of conflict.* Cambridge, MA: Harvard University Press.

Myerson, R., & Satterthwaite, M. (1983). Efficient mechanisms for bilateral trading. *Journal of Economic Theory, 29*(2), 265–281.

Nagel, R. (1995). Unraveling in guessing games: An experimental study. *The American Economic Review, 85*(5), 1313–1326.

Nakamura, K. (1979). The vetoers in a simple game with ordinal preferences. *International Journal of Game Theory, 8*(1), 55–61.

Nash, J. F. (1950a). The bargaining problem. *Econometrica: Journal of the Econometric Society, 18*(2), 155–162.

Nash, J. F. (1950b). Equilibrium points in n-person games. *Proceedings of the National Academy of Sciences, 36*(1), 48–49.

Olson, M. (1965). *The logic of collective action: public goods and the theory of groups.* Cambridge, MA: Harvard University Press.

Palfrey, T. & Rosenthal, H. (1983). A strategic calculus of voting. *Public Choice, 41*(1), 7–53.

Parfit, D. (1984). *Reasons and persons.* Oxford, UK: Oxford University Press.

Piccione, M., & Rubinstein, A. (1997). On the interpretation of decision problems with imperfect recall. *Games and Economic Behavior, 20*(1), 3–24.

Plott, C. R. (1967). A notion of equilibrium and its possibility under majority rule. *The American Economic Review, 57*(4), 787–806.

Powell, R. (2004). The inefficient use of power: Costly conflict with complete information. *American Political Science Review, 98*(2), 231–241.

Putnam, R. D. (1988). Diplomacy and domestic politics: The logic of two-level games. *International Organization, 42*(3), 427–460.

Rawls, J. (1971). *A Theory of Justice.* Cambridge, MA: Harvard University Press.

Robbins, L. (1938). Interpersonal comparisons of utility: A comment. *The Economic Journal, 48*(192), 635–641.

Roemer, J. E. (2002). Egalitarianism against the veil of ignorance. *Journal of Philosophy, 99*(4), 167–184.

Rousseau, J. [1762] (1968). *The social contract,* London, UK: Penguin.

Rousseau, J. [1754] (2000). *Discourse on the origin of inequality.* Oxford, UK: Oxford University Press

Rubinstein, A. (1982). Perfect equilibrium in a bargaining model. *Econometrica: Journal of the Econometric Society, 50*(1), 97–109.

Saari, D. (1997). The generic existence of a core for q-rules. *Economic Theory, 9*(2), 219–260.

Samuelson, P. A. (1958). An exact consumption-loan model of interest with or without the social contrivance of money. *Journal of Political Economy, 66*(6), 467–482.

Schelling, T. C. (1960). *The strategy of conflict*. Cambridge, MA: Harvard University Press.

Schwalbe, U. & Walker, P. (2001). Zermelo and the early history of game theory. *Games and Economic Behavior, 34*(1), 123–137.

Sen, A. (1974). Choice, ordering and morality. In S. Körner (Ed.), *Practical Reason*. Oxford, UK: Blackwell.

Shapley, L. S., & Shubik, M. (1954). A method for evaluating the distribution of power in a committee system. *American Political Science Review, 48*(03), 787–792.

Shepsle, K. A. (2006). Rational choice institutionalism. In R.A. Rhodes, S. A. Binder, & B. A. Rockman (Eds.), *The Oxford handbook of political institutions* (pp. 23–38). Oxford, UK: Oxford University Press.

Surowiecki, J. (2004). *The wisdom of crowds: Why the many are smarter than the few and how collective wisdom shapes business, economies, societies, and nations*. New York, NY: Doubleday.

Taylor, A. (2002). The manipulability of voting systems. *The American Mathematical Monthly, 109*(4), 321–337.

Taylor, M., & Ward, H. (1982). Chickens, whales, and lumpy goods: Alternative models of public-goods provisions. *Political Studies, 30*(3), 350–370.

Vickrey, W. (1961). Counterspeculation, auctions, and competitive sealed tenders. *The Journal of Finance, 16*(1), 8–37.

Von Mises, L. (1990). *Economic calculation in the socialist commonwealth*. Auburn, Ala.: Ludwig Von Mises Institute, Auburn University.

Von Neumann, J. (1928). Zur Theorie der Gesellschaftsspiele. *Mathematische Annalen, 100*(1), 295–320.

Walter, B. F. (2009). *Reputation and civil war: Why separatist conflicts are so violent*. Cambridge, UK: Cambridge University Press.

Young, H. P. (1988). Condorcet's theory of voting. *American Political Science Review, 82*(4), 1231–1244.

Young, H. P. (2001). *Individual strategy and social structure: An evolutionary theory of institutions*. Princeton, NJ: Princeton University Press.

Zermelo, E. (1913). Über eine Anwendung der Mengenlehre auf die Theorie des Schachspiels. In E. W. Hobson & A. E. Love (Eds.), *Proceedings of the fifth international congress of mathematicians (Cambridge, 22–28 August 1912)* (pp. 501–504). Cambridge, UK: Cambridge University Press.